SWEET LIBERTY:
TRAVELS IN IRISH AMERICA

JOSEPH O'CONNOR

SWEET LIBERTY:
TRAVELS IN IRISH AMERICA

PICADOR

First published 1996 by Picador
an imprint of Macmillan Publishers Ltd
25 Eccleston Place, London SW1W 9NF
and Basingstoke

Associated companies throughout the world

ISBN 0 330 33322 4

9 8 7 6 5 4 3 2 1

A CIP catalogue record for this book is available from
the British Library

Typeset by CentraCet Limited, Cambridge
Printed by Mackays of Chatham plc, Chatham, Kent

In memory of Thomas O'Connor and Ellen O'Neill of Francis Street, Dublin, who made the hopeful journey from Ireland across the Atlantic in the 1930s, survived the years of the Great Depression and later returned to their home city, thus allowing their grandson to be born, like each of them, a Dubliner.

ACKNOWLEDGEMENTS

Many people helped me in the course of researching and writing this book. The list of thanks must begin with Marie O'Riordan and Sean O'Connor, each of whom generously – not to say heroically – accompanied me on various difficult bits of the trip. Colm Tóibín is responsible for planting the idea of the book in my mind, and I am grateful to him and to Catriona Crowe for their support. Thanks for many assistances, encouragements and insights are due to my agents, Carole Blake and Conrad Williams at Blake Friedmann, and to Dermot Bolger, Rachel Heath, Edwin Higel, Philip Kampff, Peter McDermott, Peter Straus and the late Jonathan Warner. Thanks to Anne-Marie Casey for all her encouragement while the book was being completed. Thanks to John, Eoin and Eimear O'Connor for their help, and to Viola once again. Thanks to Vincent Browne, the former editor of the *Sunday Tribune*, Dublin, and to his successor, Peter Murtagh, for inviting me to cover the 1994 soccer World Cup in the USA, during which I learnt a little more about America and a lot more about hangovers. Thanks to the staff at the Computer Hospital, Dublin, for idiot-proof technical advice. Thanks to the AP Watt Literary Agency. And thanks once again to Bernard and Mary Loughlin at the Tyrone Guthrie Centre at Annaghmakerrig, Newbliss, County Monaghan, Ireland, for their kindness and hospitality while the book was being edited.

Item, yf any man hath many Iorneys to take by land or by water, let hym haue an eye rounde about hym, for Force is lykely to exceede in all places, and Violence already shaketh his head, and frowneth vpon Trauaylers: but Warinesse and Courage, are the best spelles agaynst such Sprites and Goblins.

Thomas Porter, An Almanacke Or Prognostication For The Yeere MDLXXXV.
(Carried on one of the earliest voyages to the American continent from Europe.)

CONTENTS

How the West Was Won

When I was a young child my family used to go on holiday most years to Connemara, a stark and hauntingly lovely place in the West of Ireland. Every July or August my father and mother would pack me and my screaming sisters and my wailing brother and various bewildered family pets into the back of the car and we would drive the four long hours from suburban Dublin to the heart of wilderness Ireland, pausing on the way just long enough to allow one or other – or sometimes both – of my sisters to throw up spectacularly on the side of the road, which, invariably, they seemed to do in the small town of Kinnegad, County Westmeath. I've never quite got over this last fact.

Kinnegad is a pleasant little town, with a nice late-nineteenth-century church and agreeable pubs and a wide main street, but my poor sisters left the semi-digested contents of their stomachs on that main street so often in the course of those hot and distant summer afternoons that Kinnegad is forever tainted in my memory. Indeed, in more recent years, I have rarely been able to pass through Kinnegad without wanting to throw up myself, perhaps as some half-hearted gesture towards getting in touch with my distant past, or my inner child, or both.

And this strange process works in reverse also. With an almost Proustian pang of memory, whenever I see one of my sisters vomiting these days – which, I should stress, tends to happen a little less frequently than it used to – I think of that small and commodious town in the midlands of Ireland, where you slow down and get into the left lane and make the turn on to the Galway road, the road to Connemara. This is a very odd thing. But anyway, you don't want to know my problems.

The drive over to County Galway was always fantastically exciting. The very names of the little towns through which we passed seemed to us children an incantation of the most powerful magic, as we chanted them and screamed them and drove our poor father towards wondering whether he should just swerve into the path of the oncoming traffic and end it all in dramatic and explosive fashion. After Kinnegad came Pass of Kilbride, Rochfortbridge, Tyrelpass, Kilbeggan, Horseleap and Moate, and then Athlone, the big town in the dead centre of Ireland. There we would stop for drinks and sandwiches, and then drive on, through Ballinasloe, Aughrim, Kilreekill, Loughrea, Craughwell and Oranmore, into Galway city, then through Salthill, where the amusement arcades buzzed and beeped and rattled all along the seafront and then, tired and dazed with anticipation, we would turn left again and out on to the Barna road which led along the Atlantic coast and towards Connemara.

When we got to the edge of Connemara we would sometimes spend a night or two in a place called the Bridge House Hotel in the tiny town of Spiddal. And we liked doing that, my brother and sisters and myself, because sleeping in a small-town Irish hotel seemed the most exciting thing in the entire known universe back then; the squeak of rusty beds, the smell of clean starchy sheets, the snuffle of half-suppressed laughter in the adjoining rooms, the salty stewish aroma of hotel cooking, the floorboards creaking in the middle of the night, the distant cacophony of a group of drunken yobbos singing off-colour come-all-ye's in one or other of the bars across the street, the redolence of stale Guinness or cigarette smoke exuded by the thick carpet in the television lounge. The presence in the hotel of young and attractive and previously unencountered foreign members of the opposite sex, the colourful rumours one might hear about which members of staff were doing what with which, and when, and with what equipment. To a young child, the Bridge House Hotel was a paradise of sensory delight. We loved it.

One of most important attractions of the Bridge House Hotel was that often there would be Americans staying! They were exotic creatures, these Americans. We regarded them as the rarest of hothouse flowers. The men would invariably be dressed in suits of the loudest check and shirts of electric, pool-table green. Sometimes they wore wide-brimmed Stetson hats so that they looked a little like cowboys, but they were usually so fat that if any one of them had sat on a horse the unfortunate beastie would have required major surgery immediately afterwards. The women wore fabulous dresses and tartan scarves and trouser-suits so astoundingly florid that they would have given Dame Edna Everage one of her famous heads. More like pantomime dames than real women, they wore more make-up on their faces than David Bowie in the Ziggy Stardust years. They dressed like nobody we had ever seen before, and the pleasure we got from simply looking at them was enormous.

They were loud and exuberant and self-confident and bold, these great-grandsons and -granddaughters of the poor Irish emigrants who had fled the West of Ireland to escape famine and misery and death. They were big spenders and big tippers. They drank a lot and talked a lot, they knew all the words of the more sentimental Irish songs, the ones with Irish placenames in their titles. 'Galway Bay', 'Fare Thee Well, Enniskillen, Fare Thee Well for a While', 'Come Back Paddy Reilly to Ballyjamesduff', 'Where the Mountains of Mourne Sweep Down to the Sea', 'I Wish I Was in Carrickfergus', 'Adieu to Innisfail'. They knew them all. There is an ancient ballad form called *dinnseanchas* in the Irish poetry tradition. *Dinnseanchas* songs are songs about places; similar songs appear in the oral traditions of most displaced peoples. This profound yearning for a meaningful sense of place is so strong in the Irish psyche that it has survived centuries of exile; what I was hearing in the late 1960s in the bar of the Bridge House Hotel were Americanized versions of *dinnseanchas* songs brought the long way home.

Most of these songs referred to places I had never seen in my life, but as a young child I couldn't help thinking how fabulous and exotic they must have been if anybody could miss them so much. I remember once hearing a song which began, 'Here's a health to you, bonny Kellswater/Where you'll get all the pleasures of life/Where you'll get all your fishing and fowling/And a lovely young lass for your wife,' and I remember that I tried to imagine just exactly how bonny must bonny Kellswater have been to inspire such an affectionate tribute. In some odd way, I think I was actually introduced to the magic of rural Ireland by these American tourists and their sentimental songs.

As the night wore on, the songs the Americans sang would become more pugnacious. They would start into rebel songs like 'O'Donnel Abu' or 'The Rising of the Moon' or 'Wrap the Green Flag Around Me Boys'. There would then follow doleful laments named for the great martyrs of Irish republicanism – 'Kevin Barry', 'Sean South of Garryowen', 'Kelly the Boy from Killane', 'God Save Ireland Cried the Heroes', 'James Connolly, the Irish Rebel', 'Bold Robert Emmet, the Darling of Erin' ('Bold Robert Emmet, he died with a smile./ Farewell companions, both loyal and daring,/ For I've laid down my life for the Emerald Isle.') The Americans would sing these songs in the bar of the Bridge House Hotel late at night, and quite often, as they did so, there would be tears in their eyes.

Some of the Irish grown-ups present seemed to find all this faintly embarrassing, and they would try to sing happy Irish drinking songs of the sub-genus diddly-eye. Sometimes, I think they would even resent these lachrymose and passionate Americans, who would jet into Ireland once a year and tell us all how to liberate ourselves through armed struggle and popular revolt before jetting back out again to a ranch in Texas or a Californian condo. This was Ireland in the late sixties and early seventies, when once again there was bloodshed and slaughter on the streets of our cities, and it was becoming clear that the simple solutions which the old songs proposed were not viable any more. But, at the time, I must confess that I loved the way the Americans went on. I loved their bravado, their shamelessness, the heady ease of their unthinking extremism. They were patriotic about Ireland and America in equal measure. They strutted around the Bridge House Hotel and the town of Spiddal as if they owned both, which, of course, they did not. But they might as well have. You felt that they could have done so, if they had really wanted to. That was the aura these plump, generous, brash, dewy-eyed Americans had. You felt there was nothing in Ireland they couldn't buy.

When we did not stay at the Bridge House Hotel, my family stayed in a house about fifteen miles beyond Spiddal, a little house in the blasted and rocky countryside around Inverin in the Connemara Gaeltacht, where the Twelve Bens Mountains loom out of the mist like benevolent giants, and the trees, lashed and battered by the Atlantic storms, grow at every possible angle to the ground, except the perpendicular. This was the heartland of Connemara, the last remaining vestige of the Gaelic, Roman Catholic and rural Ireland for which the dead heroes in the sad songs had fought. Here was a place where people could not get BBC or ITV on the television, where to have running water was considered something of a luxury. Here was a peaceful and tightly knit community where people still spoke Irish as their first language.

The house we stayed in was only slightly bigger than all the other houses on that long serpentine boreen. It was so pretty that it looked almost unreal; it looked like the kind of house you would see in a dream, or on a postcard, or in the John Ford film *The Quiet Man*. It had a green slated roof and whitewashed walls, a great black pot perpetually boiling over a turf fire in the kitchen, huge copper pans and saucepans and religious pictures hanging on the stone walls. Outside in the yard there were donkeys and hens and dogs, and there were dry stone walls around all the adjoining fields.

As a young child, my father had stayed in this house often. His parents had sent him there every summer from the working-class suburb of Crumlin in Dublin, to learn Irish. He had developed a love of that poetic and mellifluous language, had befriended the family and continued to go to Connemara as a teenager. He had been there with my mother in their courting days, and after they had got married and had children they had continued to go almost every year, and to bring us with them. We loved Connemara as much as my parents had, although thinking back now, I can see that these annual jaunts were not just holidays. I think my parents wanted us to see how hard some people's lives were in Ireland. They weren't ever boring or morbid about it; they just wanted us to know that a day's drive away from where we lived, people had to cut turf by hand and get their water, in all weathers, from a well. But like many Irish people, I think my mother and father also had the feeling that the West was in some unquantifiable but equally undeniable sense the real Ireland. They wanted us to have some notion of what it meant to be Irish, to give us just a fleeting annual glimpse of an identity we could never have found in Majorca or Rimini or Disneyland or the other distant places to which our more posh schoolfriends went every year.

As the eldest child, I was sometimes treated differently to my younger siblings. Sometimes at night, on these wonderful trips to Connemara, my father would take me down the road with him to the local pub, and I would love it when he did that. I can still clearly remember the almost frantic excitement of walking down the boreen in the middle of the night with my hand in my father's hand, just the two of us together, and the incredible blackness of the sky. I can remember the babble of the river which ran along the edge of the road, the intoxicating smell of heather and turf, the tang of Atlantic salt in my mouth, the air so crisp that you felt you could take big crunchy bites out of it. I can remember squeezing my father's hand at the moment when we would see the yellow lights of the pub glinting in the distance. And when we got there, I can remember the blast of hot moistness that would hit my face when we opened the door and went in, and the sound of traditional music and the smell of drink and smoke and the hubbub of people conversing in Irish.

Irish is a beautiful and musical language. Its natural rhythms are nonchalant, relaxed and discursive. With its long vowels and elisions and sibilances, the cadences of spoken Irish sound like English spoken by rural Irish people, only even better. To this day, we are not terrific at languages in Ireland. We are getting a lot better, but up until recently if an Irishman tried to learn French or German he all too frequently ended up spraining his lips. But if an Irish person sits you down and speaks to you in Irish, you could listen to the sound for hours, even if you have absolutely no idea of what is being said.

Apart from the sound of the Irish language, I have to confess that the pub itself was invariably boring. After a time, some old man in tweeds and wellingtons would stand up and stick his finger in his ear and begin to whine out a song, his breath chugging and wheezing, his body rocking back and forth as he sang. And after this, some old woman would tell a long and rambling story, usually about banshees, Cromwell or the souls of dead fishermen turning into seals. I do not mean to be flippant about this. It was a serious celebration of a resilient and mercilessly oppressed people's culture, and it was the kind of thing for which I would be prepared to pay out actual money these days. But back then, as a young suburban Dublin child, I despised it. For some odd reason I was more comfortable with the American tourists' sententious and maudlin version of the Irish folk tradition than I was with the real thing. When I think about it now, I remember only tedium and misery, punctuated by flickers of unadulterated boredom.

But then, one night in that pub, a strange and unforgettable thing happened to me. I remember that it was quite late. Tired and restless, I was sitting on an upturned lemonade crate at the foot of an old woman who came from the area. This old woman had that kind of statuesque beauty which is quite common in Connemara. It is said that centuries ago a large number of ships from the Spanish Armada got lost and were wrecked on the Galway coast, and the damp and discombobulated survivors, wisely enough, decided to stay and marry the local girls rather than return to the delights of the military life. As a consequence, many of the true Connemara people have dark skin, almond-shaped eyes, a haughty Iberian grandeur about their bearing. Anyway, this old woman could see that I was bored, I suppose, and she began to talk to me. Where was I from, she asked, and when I said Dublin she sighed, 'Oh, Dublin, an baile mór,' which means 'the big city' in Irish. Then she looked at me again, her dark eyes glittering, and she asked me in English what Dublin was like. I laughed at her, sure she was trying to catch me out, or make me say something stupid. But she smiled at me kindly, and she told me she had meant just what she said. What was Dublin like?

I knew, because somebody had told me, that this old woman was very well travelled. I knew she had been to America and had spent many years there. I asked her about this. She had lived in Boston, she explained, had met her husband and got married there, and then they had lived in Queens, New York for a time. But she had never been to Dublin in her life.

I could not believe this, but she assured me that it was true. I was amazed. How could any Irish person never have been to Dublin? I tried to tell her what Dublin was like, but I could not really concentrate because I was so shocked. I could not get a clear picture of Dublin in my mind, because it was so familiar to me. What a preposterous question she was asking. Surely to God, everyone would know what Dublin was like? Slowly she coaxed me into telling her all about it. What was our house like? Did it have a garden? Were there other children to play with on the road and did we have a dog? Did I sleep in a bedroom by myself or with my brother? How many children were in my school? And what would a person do in Dublin? Were there parks? Wasn't there a zoo? Which animals lived in the zoo in Dublin? Were there tigers, for example? Were there giraffes? Had I ever seen a hippopotamus?

I answered all of her questions as best I could. Then she asked me, I recall now, whether there were any black people in Dublin, and I said there were hardly any. She had known black people in America, she said, and they had it very hard over there. They were lovely people to look at too, she said; their skin was the colour of ebony, which, she explained, was the dark wood on the black piano keys. She said some of the black people you would see were so black that they were nearly not black at all, that they were almost a shade of dark blue. She said that when you saw a person like this your heart would marvel at the creation of God, who could make people so beautiful to behold. 'Fear gorm', she told me – the Irish word for a black man – literally means 'a blue man'.

America was a great country, she explained. A person would see Chinamen and black men and Indians and Jews and Mexicans and people from all over the whole world in America. And as for the Irish! Well, there were people from every county, from every parish and town in Ireland in America. There were more Irish people over there than there were in the whole of Ireland, she told me. I would have to go to America myself when I grew up, she said, because Ireland was a very small place to live. Ireland was a good place, she continued, 'and, of course, it's our own place' but it was an interesting thing for a young person to see life as it was lived in a big country, and she was glad that she had once had the opportunity to spend time in America. Living in a big country, with plenty of space, was good for people, she said.

I was breathless with excitement listening to this old lady. In those few moments, the balance of Ireland tilted in my mind. I stopped seeing Ireland as a place which revolved around Dublin, and I began to see it as a place which revolved around America. The map of the world shifted, too, in my childish imagination. No longer just off the coast of Britain, Ireland was now just off the coast of Massachusetts. To be honest, I still think of it a bit like that. And I suppose seeing Ireland a bit like that is what this book is all about.

From that night on, I was captivated by America. When we came home from our holidays in Connemara I watched American television programmes and American films with a new and ferocious interest. The sweeping plains around the Bonanza ranch, the urban avenues through which Starsky and Hutch raced in pursuit of cunning and wild-eyed ne'er-do-wells, became as important to me as the roads and avenues of the south Dublin housing estate where we lived. I hung an enormous map of America on my bedroom wall. I would look at it every morning when I got up, trying to learn how to pronounce the strange and glamorous names of American cities. How did you say 'Albuquerque'? What about 'Roanoke', 'Terre Haute', 'Des Moines', 'Baton Rouge'? I found books and magazines in the house with photographs of the American landscape. I suppose they would have been publications like *National*

Geographic and *Readers' Digest*, sometimes *Time* magazine, to which I think my parents must have had a subscription. I cut out pictures of the Grand Canyon, the Rocky Mountains, Niagara Falls, the skyscrapers of New York, the great wheatfields of the Midwest, the Mississippi River meandering into the Gulf of Mexico at New Orleans, and I pasted them into a scrapbook. My bedroom became an America to me. My own private America. I thought there was nowhere in the world as beautiful as this fabulous and distant land.

Time passed and my obsession deepened. I often thought about the old lady and what she had said to me: Ireland was too small; it was interesting to see the way life was lived in a big country. I wondered exactly what she meant. In school, I affected American speech patterns when we played in the yard, or on the bus home. I was always the drawling cowboy, the wisecracking Chicago gumshoe, the all-conquering spaceman who had planted the stars and stripes on the moon. I must have driven the poor bus conductor crazy, blithely addressing him every morning as 'pardner', 'Hoss' or 'Mac' or 'Mission Control'. He, meanwhile, addressed me every morning as 'you dirty lookin little bollix'.

Every St Patrick's Day in Dublin, I would go with my family to watch the parade, to get a look at the Americans who had come all the way over to Ireland to march and celebrate our freedom with us. I would look at the place names on their banners – Boston, Indiana, New York, Chicago – and those place names to me had the evocative power of the purest lyric poetry. And then one year – I cannot remember which one exactly – while watching the parade, I noticed a banner which read 'Dublin, Texas', and another which read 'Dublin, Ohio'. When I remarked upon this to my father, he said that there were quite a lot of Dublins in America. The Irish who had gone over there had named their new homes after the capital of Ireland, he said. There were seven or eight Dublins in America, he thought, perhaps even more. Were they like our Dublin, I asked him, and he said he didn't think so. But still, I didn't care that they were different. There were other Dublins in the world! There were Dublins in America! This, to me, was the most remarkable thing I had heard since a boy called James Downey told me the facts of life at the back of the school chapel one morning after early mass.

I have to confess that at this stage my interest in America was not purely geographical. I was by now a pubescent youngster, my face as speckled as the spar-spangled banner; and the inhabitants of these transatlantic Dublins – at least, the ones who came over to see us in Ireland – really did look like they were worth getting to know. I can see them still, these tanned and stunningly beautiful teenage girls from Dublin, Texas or Dublin, Georgia prancing and high-kicking down O'Connell Street in green and white bodices and miniskirts so short that they were actually like long sweaters. I can see them waving, blowing kisses to the crowd, grinning their orthodontically perfect grins, sashaying along to the strains of 'I'm a Yankee Doodle Dandy' or 'You're a Grand Old Flag' or 'Give My Regards to Broadway'. Let me assure you, I was gripped. My adolescent sexual urges were whipped into action by the sight of those goose-pimpled transatlantic limbs. Ever since I was eleven or twelve, I have been unable to hear the sound of an oom-pah-pahing sousaphone without breaking into a hot sweat and getting an immediate erection. (This is one reason why I attend the circus only rarely.)

Anyway, I'd better calm down. What I am trying to tell you really is that in time, I began to associate America with glamour and sex, with magic, beauty, possibility and scale. Even the native musics of America – the harrowing blues, the soaring gospel, the visceral country and western, the anarchic jazz and the wild, exuberant rock and roll – seemed in some way to be full of space, seemed to be as expansive and epic and important as the landscapes and attitudes and immigrant experiences that had shaped their formation. This was what we joked about growing up in Ireland, the sheer size of America, how America was the biggest place in the world. A Texan rancher comes to Ireland and meets a Kerry farmer. The Texan says, 'Takes me a whole goddam day to drive from one side of my ranch to the other.' The Kerry farmer says, 'Ah sure, I know, sir. We have tractors like that over here too.' There were a lot of jokes like that, but they contained the seeds of a profound truth. Ireland was small. America was big. America was the place to be.

I suppose I began to associate America with success. Because to make it in Ireland was then – and is now – to make it in America. Every single family in Ireland has in its history people who emigrated, to England, or Canada, or Australia. But the uncle who made it in America, now he was the guy people really got worked up about.

One summer in the mid-1970s, we went back to the Bridge House Hotel for what would turn out to be the last time. We didn't know, as we arrived in Spiddal and looked around and did all the things we had always done as a family, that my parents' marriage was almost over, and that they would decide to separate shortly afterwards. Even if I had known this I'm not too sure what I would have said. I was having my own emotional problems. On my first afternoon in Connemara that year I met an American girl and satisfied what was by now a major ambition – I managed to fall desperately in love with her.

Judy Dowling would not really have made the Dublin, Georgia cheerleading team. She was a tall and impossibly lanky redhead with a brace on her teeth, Buddy Holly spectacles, appalling acne and a penchant for trapping frogs, inserting straws in them and briskly blowing them up. But I kind of liked that about her. I felt Judy was a bit of a sport. She was thirteen years old, and, as such, she seemed incredibly advanced. At night we went to ceilidh dances together in the local school hall, and held hands on the way home afterwards, sometimes pausing by the soft light of the Connemara moon to check one of her frog traps. It was all very sweet. In the long hot afternoons we went for long walks on Spiddal beach, which we spiced up considerably by dropping large flat rocks on the jellyfish which lay stranded and helpless in the shallows.

Gradually, Judy and I got closer. One day she asked me if I had ever kissed a girl and I said yes, of course I had, lying through my yellowed teeth. Judy seemed to be interested in this. She then asked me if I had ever kissed a girl and put my tongue in her mouth. I confessed that no, I had not, and she nodded and tutted and laughed gaily. From then on, it began to be intimated quite frequently that Judy had been around the track a good deal more than I, carnally speaking, and that if I played my cards right, next time she was doing a lap I could sit in the passenger seat and read the maps.

One night near the end of our holiday Judy came up to me in the television room of the Bridge House Hotel while I was playing with my sisters and my brother. She asked what I was doing the next day and I told her I had no plans. She would be going to the beach at three o'clock, she said. She repeated this. Something in her lingering glance gave me the impression that if I was prepared to take time out of my busy schedule and meet her behind the lifeguard's hut, I would go home a happy boy, and we would not be talking sand-castles. I can tell you, I did not sleep at all well that night.

Next day, I was down at that lifeguard's hut about half an hour before the appointed tryst, shaking with nerves, my tongue as dry as a Teheran discobar. As I stared at the hands of my Mickey Mouse watch, the minutes seemed like hours. Finally, I saw Judy in the distance, ambling slowly down the beach, a vision of clumsy loveliness. She sauntered along with her hands in the pockets of her pink shorts, and by the time she got to where I was standing, I was practically fit to be hospitalized. She smiled at me. She winked. She spat the nodule of well-masticated chewing gum from her beautiful willing mouth. She touched the side of my face. She rolled up her sleeves. She said, 'Let's go.' I took a deep breath and gratefully staggered forwards, into the arms of America.

Well, things went downhill from there. Judy was a good ten inches taller than me, which made life a little difficult. While I might have had no ethical ambivalence whatsoever about burying my head in her chest, Judy was an absolute lady, with a keen sense of how these things should be taken in clearly defined stages. A French kiss was what was on offer today, she explained, and not very much more than that. Sweating and stammering with anxiety, I made it clear that the problem was one of relative height and not dubious morality. She seemed to accept this. So I stood on tiptoes and she stooped. But when the time came for our moment of passion I made the unforgivable tactical error of getting the tip of my tongue stuck in her dental brace. It was absolutely horrendous. It was agony. Judy and I were bonded together by something more than love. I tottered around Spiddal beach dragging her with me, hot tears of pain spilling from my eyes.

By the time I finally managed to disentangle myself, Judy seemed inexplicably to have lost that lovin feeling. She was silent for a while. She kept staring out at the sea as though some interesting noise was coming from it. When finally she spoke, she made it abundantly clear that she felt our relationship was not going to be as mutually fulfilling as she had once hoped. She did not want us to be boyfriend and girlfriend. She told me that I was a very nice person, and that she liked me very much, and that she was sure we could have a very special and unique and meaningful friendship which we would both always treasure. She told me, basically, to fuck off and die roaring. She then strolled down to the shoreline as though nothing at all had happened, pulled a pack of cigarettes from the waistband of her shorts, lit one, picked up a large flat rock and dropped it on a jellyfish. Watching all this, I felt that the jellyfish had got off lighter than me. I was absolutely crushed.

I do not mind telling you that I ran back to the hotel in tears that afternoon. And that afternoon, in the television room of the Bridge House Hotel, something odd was happening. The little room was completely full of people. All the Americans were there, in their green suits and Aran sweaters, and they all seemed to be smoking. The President of America, Richard Nixon, was resigning from office. I remember staring at his image on the screen, as he stalked from the White House, stepped into a helicopter, made one final defiant V-for-Victory sign towards the cameras and disappeared into the clear Washington sky. I remember the stunned looks on the faces of the Americans in the room. I did not really understand what they were talking about, but Richard Nixon, the President of America, seemed to be a bad man now. How could you be a bad man and be the President of America, I wondered, but I felt that the question was so stupid that it could not be asked out loud. I didn't realize that Americans all over the world were asking themselves the same question. What I did realize was that America was a little more complex than I had previously imagined.

This is a thought which has reccurred frequently since that day. OK, sure, America has its faults. I'm thinking of carcinogenic hamburgers, of Little Jimmy Osmond, of Ronald Reagan waging a covert and vicious war against the democratically elected government of Nicaragua and still managing to leave office as the most popular president ever. Hey, nobody said it was perfect, right? But warts and all – and I'm not talking about Judy Dowling's face here – the United States of America is still one of the greatest experiments in mass idealism since the dawn of human history.

When I was in my second year at University College Dublin, a Labour Party man called Barry Desmond was Minister for Health. One of the really progressive things Bazza wanted to do was to take the free medical card away from students. OK, OK, so I know it's not exactly the bombing of Guernica, but, hey, we were young at the time. We didn't like this idea one bit.

We all met in Trinity College. There was going to be an occupation. Our leader told us to be inconspicuous. So fifty of us students took our banners, our bullhorns and our balaclavas and we marched down to Barry Desmond's office, looking every bit as inconspicuous as Carmelite nuns in a sado-masochistic massage parlour. Once we had penetrated Barry Desmond's office, we all sat down on the shag pile carpet and waited for something revolutionary to happen. I had taken along my cigarette lighter so that if anyone struck up a sudden chorus of 'We Shall Not Be Moved' or 'Blowing in the Wind' I could hold it up in the air and wave it meaningfully from side to side. I was very optimistic in those days.

The police arrived. They were quite angry. They said they would 'do whatever was necessary' to get us out. We scoffed heroically. We would be here, we said, until all of our demands were met. They asked what these demands were. There seemed to be a bit of confusion at this point. Personally, in addition to having Ireland immediately declared a thirty-two county socialist republic, I also wanted to have the television adaptation of *Brideshead Revisited* repeated on a Monday night. Anyway, while we argued and debated, the coppers left, no doubt happily reflecting on the fact that their monthly income tax payments were helping to subsidize our youthful exuberance.

Their sergeant came in then. He was a big plump man from County Cork. He parked his hefty behind on Barry Desmond's desk and folded his arms. He told us that we were all very bright young people and very lucky indeed to be getting such a good education. (He was right about one of these statements, and I leave it to perceptive readers to guess which one.) We had made our point now, he said, and then he asked us to leave in an orderly manner and we would say no more about it. We told him to shag away off to hell, him and his fascist right-wing imperialist paymasters. (Actually, I think we just said er . . . no.) The monster from Munster shook his head, very sadly. He took off his cap and put it on Barry Desmond's desk. It was an absolutely terrifying sight, for some reason, a policeman taking off his cap and putting it on a desk.

OK, he sighed, there was just one more thing he wanted to say before giving the order for us to be forcibly removed. (The phrases 'give the order' and 'forcibly removed' were quite effective, now that I think of it. You could almost hear the sound of fifty middle-class sphincters simultaneously snapping shut with anxiety.) 'If any of you get arrested today,' he breathed, 'you will never get into America.' There followed a silence which can only be adequately described as stunned. 'If you get charged and found guilty today, which you probably will be, you will have a criminal record. And you will never be allowed into America if you have a criminal record.' We looked at each other. 'Never,' he repeated, letting the word hang on the air. '*Never*. Think about that now.' He told us he would give us ten minutes to consider our position. He put his cap back on and slipped from the room with the grace and alacrity of a phantom.

Reader, no water cannon was ever so effective. There was a

stampede out of that office. Great clouds of thick dust rose from the carpet. It was like being at the back door of a brothel during a raid.

I hung on with the hard core. At the time, I was going through that peculiar stage of adolescence known as virulent anti-American-ism, so I didn't really care what would happen. What did happen was that two police officers carried me out and dumped me on the steps so hard that I nearly shattered my coccyx. That was ten years ago. I have put on a bit of weight since then. It would take the entire cast of *Hill Street Blues* to do the same job now.

That sergeant understood something very important. He under-stood the idea of America, the sheer historical importance of America to the young people of Ireland. In Chile, the police deal with uppity students by attaching electrodes to their genitals. In China, they run them over with tanks. In Ireland, they simply tell them they will never get into America. It's the ultimate threat.

I first went to America myself in the summer of 1991 with the intention of finishing a novel. I lived in New York for four months, and found it even more exciting, more bizarre, more scary, more memorable than I had ever imagined. But I don't know how many times that summer I was told that New York was not the real America, that I should one day go see the rest of the country, not just the other great teeming cities, but the America of the small towns also, and the wilderness America of prairies and deserts and canyons and lakes. I came back home to Ireland that autumn but the idea of returning one day to make this journey into the heart of the real America began to obsess me.

I knew I wanted to write a book about Irish America, but I decided pretty early on that I needed to broaden the meaning of that term. I wasn't particularly interested in green beer or inflatable leprechauns or that Reaganesque Oirish America of complacency and conservatism, sham and shamrock. Clearly, I would want to write about Boston and New York, the great centres of early Irish immigration and settlement. But I also wanted to see my own imaginary America, the Grand Canyon and the Mojave Desert and Santa Fe and all the places which had existed so vibrantly in my head, as a child growing up in Ireland. These, to me, were Irish-American places too, because I grew up with them in my dreams. At first glance it may seem strange for a book about Irish America to contain, for example, a section on Route 66, yet I always knew mine would, because for me, as a kid in the Dublin suburbs, Route 66 was as urgently real as O'Connell Street, and the fact that I had never actually been there didn't diminish its importance one bit. If anything, it probably increased it.

So one day, while planning this journey into my own Irish America, I sat down and looked at the *Encylopaedia Britannica* atlas. America seemed so huge and forbidding; I couldn't figure out the best way to approach it. Where exactly would I go? What should I see? What should I avoid? Which routes would I take? An inch of space on the map translated into three or four hundred miles of road. How could I find a way to include everything I wanted to see? I simply had no idea how or where to start the journey. In weary desperation, I turned to the index at the back of the atlas and began to flick through it. And out they leapt at me, all those American Dublins of long-lost teenage desire, from New Hampshire to Georgia to California, spread out in a meandering line across the whole country from the Atlantic to the Pacific coast. Yes, I wanted to go to Dallas and San Francisco and Las Vegas and all those other magical places. But purely for the hell of it, I decided to add all these little Dublins to my itinerary, just to see what they were like. The Dublins would be rest-stops along the vast journey, tiny oases of what I hoped would be at least a residual comfortable Irishness. As you'll see, I was often wrong about the Dublins. Sometimes they turned out to be the most foreign and unfamiliar places I had ever been in my life. Frequently the places in between the Dublins were a lot more interesting – and a lot more historically Irish – than the Dublins themselves. But I'm glad I went to see the Dublins all the same, because it made this book a story about big places and small places, and about the long stretches of highway in between, and any American story should be at least partially concerned with such themes.

Many times while I was on those unending expanses of road that old lady would come into my mind, the old lady who introduced me to the idea of America in the middle of the Connemara Gaeltacht some time in the early 1970s. She told me once that if I came to America and spent a little time there, I might learn something about the way life is lived in a big country. I think she was right. I think I learnt a lot. So, I hope you enjoy this journey as much as I did. And if by any chance Judy Dowling is reading this now, I just want to say that I forgive you for everything and I don't resent you at all, you scrawny-faced, four-eyed, buck-toothed moose from hell.

PART 1

THE GREENFIELDS OF AMERIKAY

Dear Father and Mother, pen cannot dictate the poverty of this country at present. The potato crop is quite done away with all over Ireland. There is nothing expected here, only an immediate famine. If you knew the danger we and our fellow countrymen are suffering, if you were ever so much distressed, you would take us out of this poverty isle . . . For God's sake take us out of poverty and don't let us die of hunger.

Letter from Mary Rush, County Sligo,
to her parents in Quebec, 1846

Our ship at the present lies in Derry Harbour
To bear us away o'er the wild swelling sea.
May heaven be her pilot and grant us fond breezes,
Till we reach the greenfields of Amerikay.
Oh, come to the land where we will be happy;
And don't be afraid of the storm or the sea.
For it's when we get over we will surely discover
That place is the land of sweet liberty . . .

From 'Come to the Land of Sweet Liberty',
traditional Irish song, nineteenth century

I was born here. My children were born here. What the hell do I have to do to be called an American?

Joseph P. Kennedy, quoted in the *New York Times*,
28 January 1957, p. 26

CHAPTER 1

A Good Ride in Boston

[In America] the labourer can earn as much in one day as will support him for a week. The richest land in the world may be purchased here ... for $1.25 an acre – equal to 5s 3d ... If I could show them [in Ireland] the splendid prairie I am looking on, extending in wild luxuriant verdure far as the eye can reach – how different would their situation be from what it is! How gladly they would fly with their families!

Letter from Irish immigrant,
name unknown, January 1848

After some stormy weather, the shores of the new world hove into sight. The port of Boston was our disembarking place, and the wharf in East Boston where we landed was of a miserable forbidding aspect. Dire poverty was to be seen all round, such wretched, horrible tenements with ragged, dirty, hungry-looking children playing in the ash heaps of a nearby railroad. It created a bad impression on me on the spot. Thinks I to myself: 'Is this the great country of "peace and plenty" there is so much talk about?'

From the diary of Tim Cashman,
Irish immigrant, 1840s

It is a curious thing, but I was raised an Irish Catholic, and yet the only time I ever pray these days is on an airplane. It is odd. On terra firma I am a pagan and hedonistic rationalist who can dismiss millennia-old belief systems with a scarcely discernible raising of one eyebrow. In the air I am saying the rosary with a mumbling white-knuckled fervour which even His Holiness the Pope would find a tad eerie. Soon as those wheels leave that tarmac my sangfroid deserts me and I am wearing the glaze off those beads. Being on an airplane is a thing I find profoundly scary. I'm not just talking about the bright orange skin foundation worn by air hostesses the world over. I'm talking about the actual flying. Hey, I know it doesn't make sense. I know airplane travel is safe. I know you have a statistically higher chance of being kicked to death by a donkey or battered into the next world by fundamentalist Armenian terrorists than you do of dying in an air crash, but still, this is not much consolation when you're plummeting towards the earth in a metal box travelling at eight hundred miles per hour and you haven't even had the chance to open your duty-free purchases. So what I'm saying is, usually I pray on airplanes.

But I felt relatively safe on the flight from London to Boston that day. This was because the plane was full of nuns. That was the weirdest thing about the journey over. Sixty or seventy or seventy-five nuns on the plane, all in full uniform, if that's what you call it. I mean wimples, you know, and dark grey cardigans and sandals. They were all wearing wimples, and laughing together. Wimple: it sounds like something you should be eating for breakfast, with maple syrup or melted butter poured over it, but no, it is actually the garment a nun wears on her head. And, hey, if you ever get close to a nun – and you never know, the Catholic Church is changing a lot these days – the very last thing I suggest you do is ask permission to eat her wimple first thing the following morning. Say that to Mother Teresa of Calcutta some time and see how she responds. A swift knee in the solar plexus from the world's only living saint is certainly something a person could eat out on. But anyway.

You would have sworn that the plane was coming from Lourdes, or Heaven, there were so many nuns on board. It was like a scene from *The Sound of Music* crossed with a scene from *Airplane*. There were nuns everywhere. Standing in the aisles, queuing up to get into the cockpit, queuing up to use the bathroom, they were practically strapped to the wings. I'm serious. A queue of nuns, waiting to use the bathroom. That doesn't sound off to you? Look, I'm basically an Irish Catholic, all right, and even though I'm lapsed there's some things you never get over, one of them being the sure and certain knowledge that nuns are not supposed to use the bathroom. Nuns do not have bladders. Nuns are not supposed to urinate. Or if they are, they're certainly not supposed to queue up to do so. I felt uneasy looking at them.

I felt a bit uneasy anyway. I did not really know what I was doing on this plane. I had never been to Boston before in my life and I knew absolutely nobody there. This is supposed to be one of the _____ of solitary travel – the faltering step into the unknown, the seizing of fate by the scruff of the neck and the shaking of happenstance until it falls down on the floor and whimpers for mercy – but frankly it doesn't appeal to me very much. My idea of foreign adventure is sunbathing on a Spanish beach without wearing my socks, and maybe, if I am feeling utterly reckless, having a tequila sunrise on the hotel balcony afterwards. With one of those little pink paper umbrellas in it, please.

Still, Boston was the only logical first stop on my journey across Irish America. This was the city that the Irish had made most profoundly their own, and so I had to see it. In addition, there was a Dublin in New Hampshire, a relatively short journey from Boston. This would be the first of the nine American Dublins I would visit.

But with the possible exception of a bad attack of diarrhoea or the early recorded works of Emerson, Lake and Palmer, nothing quite so efficiently saps enthusiasm and energy as long-distance air travel. Half an hour into the flight I was already bored out of my mind. I had read the in-flight magazine. I had experimented with repeatedly flashing the reading light over my seat to the extent that my section of airplane was rapidly beginning to acquire the ambience of a 1970s discotheque. I had even tried inviting my neighbour to play glove puppets with the attractive pair of woolly socks which the airline had so thoughtfully provided. (I interpreted her glacial zombie-esque stare as a polite no.)

I sat squeezed into my tourist class seat and tried to read a book, but I couldn't concentrate. This was a book I had found in a London bookshop. It was full of bizarre statistics about America. It is difficult to generalize with any accuracy about Americans, but one thing you can say without fear of contradiction is that they seem to be addicted to three things: soap operas, food additives and statistics; next to Ms Madonna Ciccone's chest their beautiful country must surely be the most thoroughly measured entity on the face of the planet. I had bought this book thinking it might somehow come in handy, but reading it now, in detail, I could see that in point of fact it would be completely useless. I mean, I suppose there was a certain fascination in knowing that in the entire United States, Florida has the highest number of boating accidents per year (1,019) and that Ohio has the lowest (168). It was fleetingly diverting to note that Wyoming has 172,852 antelopes within its proud borders, whereas Oregon has only 15,780, and poor old Arizona, with a mere 1,147, is practically antelopeless. And to read about the circumstances in which Americans had committed adultery (Casual meeting: 28 per cent; Growing friendship: 10 per cent) was admittedly thought-provoking. Twelve per cent of respondents had ticked the box marked 'Just happened/ Accident'. I sat on that plane for a good ten minutes wondering how in the name of Jayzus you could commit adultery by accident. Now, that I would like to see. That is something to which a person could sell tickets.

When I had finished leafing through the book, I watched a little of the in-flight movie. I can't remember its name now, but it had a one-word title, and it was a sequel. Perhaps it was *Bludgeon II* or possibly *Stab III*. It certainly was not *Henry IV, Part II*, that much I recall. Nevertheless it was a thoughtful and complex piece of work, involving lots of Arabs being blown up by laconic Americans with big muscles, a small vocabulary and a very limited grasp of contemporary multicultural concepts. Actually, it was a criminal waste of good celluloid and I had seen a better film on teeth. But whenever the Arabs got bombed or shot, the Americans around me cheered and made that high-pitched whooping sound that redneck imbeciles make while sodomizing sheep or enjoying country and western concerts, and as I have never been able to make that sound myself I suppose I was impressed by their enthusiasm.

All the Arabs in this film were smoking, and I smoke too. And every time another Arab whipped out a cheroot and lit up and spat on the floor and cursed Yankee imperialism and sniggered wickedly, I found that I was getting a longing to smoke, although not to do any of the other things he was doing. But despite my pleas and offered bribes to the ground staff at Dublin airport, I had been placed in the non-smoking section. I wondered what to do about this. I was not sure that I could sit through much more of this abysmal film without the aid of poisonous chemicals, and so it was that after a while I managed to tear myself away from the screen and out of my seat. I wandered down the back of the plane to see if there was a spare place in the smoking section. There was. It was beside a nun. A smoking nun. Good God almighty, my first day of travel adventure, and already I had seen sights so bizarre they would have given the famous Mr Ripley a heart attack.

Sister Marie Bernard was a very nice middle-aged woman from County Limerick. She told me that she and the other sisters were on their way to Boston to do community work in the inner city. This was something they did every year, she said, it was a bit of a holiday for the sisters. I marvelled at Sister Marie Bernard's idea of a holiday. Dodging Uzi bullets and wild-eyed crack dealers would not be everybody's idea of fun, I said, and she laughed tolerantly. It wasn't at all like that, she told me. The people in the inner city of Boston had their problems, like anyone else, but really they were wonderful, especially when you considered how badly they had always been treated. 'I don't know how they haven't had a revolution,' she said. Perhaps things would be better for them if they did have a revolution, I suggested. She looked at me with an expression which was truly and utterly saintly but simultaneously disapproving. In nun school, as every Irish Catholic knows, you are trained to do this expression in the first week.

She then asked me why I was going to Boston and I said that I wanted to write a book about all the Dublins in America. She said that this sounded like an interesting thing to do, and I replied that I hoped it would be. Sister Marie Bernard had been to one of the Dublins herself, she told me, Dublin, Georgia. She couldn't remember very much about it, except that it had been very hot, and that her husband had found the heat a little difficult to get used to. At this point I kind of wondered what to say. My knowledge of the finer points of canon law is not exactly what it might be, but one thing I did recall from my Catholic childhood was the general principle that nuns are not supposed to have husbands. I suppose my expression must have given me away. Sister Marie Bernard laughed lightly and told me that her husband had died some years ago, and that she had entered the convent then. Her husband, a teacher, had been very interested in American history and they had often gone to America for holidays. 'Massachusetts is a fascinating place', she said, because it is 'so full of history'.

Sister Marie Bernard was correct, of course. Massachusetts was a good starting point for an American journey, because in several important ways this was, after all, where the idea of modern America began. It was to Salem, just a donkey's roar down the road from Boston, that the first English Puritan settlers made their way in 1630, nobly intending to set up a Utopian city-state run exclusively on Christian principles. Things went a little downhill from there, however. Almost before the Puritans had unpacked their suitcases and found a good beach, they began to express their Christianity by tying up any teenage girl who showed too much of an interest in the local herbs and burning her at the stake for witchcraft.

Unfortunately for the Puritans, but fortunately enough for the rest of us (especially the herbalists), a society run exclusively on Christian principles was not everybody's idea of a good time. Having done all the hard work of moving to Massachusetts, robbing the Indians blind and settling the land, in time the Puritans were to see Boston become a haven for lefties, rebels, cranks, alcoholics, vegetarian troublemakers and general good-timers from all over Europe, and the region which the Holy Joes had christened, with sublime bloody nerve, New England, became a hotbed of radical revolutionary activity.

But there were consolations for the Limeys. What is sometimes called in textbooks 'the intellectual rigour of the Protestant tradition' (ho ho) took hold, and would come to leave its mark on Massachusetts for ever. In between torching virgins and stitching enormous capital A's on harlots' tits, the Puritans got around to setting up Harvard University in 1636, thus ensuring that whole generations of middle-class American teenagers, if they could not actually afford the astronomical tuition fees, could at least purchase tasteless sweat-shirts with 'Harvard University' printed on them, thinking that this made them look cool as fuck, when actually it made them look like lobotomized rejects from a Beach Boys audition.

In the nineteenth century, of course, New England became something of a literary mecca. Boston was to writers what Dublin, Ireland is now to pop stars. Melville, Poe, Hawthorne and Thoreau all strolled its elegant streets, swapping epigrams, trying to be smartasses and generally putting each other down. You were nothing in fin-de-siècle Boston if you hadn't published a novella about birth or at least a slim volume of turgid poetry written while wearing velvet trousers.

Apart from dewy-eyed dandified wordsmiths, the other big group which invaded Boston in these years comprised poor Irish immi-grants fleeing the potato famine back home. They took to Boston like Hollywood Indians to potent hooch. Throughout the terrible years of the mid nineteenth century they flooded into the city, along with Italians, Portuguese and huge numbers of liberated slaves. The outsiders were not always received hospitably by the good Christian folks who ran the city. In fact, the early decades of Irish immigration saw waves of mass protest, race hatred and violence in the city. Boston likes to pretend it is a haven of tolerance and brotherly love, but like every American city it has its bloody past. The Puritans were about as fond of the Irish as King Herod was of toddlers, and they made their feelings known as often as they possibly could.

But let us not be ungenerous. At least since the days of the Kennedy administration, modern Boston has had a reputation for progressive politics and reforming zeal. It hasn't always worked but, darn it, at least they've tried. And, hey, let's face it, any state that could actually elect Michael Dukakis governor at least has a remarkable sense of comedy. So I was glad I was going to Boston. I thought that going to Boston made sense, and Sister Marie Bernard agreed with me. The most important thing you need when you're travelling, she said, is some vague kind of idea of what you're trying to do. When she said this, I must admit, I began to get a bit of an uneasy feeling.

It was too late to stop now. The plane landed and rolled in to the terminal and the first thing I noticed when I disembarked at Boston airport was an enormous Irish flag flying over the arrivals building. I couldn't see an American flag anywhere, just this enormous green, white and orange tricolour. For one unspeakable moment, I thought the plane had been accidentally turned around in mid-flight and flown back to Ireland. If you could commit adultery by accident, after all, just about anything was possible.

We all went into the building and queued up at the immigration desk. I noticed while I waited in line that visitors who were black or brown in aspect seemed to be questioned for a much longer time than visitors who were white, tanned or pink. The immigration officer was a pleasant woman who told me she had Irish ancestors. Her great-grandfather's name was Boyle and he had emigrated to America 'when you guys had that potato famine over there'. She told me all about her great-grandfather, how he had come to Boston with only the clothes on his back, started his own construction company, lost everything, started again and died a very wealthy man. 'He never forgot Ireland,' she said, and I assured her on behalf of the nation that I was glad to hear it. 'Yes,' she said, 'he never forgot the old country.'

Officer Boyle admired my Irish passport for a while, and asked me to read out some of the Irish words printed thereupon. I tried my best to do this, and although my Irish is pretty crap, I think I managed to impress her. She told me that her parents had taught her to say the Hail Mary in Irish, which she then did, even though I could not remember having invited her to do so. *Se do bheatha, a Mhuire, a ta lan de grasta. Ta an tiarna leat* . . . It sounded odd in a Boston accent, but she was so happy saying it that I suppose I felt kind of touched. She recited the entire Hail Mary and then she asked what the purpose of my visit to the United States was, and I said vacation. She must have talked to me for a good five minutes then, telling me which museums and art galleries were worth seeing in Boston, and which bars were fun, and which were not, and which were downright dangerous, and where you could buy cheap souvenirs. Officer Boyle was clearly a good time gal. She tore a page out of her notebook and scribbled some addresses and telephone numbers on it. She was really lovely.

I collected my luggage from the baggage carousel and went outside. It was a beautiful sunny day, even though the early November air had not so much a bite in it as a viciously bloodthirsty snap. I saw Sister Marie Bernard just down the way, getting into a bus with all the other nuns. She waved at me, and I waved back. She blew me a kiss. I was glad that I had met her. I felt that she would bring me luck.

After a few moments, an enormous black taxi pulled majestically up to the rank. It was a Cadillac or a Chevrolet, one of those big mothers anyway, and I got into the back of it, sliding and slithering around the seat, and I explained to the driver that I wanted to go to Tremont Street. 'Can I go witcha?' the driver quipped. He was the size of a baby elephant and he was chewing gum and wearing mirrored sunglasses and a luminous yellow sports shirt which displayed his pendulous breasts to some effect. I did my best to perform a smile. 'I said, can I go witcha?' he repeated. Just what I needed after eight hours on a transatlantic flight beside a smoking nun. A comedian.

'So, warez ya from, bud?' he asked, as we pulled away.

'Ireland,' I said.

'Get da fuck outta here,' he laughed, 'me too. Mahoney's the name.' He pronounced it Ma-hoe-nee, the way nobody in Ireland has ever pronounced it.

'Oh really,' I said.

'No woyd of a lie,' he said, 'till the day that I fuckin die,' and he laughed then, as though what he had just said was hilarious. We drove out of the airport and he switched on the radio.

The radio was playing a chat show, and the disc jockey kept barking, 'Today, folks, what we're gonna talk about is, what makes ya happy. What makes ya happy, that's what I wanna know. What makes ya happy? Just gimme a call, right here, right now, and tell me, what makes ya happy? What tickles ya? What gives ya the yuk-yuks? Is it food? Is it sex? Is it food and sex togethah? Is it other people? Is it yaself? What is it? What makes ya happy? Call me up. Tell me. I'm waitin.' This was the first important thing I learnt about Americans on this trip. They seem to be very interested in being happy.

We came to an intersection above which was a large signpost announcing 'BOSTON: THIS WAY'. Mr Mahoney stopped his taxi and began to look thoughtful. He glanced at his watch, then at me, then at his watch again. He said that he really felt it would be better not to take the highway, because the rush-hour would be starting soon. He was aware that there didn't seem to be any traffic whatsoever just now, but when you knew Boston traffic as well as he, Mr Mahoney, did, you got to know how deceptive and sneaky the rush-hour could be, and he really felt that it would be better to 'take a little fuckin detour'. God damn my eyes for a naive sucker, but I agreed. Thus began an extensive and circuitous tour of Boston's outskirts. My first time in Boston and I had already met a dishonest Irishman. (He was probably a city councillor.) I suppose I should have been delighted with myself.

But I wasn't. 'What makes ya happy out there?' the radio kept saying. 'What makes ya happy? Come on, call up the station and tell me.'

'Ya know what makes me happy, bud?' Mr Mahoney asked.

'Tell me,' I said.

'When the fucken wife goes to her mother for the weekend,' he laughed. 'That makes me fucken delirious.'

'Does it?' I said. 'Really, Mr Mahoney?'

'Jeez, the fucken mother-in-law,' he said. 'Ya gotta meet this woman, I'll tell ya, bud. She got a face like a burgled fucken bank. The other night she fell asleep on her fucken stoop out back of her fucken house and her fucken dog buried her, you know what I'm sayin here?'

Up and down the back-alleys we sped, Mr Mahoney all the time regaling me with secondhand one-liners about the many and apparently considerable failings of his mother-in-law, and tender stories of how his grey-haired old mammy from County Donegal used to place a set of rosary beads under his pillow at night before rocking him to sleep with an Irish lullaby. It was a great pity, I soon came to feel, that she had not smothered him with the pillow instead, or strangled him with the rosary beads, but I did not say this because I thought it would not make Mr Mahoney happy. Anyway . . . there are some very interesting power stations, gigantic industrial estates and filthy rundown local authority housing projects in the suburbs around Boston, let me report, and I saw every single one.

To say the route was a little indirect would be like saying that President Ronald Reagan was not exactly a Mastermind finalist. We crawled around the edge of the city for a good hour and after a time I had the distinct sensation that we were driving in circles. Either Mr Mahoney was ripping me off or he was the kind of person who could not find his own arse in a darkroom. The guy on the radio kept screaming, 'What makes ya happy, huh? Call me! Lemme know out there, what makes ya—' When we eventually got to Tremont Street Mr Mahoney tried to charge me seventy dollars for the pleasure of his company. I told him that this certainly did not make me happy. I then told him there were two chances of me paying him seventy dollars: fucking slim, and fucking none. Next I did my level best to disabuse him of the notion that I had come down the fucking river on the last fucking canoe. Then I think I said something about his mother. He said he would call the police. I said we would go into the hotel and call them together. This seemed to calm him down. He said that he would accept fifty dollars, and after I had finished laughing and slapping my thighs I said that I would give him forty, and that he should get down on his lousy stinking knees and thank God and all the blessed saints that I was in such a good mood.

After Mr Mahoney had opened his trunk and kindly allowed me to remove my own suitcase, I ambled into the hotel, checked in at the desk and went up to my room. It was big and airy and there was a bunch of plastic exotic flowers on the windowsill. There was also a telephone on the bedside table. Now, I love hotel telephones, I don't know why. I don't think I have ever truly come to the realization that hotel telephones do not actually allow the user to make calls for free. So I stared at this telephone for a while in much the same way that a recovering dipsomaniac would stare at a quart of gin in a glass case and I wondered who I could call on it. In the end, I picked it up and dialled the Speaking Clock. Sad, but true.

After a while I realized that having a conversation with the Speaking Clock would not make me happy, and so I hung up the phone and went into the bathroom where I checked out the little plastic bottles full of shampoo, shower gel and shoe polish. There was also a strange sort of polythene bag wrapped up in a cardboard box. At first I thought it was a modern American contraceptive device, but eventually, after a good deal of quite detailed experimentation, I realized that it was actually a shower cap. I put it on my head and peered at myself in the mirror. It made me look like a depressed Martian. Then I came back into the bedroom and discovered that there was a minibar cunningly concealed in the wardrobe. This, I must say, did make me happy.

I had a large gin and tonic, and then another one, and next I put on my coat, went downstairs and strolled outside. The day was cold and crisp and fresh, and as I walked around I kind of liked what I saw. Central Boston appeared to be a pleasant place, clean as Switzerland and green as a cowboy's teeth. It seemed to be organized with intelligence, grace and charm. If Boston was a movie star, I thought, it would be Cary Grant. The place was practically wearing spats and a tux.

One interesting thing is that Boston looks like no other American city. Over the centuries it has radiated out from Boston Common, which was claimed as common land in 1634 and has stayed that way ever since. You can see everything of historical interest in a fairly

short time – which is always a good thing, in my book – because it
is all laid out around you. This is the real pleasure of Boston. It was
built long before cars began to define the shape and appearance of
modern American cities, and as a result it is a joy to walk in and an
appalling nightmare in which to drive. If you ever find yourself in
downtown Boston and have an hour to kill, just stand by the side of
the street and watch for a while. You will notice that there are
thousands of old men with long white beards driving around the
city's cruelly confusing one way system and weeping openly. Most
of them left their homes to go and vote for President Kennedy in
1959 and have never found their way back again.

I went up to the common and waited for something quirky or
interesting enough to be included in a travel book to happen to me.
Nothing did, so I thought I would fill in the time by doing a little
sightseeing. The Boston Visitor's Centre is at the north end of the
common, and this is where the famous Freedom Trail begins. As
you stand here facing up Tremont Street with the golden dome of
the State House on your left, Quincy Market and the dock are
slightly ahead of you down to the right. Behind you is Beacon Hill,
once known as 'Mount Whoredom', before being yuppified in the
late nineteenth Century. This is where Boston millionaires live now,
and it still looks every bit as forbiddingly posh as it must have when
Henry James dubbed it 'the most prestigious address in America'.

I set out to walk a bit of the Freedom Trail, which is helpfully
marked by a thick line of red brick on the sidewalk, and also by a
veritable multitude of trashy souvenir sellers and hotdog hawkers. If
you can escape from this human pondscum, the trail is a fascinating
way to pass a few hours. Charles Bulfinch's State House is really
quite an impressive pile. Nearby, Park Street Church is where the
movement began to liberate America's slaves. (Massachusetts itself
was the first state to abolish slavery, in 1793.) A statue of Benjamin
Franklin marks the site of the city's first public school, and this is
worth seeing because poor old Mr Franklin looks for all the world
like a desiccated muppet. The Old South Meeting House down the
way is where Samuel Adams addressed the patriots who were about

to attend the Boston Tea Party on 16 December 1773. (This was the occasion when a group of republican conspirators threw China tea into Boston harbour, thus provoking the British authorities to shut down the port and place the city under martial law. Touchy, touchy, huh?) The Declaration of Independence was first read from the balcony of the Old State House, built in 1712. Close by is a ring of black cobblestones, commemorating the shooting of five civilians by British soldiers on 5 March 1770. The Globe Corner Bookstore (on School and Washington Streets) stands on the site of the first *Boston Globe* offices, much frequented by Longfellow and other literary lovelies. Just down the way, the Old Granary Burying Ground, on the corner of Park Street, contains the mortal remains of Samuel Adams, John Hancock and one of the most famous Bostonians ever, Paul Revere.

The late Mr Revere was a Boston patriot and republican, a silversmith by trade, who, when he was not knocking out charm bracelets and attractive teapots, entertained an ambition to be regarded as a bit of a dashing blade. Thus, on the night of 18 April 1775, he rode out of Boston down what is now Massachusetts Avenue, racing through Cambridge and Arlington and into the pages of American history to warn the patriots gathered at Lexington of an impending British attack. Close behind him was a force of over six hundred heavily armed Crown soldiers who were, in a very real sense, open for business.

Although Revere's route has since been bizarrely turned into a series of unpleasant grey motorways, the various scenes of the first encounters of the Revolutionary War remain pretty much as they were on that mythic night. The Town Common at Lexington was where the British first realized they might have a bit of a problem on their hands. The brave and unfortunate minutemen were no match for the seriously tooled-up Limeys, however, and the minute-man statue on the common commemorates the eight Americans who died. There were no British fatalities at Lexington, but by the time they marched on Concord the next morning the locals were ready to rumble. In a bloody battle in the town itself, and through the surrounding streets, three hundred young British conscript soldiers were killed. The nearby Minuteman National Historic Park commemorates all those who died. A quarter of a mile down the road is the Hancock Clarke House Museum, where Samuel Adams and John Hancock were awakened by Paul Revere in what must have been one of the most abrupt alarm calls in modern American history.

This was all kind of nice, but I wanted to get a look at modern Boston too. So I bussed back into town and turned down a few side streets and walked on, feeling content enough now to get a bit lost. I had absolutely no idea where I was or where I was going, but before too long I ended up in Chinatown, and for some reason which I fail to understand this made me feel relatively safe. I wondered about trying not to look like a tourist – a little difficult, really, for a Caucasian in Chinatown – as I gazed in the windows of the jewellery shops and restaurants and cafés. After a while I noticed a covered market just off one of the side streets and I decided to go into that and take a look around.

The aisles of the market were very busy. Vegetable sellers were shouting from their stalls. Women were sweeping the aisles, sending great clouds of sawdust into the air. Bulging boxes of jeans and T-shirts and colourful dresses were being unloaded. There were crates of bananas and grapes and plump oranges. There were chunks of pork and long strings of sausages. Bloated wriggling fish in crates gulped at the dry air. There were black fish and red fish, crabs and shrimp, lobsters in greasy-looking tanks, scaly slimy creatures with tiny eyes and huge bulging mouths. There was an enormous frozen cube of black squid. I ambled around the stores, looking at these ghastly fish. There were things on those slabs that would have made Rod Steiger look pretty.

When I came out of the market I was feeling a little ill. I went into a Chinese café and ordered a coffee with a glass of water. The waitress said they had a special on Chinese carrot cake. I told her I didn't like carrot cake. She told me it was really nice, and that I should try it. I said I didn't want any, and she looked personally crushed. When she brought me the coffee she had another go at persuading me, and I said no again. She went back to the counter with her head hanging low. As I sat there sipping my coffee and feeling vaguely guilty I noticed that she kept staring at me. I tried to smile at her. Her upper lip seemed to quiver as she looked away.

At this point, an interesting thing happened. A young man in a bloodstained apron came out from the kitchen with a cleaver in his hand. He began to engage the waitress in conversation, in a language which I presumed was Chinese. She pointed over at me and said something and he shook his head and sighed. I do not know what they were saying, of course, but I feel almost certain that my inexplicable reluctance to eat carrot cake was at least touched upon briefly. He glared at me for several moments. Had he come one millimetre closer to me with that cleaver in his hand, I'll tell you, you would have seen me order a slab of that carrot cake and shovel it down with some considerable speed before – *mmmmm!!* – asking for more.

After a time I had enough of this. I paid my check, came out and began to stroll around again. The streets were busy now; it was after five o'clock and people were getting off work and rushing through the drizzle. Suddenly thunder boomed and the rain poured down. I ran around a corner looking for somewhere to shelter and there, just in front of me, I observed an adult cinema, with posters of naked and well endowed young individuals on the walls. Heck with it, I thought, I'm supposed to be having new experiences. I marched straight up to the ticket booth.

The woman sitting behind the desk was the size of a baby walrus. She was reading a copy of the *National Enquirer* and eating a hamburger which looked like it contained a whole calf. She had on a pink sequined blouse which could comfortably have accommodated the Moscow State Circus. I knocked on the glass. She glanced at me as though she had just woken up. I said nothing. She peered at me in bovine silence as she attractively munched lumps of her burger. People say that you are what you eat, and if there was ever living proof of that wise adage it was this woman. She practically had horns and a swishing tail. I could not see her arse from my vantage point, but it would not have surprised me greatly to find the Ponderosa Ranch brand stamped upon it.

'One ticket, please,' I said.

She pursed her lips and snuffled. She wiped her mouth with the back of her hand. 'Yooo want shorts?' she mooed.

'I don't exactly know,' I said. 'Will I need them?'

She didn't even grin. 'Yoooo want shorts or yoooo wannna feature?' she clarified. 'Theatre four is five minute shorts, other three's features.'

'What are the features?' I enquired.

'Let's take a looook,' she said, scrutinizing her notebook. 'Theatre one, *My Tits Are on Fire*. Theatre toooo, *Come with the Wind*. Theatre three is a triple bill, *Star Whores*, *Planet Domination* and *Teenage Space Nymphos Take It up the Hot Ass and Beg for More*.'

'*Up the Hot Ass*?' I clarified.

'*And Beg for Moooore*,' she assented.

'I think I'll go for the shorts,' I said.

'S'up to yoooo,' she said and wiped her face again with her right front hoof.

So it was that I paid out seven dollars and went into my first ever 'adult' cinema. The interior was small and dark and it smelt overwhelmingly of disinfectant. Exactly what that odour was trying to disguise is anybody's guess, but it seemed to me that the problem couldn't possibly have been very much worse than the solution. Up on the screen a naked blonde woman was writhing and moaning, as though in the grip of some terrible intestinal parasite. I groped around in the murk looking for somewhere to park my own hot ass, and then almost spoiled a beautiful moment by practically sitting down on a punter's knee. At least, I think it was his knee. In any case, he playfully redirected me with a helpful 'Stroll, motherfucker,' so I wandered up towards the front, found another seat and settled in to enjoy the show.

On the screen there was now a fifteen-foot-high close-up of a vagina being repeatedly penetrated with a carrot. It was quite an arresting sight. I mean, I had never actually seen a fifteen-foot vagina before. The clitoris was the size of a rugby ball, for God's sake! The colour control was turned up way too high so that the vagina was as pink as a teddy-boy's socks and the carrot was so orange that it would have made an orange look like a lemon. I burst out laughing and there was a chorus of angry 'shshshs'. I tried to watch with a straight face as the line, 'Oh yeah, baby, fuck my wet pussy with that big carrot,' was fervently repeated. I watched, my fist stuffed firmly into my mouth (which was not, I must point out, where the fist on the screen was stuffed). I was quite enthralled by what I was seeing – although after a time, I must admit, I was kind of glad I'd passed on the carrot cake earlier.

This film soon ended and was followed by another similarly artistic work. The plot lines of these films were not exactly complex, to tell you the truth. Character development, also, was rudimentary. The influence of Stanislavski was not much in evidence, and one couldn't help but feel that the principal motivation of the dramatis personae was the prospect of getting a very large cheque at the end of what I must call, perhaps unfortunately in the circumstances, 'the shoot'. Suffice it to say, these people would have made Minnie Mouse seem like Lady Macbeth for depth.

After two or three short films had been shown there was an advertisement from a civil liberties group, showing the Stars and Stripes waving softly in the background while a black man in cowboy boots and a Caucasian woman in a ripped leotard fucked the living daylights out of each other in the foreground. There was a solemn voiceover about how it was every American's right to watch material of his or her own choice and how America was the greatest society on the face of the entire planet for this reason. Poor deprived countries all over the third world, it was implied, were crying out for the right to watch vaginas being penetrated with carrots. I did find this a little difficult to take, as it were. If you were to show your average ravenous Somalian a carrot, I remember thinking, he could probably think of a lot of things to do with it, before finally rocketing to the inevitable conclusion that it ought to be repeatedly inserted into a vagina. After a while the woman on the screen began to claw her partner's back and moan, 'Oh Jesus, I'm coming, I'm coming, I'm COMMMMMMINGG,' and the words 'State Censorship: Coming Soon' flashed up on the screen. When the advertisement finished there was a round of heartfelt applause from the audience. There followed a short film about Santa Claus and the elves in his toyshop which, I must say, radically redefined the traditional yuletide myth. Certainly, when Father Christmas put on his rubber gloves, it was not to do the washing up.

People will tell you that pornography is boring, and it is. Watching other people having sex is about as interesting as watching them eat spaghetti, that is to say, very interesting for about four and a half minutes and then suddenly not very. Before long I found that I was passing the time by counting the carbuncles on the leading characters' bottoms. Also, the music in porno films is amazingly irritating, sounding exactly like the music you hear on video games, or in lifts, just not quite as good. I did my best to concentrate, but the fact that in the row in front of me I could now see that an elderly man was masturbating frenziedly, his eyes rolling, his long tongue hanging out of his dribbling gob, did not help matters much. Although I must confess, I did have to admire his stamina. He had the kind of wrist that a concert violinist would kill for.

After about half an hour of this I left the cinema and walked slowly back towards the hotel. The rain had stopped and even though the night was quite cold, the streets were still full of people. It was about eight when I strode into the lobby. For some reason everything seemed to be closed. The bar, the restaurant, the swimming pool, everything. At the end of the corridor the bell captain was energetically leaning against a wall and scratching the boils on his neck. I approached and tried to address him. It was then that I ran up against that greatest of barriers to the unwitting traveller, the Massachusetts accent.

'Do you know a good place to go for a drink?' I said.

'You waanna baa?' the bell captain said.

'What?' I said, suddenly feeling that I was being addressed by a distressed sheep in semi-human form.

'They's a first claaaass baa near Haavaad Yaad,' he said.

'Huh?'

'Haavaad Yaad. The Haavaad Yaad Baa. You can paak ya caa outside the baa,' he explained. 'In the yaad.'

'Sorry?' I said.

'It's not too faa,' he said. 'If you're going by caaaa.'

Soon, a young man in a waiter's outfit came over and began helpfully to translate what the bell captain was saying to me. Eugene (not his real name) turned out to be from Kinnegad, County Westmeath, the town in whose pleasant streets my younger sisters had deposited a veritable Everest of vomit over the years while en route to Connemara. I didn't tell him about this straight away, because I thought it might not make him happy. And I was so happy myself to encounter a hotel employee who did not have the vocal intonation of either Shari Lewis or Lambchop that I did not want to presume on his affections.

It is always an odd thing for an Irish person to meet another Irish person in a foreign country. We Irish have a reputation for being friendly to foreigners when they come to Ireland, and indeed we are. But we are not particularly friendly to each other. Put an Irishman on a spit, wrote George Bernard Shaw, and you will quickly find another one to turn him. And while things may not be quite as bad as all that, it is undeniably true that there are suburbs of Dublin and small towns in rural Ireland where the conversation dies with Wild West movie speed when a stranger walks into the pub.

Out of Ireland, however, the Irish bond like strips of velcro. It is very strange. I suppose it is a little like meeting a person who suffers from the same embarrassing skin disease as oneself. It is not that you like them necessarily, it's just that there's so much you don't have to bother explaining. Thus it was that a mere ten minutes after I had met Eugene, I found myself sashaying down Tremont Street with him, in search of a pizza and a beer.

The first establishment we tried was completely empty, except for a huddle of scar-faced and vividly dressed youths listening to rap music on a ghetto blaster, and an old man lying face down on the floor with a K Mart shopping bag on his head. I suggested we might give it a miss and Eugene nodded his agreement. We walked to the end of the street where a twenty-four-hour drugstore was open. There was a hot food counter at the back. We ordered something called a Hawaii-Five-O pizza, and parked ourselves on the steel chairs waiting for it to arrive.

While we sat there shivering under the air-conditioning machine – for some reason it was on full blast – Eugene asked me what I was doing in America. This, I told him, was a very good question indeed. I explained that I was writing a travel book about all the Dublins in the United States, and the various places in between them.

'A guidebook, is it?' Eugene said, his lips turning blue.

'Well not really,' I said, blowing on my thumbnails. 'It's, you know, travel writing.'

'What's travel writing?' Eugene said.

That was another astoundingly good question. I found myself wishing, for perhaps the first time in my life, that I was Paul Theroux. Eugene was giving me cause for some pretty serious self-analysis.

'It's where you just wander around a place,' I said, brilliantly, 'and you write down your impressions and what happens to you in a book.'

'You're fuckin joking me?' said Eugene.

'No,' I tittered nervously.

'And would people buy a book like that?' he gasped, astonished.

'This is the theory,' I said.

'Sweet mother of holy fuck,' he said. 'I might write a fuckin book like that myself one day.'

The Hawaii-Five-O pizza turned out to be a soggy lump of dough with half a gallon of coagulated tomato puree and three bluish pineapple chunks on top. It was about as tasty as eating a toilet roll. Eugene wolfed his down and suppressed an appreciative belch. He then ate half of mine.

Outside again, the wind had started to whip up, but it was a good deal warmer than it had been in the delicatessen. Scrags of newspaper danced down the street, and a garbage can overturned with a clanging sound, spilling its contents. It was all very Martin Scorsese. Eugene suggested that we proceed directly to a bar he knew. Some of his friends would be coming along later, he said, and there might be a bit of crack.

'Ha, ha,' I said. 'That's gas, isn't it? That phrase.'

'What's gas?' Eugene grinned.

'Well, when we Irish say a bit of crack they don't understand. Irish crack, like. The Americans think we mean drugs.'

'That is what I mean,' Eugene said. 'There might be a bit of crack going. Or Ecstasy.'

We strolled on in silence. 'You're not into that, no?' Eugene said.

'Ah yeah,' I lied. 'Yeah, sure. Occasionally.'

'Just say if you're not,' Eugene said. 'That's game ball.'

My voice became a shrill and shrieking falsetto, so casual did I sound. 'No sweat, daddy-oh,' I said. 'I think pot is groovy.'

'I'm only messin with you,' Eugene laughed, playfully slapping me on the shoulder. 'I don't take crack.'

'Neither do I,' I said.

'I do take E though,' he said. 'I might try to score a few later on.'

'Yeah, great,' I said. 'Whatever. Groovy. Far out. Gone.'

But I was a little nervous about this, I have to admit. My own total experience of the drug culture happened one night in college where I smoked a marijuana joint, inhaled, fell asleep and woke up ten hours later with a slight headache and an intense desire to eat an entire bowl of sugarlumps. Where in the name of Christ was Eugene leading me? In my mind's eye, I envisioned a dark, filthy, graffiti-sprayed basement full of used needles and flailing young men with hysterical giggles and mournfully fallen women called 'Sugar' in low-cut red dresses. I saw the doors being kicked in by the cops, each of whom bore a disturbing resemblance to Howard, the neo-fascist leader of the SWAT team in *Hill Street Blues*. I saw them brandishing their pistols and nightsticks and crying out, 'Freeze, you Irish dogbreath motherfucking scum.' Be assured, gentle reader, it was not a pretty sight.

I did not particularly want to spend my first night in Boston being harassed by violent lunatics and half-drunk psychopaths in the basement of the city jail. And that was just the police officers! God and his Holy Mother know what the *prisoners* might have done to me. Still, I hung in there. Travel writing, I thought, it's dirty work, baby, but I guess someone's gotta do it. Here we go, into the wide blue yonder. Damn the torpedoes. Bruce Chatwin, eat your heart out.

The bar was called something authentically Irish like the Purple Shamrock or the Neon Banshee, and it was very full. There were posters of many famous people from Irish history – Michael Collins, Eamon de Valera, Bobby Sands, Mickey Rourke – on the walls and behind the bar there was a map of the country covered in Celtic crosses, little harps and laughing leprechauns. It looked just like home, I thought. Eugene ordered a couple of beers. The barman referred to him as 'Scout', I noticed (which was also not his real name). We sat on the high stools by the bar and began to drink.

Up on the stage, a young woman with long thin blonde hair was strumming a guitar and belting out a martial Irish song. She kept waving her long hair from side to side. I had the distinct impression that the hairdo had cost her a lot of money. She clearly thought that it made her look like Cindy Crawford, whereas in point of fact it made her look like Garth from *Wayne's World*. Eugene's fingers drummed rhythmically on his beer bottle while the singer sang:

Armoured cars and tanks and guns
Came to take away our sons,
But every man will stand behind
The men behind the wire.
Through the little streets of Belfast
In the dark of early morn

British soldiers came marauding,
Wrecking little homes with scorn;
Heedless of the crying children,
Dragging fathers from their beds,
Beating sons while helpless mothers
Watch the blood pour from their heads . . .

Now isn't that just what you want to hear over your Budweiser? I always like a helpless mother or two instead of a pretzel. After what seemed like, oh, five hundred years or so the song segued into the Johnny Cash number 'Folsom Prison Blues', then into 'May the Circle Be Unbroken', and then, eerily, into 'Jimmy Crack Corn and I Don't Care'. Surely to God, I thought, it should have been 'The British Army Crack Heads and the Reverend Ian Paisley Don't Care'?

Eugene told me that he and his brother Vinny (not his real name) had come to Boston five years earlier to work on the construction sites. They had heard from a pal that there was good work to be had on the sites in Boston, but it turned out that the unions had the whole thing sewn up, and non-union men could not get work any more. So Eugene and Vinny had got jobs working for a furniture removal company instead. Neither of them had a work visa or a cherished green card. When I asked why not, Eugene said that they were impossible to get. I pointed out that it was becoming easier to get one all the time. The Irish government and Congressman Hugh Morrison had negotiated fifty thousand extra visas for Irish migrants to America. Eugene was aware of this, but he was also aware that the American government ran pretty thorough security checks on Morrison visa applicants. 'So what?' I said, and Eugene laughed softly, before indicating that his brother Vinny might have a few skeletons in the old closet. 'He's not exactly an altar boy,' he chuckled, before intimating that Vinny was unusually well suited to his new profession of furniture removing. Vinny, in fact, had garnered considerable experience in the whole area of furniture removal, in that over the years he had removed a good amount of it from its owners' homes without their prior knowledge or consent.

He then proceeded to tell me a lurid and unpleasant story the principal dramatic elements of which were Vinny, a lump hammer, a post office in rural England and a Ford Cortina getaway car which had developed camshaft trouble at a crucial moment. The bottom line was that Vinny had spent a number of years enjoying the hospitality of Her Majesty Queen Elizabeth in an English prison, and according to Eugene, his parents back in Kinnegad, County Westmeath (Mr and Mrs Not His Real Name), had never found out. They believed that the fruit of their loins had turned religious, and had taken to attending long silent spiritual retreats in country abbeys. They were pleased, in fact, when they did not hear from Vinny for months at a time, because they thought he was in an unusually intense bout of prayer. Little did they know he was actually in solitary confinement for biting a sizeable chunk out of a warden's thigh. 'He's a gas man,' Eugene laughed. 'He's a bit of a fuckin diehard, you know?'

Just as he was saying this, the door of the bar opened and everything seemed to go dark. Eugene's colourful brother came strolling in with an attractive young woman by his side. Vinny was about six foot six and his neck was a good deal thicker than his thoroughly shaven head. Even though there was practically a blizzard blowing outside, he was clad in jeans and the flimsiest of T-shirts. As he shambled over and sat down and said hello, it was clear that he was already quite drunk. He had gone for a few drinks after a session at the gym, he said. He explained to me that he had recently taken up boxing as a hobby. He was devoted to the Irish boxer Michael Caruth who had won Ireland's first gold medal for boxing at the Barcelona Olympics in 1992. 'He's a fuckin horse of a man,' Vinny asserted. 'He's not a man at all, he's a fuckin horse. He has balls the size of church bells, that Michael Caruth, don't you think?' I indicated that while I was in no position to comment from personal experience, I was nevertheless sure that this was indeed the case, yes.

A brisk toast was drunk to Michael Caruth's almost unfeasible testicular greatness, and then another, and another. The evening began to feel pleasantly soft at the edges.

Vinny's girlfriend was light and red-headed (whereas Vinny was red and light-headed). Alison (her real name) was from the north side of Dublin, and she was working in a travel agency in Cambridge, Massachusetts. She was more conversational than her sturdy beau, whose idea of the social graces seemed to be farting as loudly as possible and then bursting into quite hysterical laughter. I told her, in case she wanted to know, that I was writing a book about all the Dublins in the United States. She laughed. She said she hardly ever thought about Ireland now, and that she didn't miss it at all.

'So are you going to stay here in America for good?' I said.

'Are you tryin' to chat up my girlfriend?' Vinny snarled.

'No, no,' I laughed. 'I'm not.'

'You better fuckin well not be,' he said, 'or I'll dance yeh into the fuckin floorboards, all right?'

'Fine,' I said, 'sounds very fair to me. But really, I was just asking her if you're both going to stay in America?'

'Does Pinocchio have wooden bollocks?' Vinny replied, pausing only to belch between the syllables 'boll' and 'ocks'. Up on the stage the singer started doing her thing again.

Wrap the green flag round me, boys, to die were far more sweet
With Erin's noble emblem, boys, to be my winding sheet.
In life I loved to see it wave and follow where it led.
But now my eyes grow dim,
My hand would grasp its last bright shred.

At this stage, I have to tell you that there were several things I would have liked to wrap the shit-for-brains chanteuse in, but a green flag was not one of them. Half a ton of quick-setting concrete perhaps. She was really starting to get on my nerves. I began to wonder if she knew any songs that were not about people being shot, stabbed, bludgeoned, tortured or beaten up. Did she know anything by The Carpenters, for instance?

Just then, a middle-aged woman in jeans and a leather jacket came in to the bar selling *An Phoblacht*, the weekly journal of the militant republican movement in Ireland. She moved from table to table trying to sell the paper, but nobody bought a copy. I thought this was strange, and I asked Eugene and Vinny about it. They said they found the idea of buying *An Phoblacht* quite laughable, and that they had no time for 'all that Provo shite'. If this was the case, I asked, why did they frequent a pub where Irish rebel music was so popular?

They looked at each other and pursed their lips. 'Ah,' said Eugene, 'sure they're only songs. They don't mean shit.' Up on the stage the cretinous cackler now started to give it the full welly. Almost everybody in the bar was soon joining in. I did not join in myself. The song she was singing – 'A Nation Once Again' – has always reminded me of the kind of thing that went down really well over the schnapps in mid-1930s Berlin.

> When boyhood's fire was in my blood,
> I read of ancient freemen
> Of Greece and Rome who bravely stood
> Three hundred men and three men.
> And then I prayed I yet might see
> Our fetters rent in twain;
> And Ireland long a province be a nation once again.
> A nation once again! A nation once again!
> That Ireland long a province be a nation once again!

When she had finished, the singer announced that she was taking a short break, presumably to have a beer, adjust her lederhosen and plan her forthcoming march into Poland. Her imminent departure depressed me so much that I immediately ordered another round of drinks and told the waitress to make them doubles. Before she quit the stage the singer asked if anybody in what she rather charmingly called 'the audience' wanted to come up and sing in her absence.

Alison turned to Vinny and tugged on his sleeve. 'You sing,' she said.

'Ah fuck off,' Vinny replied, the silvery-tongued old devil.

'Sure, go on, Vinny,' she said. 'And I'll give you a blow job that'll leave you cross-eyed for a week.'

If Vinny did a mental cost-benefit equation at this point, he must have done it with remarkable dexterity, for he rocketed out of his seat at the speed of light and sloped up on to the stage. He tapped the microphone several times with his hand, and then he butted it playfully with his forehead. 'Anyone here got any Irish in them?' he bawled. A few people shouted back and clapped. 'Any of the girls want a bit more Irish in them?' he snickered. To judge from the ensuing silence, the jury was kind of out on that one. Quite undaunted, Vinny took the guitar in his hands and lightly strummed a few chords. 'Listen to this now, Joe,' Eugene said, as Vinny changed his mind about the guitar, put it back down on his lap, rested his hands on the strings and started to sing.

When all beside a vigil keep
The West's asleep, the West's asleep.
Alas, and well may Erin weep,
When Connaught lies in slumber deep.
There lake and plain smile fair and free
'Mid rocks, their guardian chivalry
Sing oh, let man learn liberty
From crashing wind and lashing sea.

Vinny's singing was something of a revelation. He had a really beautiful soft tenor voice. It was astonishing to hear such a gorgeous sound coming from such a bulky and frankly ugly body, but somehow that served to make it even more affecting. As he began the second verse, I noticed that people were beginning to put down their glasses and really listen to him.

That chainless wave and lovely land
Freedom and Nationhood demand.
Be sure, the great God never planned
For slumbering slaves a home so grand.
And, long, a brave and haughty race
Honoured and sentinelled the place.
Sing oh, not e'en their sons' disgrace
Can quite destroy their glory's trace.

By the time the third verse got under way, people were beginning to hum along with the tune. Up on the stage, Vinny closed his eyes and leaned in closer to the microphone. He lifted up his huge hands to request silence. He continued, then, singing softly, almost in a whisper. He really was a bit of a pro.

And if, when all a vigil keep,
The West's asleep, the West's asleep,
Alas, and well may Erin weep
That Connaught lies in slumber deep . . .

At this point Vinny took a deep breath and opened his mouth wide. The glasses on the table seemed to rattle as he bawled:

But hark! Some voice like thunder spake:
The West's awake! The West's awake!
Sing oh, hurrah, let England quake,
We'll watch till death for Erin's sake.

When he had finished singing there was a thunderous round of applause. Vinny sat still for a moment, strumming the guitar, then he stood up, put down the guitar, scratched his crotch and blushingly beamed at the crowd. 'Fuck yez all for a shower of sheepshaggers,' he said, and he shambled back over to us, sat down and farted again. His brother clapped him on the back. Alison kissed him so hard she looked like she was trying to suck off his lips.

'I sang that for you, petal,' Vinny said, and he put his enormous hand up the back of her shirt.

Sadly perhaps, Vinny did not get the chance to leave his hand there for long, because people started coming over to us and wanting to shake it. They told him he was wonderful and offered to buy him a drink, and any time they said anything complimentary about his voice he would blush and stare at his feet and murmur 'Ah, fuck off you big cunt,' or, 'Shut up now before I break your fucken face,' until they went away again.

'The Sperminator,' Eugene said, 'that's you, isn't it, Vinny? The fuckin Sperminator.'

'Ungh,' said Vinny. 'Fuck off you dirty bollix.' The Not His Real Names were obviously a remarkably close family.

More drinks were had. The singer came back and started doing Joni Mitchell songs. There are not many Joni Mitchell songs about low-level urban guerrilla warfare, so I began to feel a little better. We chatted for a while, Eugene, Alison and I, while Vinny, clearly exhausted by the emotional intensity of his performance, sat quietly in a corner speculatively picking his teeth, as I'm sure Maria Callas must have done whenever she finished singing *Tosca*. We had yet more drinks, and after a while Vinny and Eugene persuaded me to join them for a few 'shots', small glasses full of a noxious substance that tasted like industrial alcohol. After three or four of these the room started to look distinctly wobbly.

'What'll we do now?' Eugene said. 'Will we go on somewhere else?'

'Yeah,' Vinny chuckled, 'we could go and get Joe a fucken woman somewhere.'

I tittered nervously at this point. I certainly did not want to offend Vinny's generous and thoughtful hospitality, but for some reason or another I also did not want him procuring some pox-ridden dockside hooker for me. Eugene seemed to pick up on my nervousness.

'Ah, Boston's not a great town for the women,' Eugene said. 'Too many Protestants here.'

There followed a somewhat unreconstructed if highly spirited

discussion about the relative merits of Boston Catholics and Protestants as sexual partners. Vinny felt that Catholics were more
interesting carnally because they were more guilty about it. This
meant that if a Catholic was going to have sex at all he or she would
act in a completely depraved and lascivious manner, on the basis that
he or she was going to be sent to Hell anyway so they might as well
enjoy themselves. Protestants, on the other hand, were more logical
and pragmatic and cerebral, and were thus not as much fun in the
old sackeroo.

'But Boston's no good for all that carry on anyway,' Eugene said,
and he paused and poured another shot down his throat.

'I suppose you're right,' Vinny said.

'I am right,' Eugene said, then, 'Here, Joe, you know the last
person to get a good hard fuckin ride in Boston?'

'No,' I said. 'Who?'

'Paul Revere,' Eugene said. He had to explain it to Vinny.

The next morning I woke up quite early with a truly spectacular
hangover. My head was pounding, my skin felt too tight for my
body and my mouth felt like a diseased rat had died in it. I lay quite
still for a few moments trying to piece the night back together.
Then I held my hand up in front of my face and stared at it for a
moment. It was trembling and shaking as though attached to a
person with a bad case of rabies. This was not good. It was certainly
not making me happy. I tried to sit up. The room spun around in a
clockwise direction, then stopped and went into high speed reverse.
I lay back down again and tried to concentrate. What had happened
last night? All I could remember was saying goodbye to the others
at some point and stumbling around in the darkness while trying to
find my way back to the hotel. There had been more singing at
some point, I was sure. In fact I was positive that I could remember
singing my own version of that well known Irish ballad of peace and
reconciliation 'Up Against the Wall Yiz Black and Tan Bastards',
but I could not recall where, or to whom. With a sense of dull

horror I suddenly realized that I was still wearing the clothes I had put on yesterday morning in Dublin. I sat up again and looked at the spinning room. Next time it spun in my direction I decided I was going to jump.

I landed on the floor, bucking and weaving like a superannuated rodeo stallion and staggered into the bathroom where I stripped off and took a shower, without even using the thoughtfully provided shower cap. Under the hot water my flesh felt like it was being flayed off me. I got out of the shower, slithered around the floor and went back into the bedroom to get dressed.

When I put my hand on the television to turn it on I got a bracing electric shock. I hopped up and down, cursing and profaning and moaning in pain. It wasn't that sore exactly, but it was just so predictable. For some reason, I always get electric shocks in America. I don't know why this is, but it always happens. I put my hand on an elevator panel or a radio or even a car door and I get a blast of electricity up my spine. This never happens to me in any other country. But in America, whatever part of my body that should be earthing me just fails to operate as soon as I bloody touch down. It is all very annoying.

When I went downstairs for breakfast I found Eugene already hard at work in the dining room, flapping from table to table like a demented, almost extinct and certainly flightless bat. He looked like downtown Sarajevo on legs, but he was clearly determined to keep going. I ordered breakfast from him, and he told me that after I had gone home, he, Alison and Vinny had bought some Ecstasy pills and gone to a nightclub, where Vinny had tried to start a fight with a Norwegian anthropology student before falling asleep in the rest room. I told him I was sure I had done some singing at some point in the night, but he shook his head and said it must have been after I had left them.

Eugene poured me a cup of coffee and got me a newspaper. The muscles in my hands practically went into spasm as I tried to read, but I really thought that if I couldn't even read a bloody newspaper there was not much point in going on with the trip at all. I held it up in front of my face and tried to focus on one of the articles. It was a long piece about The Beatles, pointing out that former member Pete Best was now working in a career guidance office in Liverpool. Fuck me pink, I thought. Imagine taking career advice from Pete Best.

The American breakfast is a thing of beauty and a joy for ever. From time to time Europeans look down on America as an uncivilized and barbarian society, but as far as I'm concerned any country where you can have potatoes for breakfast can not be all bad. The breakfast in this hotel exceeded even my wildest expectations. The plate, when it arrived, looked like part of a travelling exhibition on what you should avoid eating if you don't want to develop a heart condition. The sheer amount of dead meat on that plate would have given Linda McCartney a terminal emotional breakdown. It took me a solid twenty minutes of hard work to do any kind of damage to the breakfast, and when Eugene finally took it away, cursing me for a big girl's blouse, there was still enough food on it to keep Oprah Winfrey going for a week. I staggered out into the day, clutching my stomach and moaning lightly.

Boston Common at seven in the morning was almost absurdly beautiful. A heavy frost had settled in the night, and the bright sun was coaxing steam from the grass. Squirrels were skipping around the trees, trying their best to look cute. They were wasting their efforts on me, however. I'm afraid I am of the opinion that squirrels are basically nimble rats who should be hollowed out and turned into children's slippers. I walked around the common and looked at all the statues of the revolutionary heroes who had founded the American republic. It struck me that there wasn't one Irish person there.

This was odd. Strolling the streets of Boston you are constantly reminded that it is still what it has been for centuries, the most Irish city in America. You see icons and images of Ireland everywhere. There are shamrocks and harps on the street signs, Irish tricolour flags at every turn, the avenues and squares have Irish names. Perhaps most movingly, there are plaques in memory of the many Irish police officers who have met violent death on the streets of the city their fathers and mothers had made their own.

I wandered up to the City Hall and reclined on the steps smoking a cigarette and staring up at that impressive façade. It seemed to have the word 'power' written all over it. I sat by myself, enjoying the early morning stillness of Boston, and reflecting on all the notorious Irish politicians who had worked in that building over the years.

As the Irish began to flood into the city in the middle years of the nineteenth century, they were not long in establishing a firm foothold. They took over the police force, state government, small-scale manufacturing and local business with truly remarkable speed. It is extraordinary to note, for example, that the worst year of the Irish famine was 1848, and that the first Irish mayor of Boston was elected a mere thirty-eight years later, in 1886.

William Shannon's *The American Irish* points out that for the early Irish immigrants, Boston proved to be quite unique. They began to arrive in large numbers in the 1840s and for decades afterwards were the only sizeable and homogenous ethnic minority in the entire city. Later in the century migrants came from all over Europe, but for a good forty years the Irish had Boston almost to themselves. The fact that they spoke English as a first language gave them an enormous advantage over other migrant groups, as did their extraordinary talent for political sharp practice and outright corruption.

The Catholic Irish in Boston quickly came almost to outnumber even the Protestant Brahmins. This put their leaders in the happy position of being able to behave more or less as they liked. But the sheer size of the Irish community must have made Boston politics more aggressive and corrupt. In other American cities, political distinctions were blurred and pragmatic compromise was not only possible but necessary. In Boston, such distinctions were always crystal clear. The sectarian warfare which characterized the city's political life took place between the Irish and the native Yankees. Nobody else even got to play the game.

Another important factor in making the Irish–Yankee struggle so pointed was that Boston – compared to New York, say, or Chicago – was an old city with a well established ruling elite. The poor old Yankees had produced most of the revolutionary leaders and literary giants of Boston society, but it was relatively easy for the immigrants to blame them for all of Boston's many undeniable ills.

The baleful role of the Boston Catholic Church was another important factor in keeping Irish-Yankee divisions so sharp, and no single individual did more to make the tension worse than William Cardinal O'Connell. O'Connell was born in 1859, the last of eleven children, to a lower-middle-class family of Boston Irish immigrants. He was a bright kid, who won scholarships and came up through the ranks of the priesthood at breakneck speed. He could have used his influence to foster reconciliation between the two communities, but he was an uptight old wanker who had pretty strong views on the subject of Irish assimilation. These he expressed in a fiery sermon style which would have made Savonarola seem like a bit of a wuss.

He regularly lambasted those Irish immigrants who had decided to play down their national identities, their Catholic religion and, sometimes, even their Irish names in an attempt to make economic progress in Boston. '[They] went over body and soul to the enemy,' he ranted, 'and sold their glorious inheritance for a mess of pottage. No sooner had they taken their places among the Protestants than they were given places which as Catholics they would never have obtained. And so some of the Murphys became Murfies . . . Delaneys became Delanos. But, be it said to the credit of the Catholics of those times, such betrayal and treason were stamped as ignominious and detestable.'

Father O'Connell had begun his priestly career working with the very poorest of the city's poor Irish, and he seems at one point to have been pretty liberal in his views on social justice. But time and the prospect of promotion changed what we might euphemistically call his mind, and by the turn of the century he was, to put it mildly, a goose-stepper.

When he was made archbishop of his home town in 1907, he

finally dropped his working-class parishioners, moved into an exceptionally vulgar palace and started hanging out at dinner parties and literary soirees with any local wasp bigwig who would bother sending him an invitation. Four years later he became a cardinal. He was now one of the most powerful men in the entire American Catholic Church.

He turned his back on the socially progressive doctrines with which the papacy was then flirting. From the comfort of his palace he lectured the poor on the evils of trade unionism, vice, drink and pornography. He used his power to have many books banned. He established a system of theatrical censorship which would have gladdened the heart of any self-respecting Ayatollah. Basically, he made the Irish the laughing stock of the Yankees, and Boston the laughing stock of liberal America. In the years when Boston Irish society should have been opening up and becoming more tolerant, it was actually narrowing in on itself, becoming meaner and more insular and more nasty, in more or less direct relationship to the inexorable increase in O'Connell's political power.

From time to time political leaders sprang up who tried to bridge what was now a very wide gap between the Irish and the Brahmins. John 'Honey Fitz' Fitzgerald was the most famous of these. He was narrowly elected as mayor of Boston in 1909 and set out to court the establishment, who always had a scarcely concealed contempt for him. Fitzgerald was a thoroughly decent fellow who genuinely believed in the multicultural ideal of America, but the bankers of Boston resisted his every attempt to better the lives of the city's poor and regarded him as an ignorant malleable fool. It was a bad tactical mistake to try to isolate and ignore him. For under Fitzgerald's troubled reign, a new generation of hard-nosed Irish politicans began slowly to grow up in Boston. The time was soon to come when the Brahmins would look back on the days of Honey Fitz with something approaching tender nostalgia.

James Michael Curley was born in a tenement on 20 November 1874. He grew up on the back streets of Boston and, apart from a few years of grade school, received no formal education whatsoever.

At the age of seventeen he took the city's civil service examination and passed. He wanted to be a civil servant, he once wrote, 'because I was lured by the prospect of retiring at the end of twenty years'.

But Curley's ambitions were to take him beyond the clerk's office. He was a tall and strikingly handsome fellow, a passionate speaker with a ferocious temper. He was possessed of the two great traditional skills of Boston Irish politicians, a genuine sympathy for the poor and a mind-blowing talent for corruption and threats.

When Curley entered the wacky world of Boston politics, it was an era when leaders regularly hired thugs to smash up rival meetings, and where the notion of a citizen voting only once in an election would have been openly scorned. The great man's memoirs are full of wistfully recalled incidents from his eventful early career. The following is not a desciption of a pub brawl, but of a selection committee meeting: 'Several times that night flying wedges of rowdies tried to crash our lines but we plugged them as they came in. John [Curley's brother] suffered a broken jaw and my cohorts and I myself took a pounding.' (Readers who are members of the British Conservative Party will find the scene familiar.)

The experience of losing his first city council election did not make Curley happy. Indeed, it was so crushing to his inner child that he resolved never to let it happen again. He was elected next time around, and for the rest of his political life – a period of some fifty years – was a huge and indomitable force in the city's political scene.

Curley was one of the first in a long line of ruthlessly clientelist Irish-American politicians. He ran a political club from where he conducted naturalization lessons, found jobs for his constituents and interceded with the police on their behalf whenever necessary. From time to time he took his frantic desire to cultivate votes a little too far. On one memorable occasion he was caught taking a civil service postal delivery examination on behalf of an illiterate Irish constituent and was promptly arrested and jailed. Paradoxically, this did his career an enormous amount of good. While still in the slammer, Curley's fame spread through the Boston Irish community and he was immediately elected to the Board of Aldermen. In later years, to many cynical observers it seemed that big Jim had actually arranged his arrest as a brilliantly contrived stunt.

On his release from jail, some of his fellow aldermen who had less imaginative approaches to helping out unemployed constituents attempted to have his election declared void. Curley's rambunctious autobiography (as quoted in Shannon's *The American Irish*) describes in gleeful detail how he dealt with this minor difficulty:

It was relatively warm for a January day, and the large window behind the presiding officer's chair was open. I took the first seat nearest Whelton [President of the Board of Aldermen] in the council chambers, and just before the meeting started stepped up to him and said: 'I understand that you propose to move that my seat be declared vacant.'

'Yes,' he said, 'I do.'

'Well,' I answered, 'I just want to inform you that if you proceed with such a motion, you will go through that window.' The window was on the second floor, and he apparently realized it would be a rather uncomfortable landing on the hard surface below. He glared at me, rapped for order and proceeded with the business of the day without making any reference to me.

Curley was a tough guy from the back streets, and the Boston Irish knew it, and loved him for it. He had no time for the gentility and moderation of the appeasing Honey Fitz. He regularly and openly derided his enemies as 'chowderheads', 'insolent, arrogant sharpies' and 'complete Goddam imbeciles'. 'You're nothing but a pack of second-storey workers, milk-bottle robbers and doormat thieves,' he once roared at a group of hecklers. 'I'll be elected mayor of Boston and you don't like it. Here I am. Does any one of you bums want to step up here and make anything of it?'

He slandered his opponents, openly spreading rumours that they were adulterers, wife-beaters, alcoholics or – his favourite insult – secret Protestants. In the 1921 mayoral campaign his opponent was

John R. Murphy, one of the most respected and genial old duffers in the Boston Irish community. Curley described him as 'an old mustard plaster that has been stuck on the back of the people for fifty years'. When this provoked uproar and condemnation, he began a quite libellous campaign undermining Murphy's well-known religious devotion. 'The counterman at Thompson's Spa told me Murphy ordered a roast beef sandwich last Friday,' he told a journalist. (Friday is a day of religious observation for Roman Catholics, when meat may not be eaten.) Curley was later forced to apologize for this terrible slur, but the damage to his hapless opponent had already been done. Curley was elected with a huge majority, and the unfortunate Mr Murphy disappeared from the Boston political scene for ever.

It is unlikely that the Boston Irish believed all of Curley's outrageous lies and cunning distortions, but they respected and admired him anyway. He fought hard and dirty, and in a world full of sharks, they were sensible enough to see that they needed a barracuda. They elected him to congress and then made him mayor. Weary of being seen as some lesser form of animal life, they wanted a leader who would hit back hard. But they also loved Curley for his frequently expressed and curiously sentimental affection for Boston's poor. (Once again I am indebted to William V. Shannon for uncovering the following typical quote.)

'My mother was obliged to work as a scrubwoman toiling nights in office buildings,' [Curley] once told an interviewer, 'and I thought of her one night while leaving City Hall during my first term as mayor. I told the scrubwomen cleaning the corridors to get up. "The only time a woman should go down on her knees is when she is praying to Almighty God," I said. Next morning I ordered long-handled mops and issued an order that scrubwomen were never again to get down on their knees in City Hall.'

It was not only the Irish scrubwomen and the mopmakers who did well under Curley's colourful administration. He spent a fortune on building hospitals, parks and schools, and, to the utter despair of the city's large Italian and Portuguese communities, would use only

Irish firms on city projects. He loathed Boston's Protestant establishment and never missed a chance to mock its leaders. 'The Irish had letters and learning, culture and civilization when the ancestors of the Puritans were savages running half-naked through the forests of Britain,' he said. When asked by a reporter to comment on the merits of a Republican opponent, Mr Endicott Peabody Saltonstall, Curley famously quipped, 'What? All three of them?' In company he often boasted that although Harvard had accepted his eldest son, he had ripped up the letter and burnt it and instead sent the boy to Holy Cross College, a Massachusetts university run by the Jesuits.

In his personal bearing, Curley had the kind of flamboyant style always loved by the poorest of the immigrant Irish. He never lost their affections, even though his own lifestyle was so wildly different from theirs. Surviving photographs show what looks like a member of the early Roxy Music, in fabulous suits, outlandish hats and garish ties. Curley boasted that his largest expense in any political campaign was on clothes. It was as though he lived out vicariously his constituents' fantasies of the American dream. When Harvard eventually tried to deal with him by inviting him to be guest of honour at its tercentenary bash, he turned up with a brass band, a fleet of bodyguards and a huge team of aides dressed in eighteenth-century military-style uniforms. All the way through the ceremony, Curley sat down the back, puffing on a cigar and chattering loudly to anybody who would listen to him.

He built himself an obscenely large mansion, full of imported Irish crystal and opulent furniture, with enormous shamrocks carved into the window shutters, and somehow survived an extensive city investigation into how exactly, as a full time professional politician, he had acquired the greenbacks to do this. I am sorry to have to tell you that there were even allegations that he had taken the occasional bribe!

Still, in between making himself very rich and rigorously promoting his spectacularly talentless sidekicks, Curley did somehow find the time to put through an enormous amount of progressive legislation. Under his reign, state employees – most of whom were the sons or daughters of the poor Irish – received a forty-eight-hour maximum working week. The widely hated system of attachment of wages for debt was made illegal, the eligibility for old-age pensions was reduced to sixty-five and tens of thousands of houses were built for the city's poor. He gave the firemen and police officers more time off, and insisted that labourers be paid for days of inclement weather. He was absolutely ruthless in his courting of the Irish vote, but, to be fair to his memory, he was not afraid to stand up to even his constituents on the rare occasions when he suffered an attack of genuine principle. He risked ostracization by many of his own racist supporters when he appointed the first black doctor to the staff of the city hospital and joined the National Association for the Advancement of Colored People.

When he finally made the Boston Protestants extraordinarily happy by dropping down dead in 1958, the city's Irish were amazed to find that Curley was almost completely broke. His estate did not even have enough money to pay off the many charitable and trade union bequests he had made in his will. It must have seemed to many as though James Michael Curley was still trying to buy votes from beyond the grave. He left a trail of Byzantine corruption behind him, but he had brought the Irish to overwhelming power in the city that had once despised them. He was condemned as a crook, a hypocrite and a liar by the conservative newspapers, but his funeral was absolutely enormous. Many of the mourners were poorly dressed, one contemporary observer sneered. They seemed to be dressed like scrubwomen.

CHAPTER 2

Irish Spring

I went up to [a prospective employer] with my hat in my hand, as humble as any Irishman, and asked him if he wanted a person of my description. 'Put on yr hat,' said he, 'we are all a free people here, we all enjoy freedom and privileges.' He hesitated a little and said, 'I believe I do' . . . and we closed our bargain.

Letter from James Richey,
Irish immigrant, early 1800s

I have met with so much deception since we landed on the shores of the New World that I am fearful of trusting anyone.

Letter from Francis Rankin,
Irish immigrant, May 1848

The morning after my night out with Vinny and Eugene I was wandering around the centre of town, trying to get rid of my hangover, when I noticed something strange in a drugstore window. There in the middle of a tasteful display of perfume, foot odour remover and anal wart cream was a large poster for an anti-perspirant product called 'Irish Spring'. I stopped and stared at this for some time. I wondered what James Michael Curley would have made of it. It seemed ironic, finding two hundred years of the Irish-American immigrant experience distilled into an anti-perspirant. I went into the store and sniffed it. It was quite something. Whatever it smelt like, it certainly wasn't an Irish spring. I mean, I know what an Irish spring smells like, and believe me, it's not something you'd want your armpits to smell like too. But I bought some anyway. One thing any self-respecting travel writer needs is a potent anti-perspirant.

I went back to my hotel room and packed my bag. I wanted to catch the bus to Keane, the nearest big town to Dublin, New Hampshire, and although I had got up very early that morning when I looked at my watch now I could see that I was running late. I called a taxi, rushed downstairs and tried to check out of the hotel. An easy enough thing to do, you would think. But you would be wrong, oh, so wrong.

The woman behind the desk was so good at her job that she practically drove me crazy. When I told her I wanted to pay my bill and leave, she printed out the check and went into what felt like a ten-minute spiel while I desperately tried to persuade her to take the credit card receipt from me. 'We sure hope you have a very nice time here with us,' she said. 'Quality, service and value are our aims here, and we hope you will agree with us that we have reached them. We'd like to bring our frequent guest package to your attention. May I give you a brochure? Thank you. You'll find a membership application with two hundred complimentary bonus points on the back. Also, if you tell a friend about us we'll send you by immediate mail a most attractive gift . . .'

When I finally managed to get away from her and out into the street my taxi driver had left, taking his taxi with him. I sprinted back inside, rang the bell on the desk and got another really BIG electric shock. I hopped around, whimpering like an anxious puppy, while the receptionist tried to call me another taxi.

Ten minutes went by with no sign of the taxi. I began to get really worried. I did not want to miss this bus, because I had been told there wasn't another one for several days. I told the receptionist to cancel the taxi. I hauled my bag back out into the daylight and began to run through the streets of Boston.

Now, I have not actually run anywhere for a period of some time. In 1985 I was staying at Annaghmakerrig, a writers' colony in County Monaghan, Ireland. One Sunday morning a number of promising young Irish painters and novelists had organized a soccer match. At a crucial point in the proceedings I had been sent somersaulting over a grassy verge, the major moments of my life flashing before me in rather lurid colour until I landed on the gravel car park below. All I remember next is the sound of the talented writer Colm Tóibín laughing his heart out at me.

Mr Tóibín later restored himself in my affections by driving me to a hospital where the doctor told me that I had broken my ankle in three places. About a week after this, I began to get the nagging suspicion that my ankle was not healing properly. It was the little things, really. The way I kept waking up in the middle of the night screaming in abject agony, for instance. I had to go back to hospital and my ankle had to be broken again and reset. The point is, my left ankle contains more steel and screws than the Golden Gate Bridge and as a result I can't run. And that morning in Boston, I was running.

I arrived at the Amtrak terminal, gasping, sweating and wheezing, my ankle throbbing with pain, and I dragged myself up to the counter. The young woman on duty there peered at me for a moment before she started to speak. She had obviously been on the same training course as the woman in the hotel.

'Good morning, sir, and welcome to Amtrak. My name is Suki and I am here to assist you with any enquiries you—?'

Somehow I managed to interrupt her and gasp that she could best assist me by shutting her fat face and selling me a ticket for the bus to Keane, New Hampshire. She nodded and smiled and said that the bus counter was at the other end of the station. I turned and limped back the way I had come, looking for all the world like Richard III with a rucksack.

Some cretinous student type was up at the counter trying to save himself fifty cents by going to New York in a mindbendingly circuitous route. 'Well, how would it be if I went via Springfield, Massachusetts and changed to the interstate bus and came down through Albany as opposed to . . .'

Ten minutes later the specky git departed clutching an armful of timetables and maps. I hopped up to the counter and tried to get in the first word, but I made the fatal mistake of drawing breath. The assistant was straight into the conversational gap like a rat up a drainpipe.

'Good morning, sir. My name is Julian, and I'll be serving you today. How—'

'Never mind about that, sweets,' I said. 'Gimme a ticket for Keane.'

He looked at his watch, then at me. He raised his eyebrows like a scolding dad in a 1950s US sitcom.

'Cutting it a bit fine today, aren't we, sir?'

'Ugh, ugh,' I panted. 'We've been here for five minutes actually.'

He shook his head. 'We here at Amtrak have a policy of requesting customers to turn up ten minutes in advance of any journey. Any failure to do so will result in—'

I grasped his hand. 'Please,' I said. 'Please, Julian?'

'I just can't do that, sir,' he said. 'You're too late.'

I gaped at him. My ankle was so sore now that there were tears in my eyes. I decided to let them come. 'My grandmother's dead, Julian,' I blubbed. 'Her funeral is this afternoon in Keane. You don't understand. I've flown all the way from Ireland to be here in time for her funeral. It'll just break my grandfather's heart in two if I'm not there. And I mean, Jesus fucking Christ, the man only has one leg!'

Julian's lip trembled. 'Oh I'm so sorry, sir,' he said. He glanced over his shoulder, sniffing. 'I suppose we can make an exception in the circumstances.'

He handed me the ticket and I threw a bundle of banknotes at him. As I cantered down the stairs at top speed I could see the bus start up and begin to pull away towards the gates.

'STOP,' I called. 'Please, stop!'

The doors opened with a dull farting sound. The driver peered down at me. He was a pleasant-looking man with a fat jolly face. 'Howdy-doody,' he beamed. 'Ya comin for a ride today?'

I clambered up the steps, showed him my ticket and staggered down the aisle, being thrown from side to side as the bus swerved and screeched out of the station. The only seat I could find was down the very back, beside the toilet. The hinge on the toilet door was broken, so that the door kept opening and closing, releasing a pungently nauseating aroma of stale human waste into my airstream before slamming closed again with a noise like a cannon going off. The seat beside me contained a young couple who were kissing and hugging and calling each other 'funny bunny'. I wasn't sure whether the toilet or the couple was more sickening.

We left Boston, passing through Cambridge and Belmont on the way. At Lincoln, we crossed over Interstate 95 which circles the city, passing the Minuteman Park. We pulled on to Highway 2 for West Concord and West Acton, crossed Blue Star Highway 495 and cruised along to Fort Devens. I was shattered with tiredness and my ankle was killing me. I tried to sleep. I felt that there had to be one physical position suitable to sleeping in this straitened circumstance, but try as I might, I could not find it. I contorted my body with more imagination than even the actors in the porn films I had seen the day before, but no matter what I did, I felt awful. I tried curling up like a foetus, my knees drawn up to my chest and my arms wrapped hard around my ankles. Didn't work. I tried sitting up straight, arms folded, leaning my head against the window. I tried lying on my back with my legs dangling out into the aisle. Eventually I fell into a coma. I had the flickering intermittent dreams of the totally hungover, lights flashing at me in darkened rooms, seeeing myself fall off cliffs, watching shapely young mini-skirted women from Dublin, Texas twirling batons on O'Connell Street. You know the kind of thing.

When I woke up I had an erection, my mouth was dry and salty, my head was pounding and I had lost all feeling in both my feet. We were passing through a town called Fitchburg. I tried to stand up but the pins and needles in my legs became suddenly worse and I fell back into the seat. The snogging couple turned and snickered at me, before resuming the process of wearing several inches off each other's faces.

We turned north on to Highway 12 and drove on, passing

through a nice little town called Ashburnham. At Wichendon we crossed the Massachusetts–New Hampshire border and shortly afterwards we stopped for a few minutes to pick up more passengers. A fat woman with appalling halitosis had slid into the seat beside me, so that I couldn't even lie down, except on her lap, which I really didn't want to do. We drove on through Fitzwilliam and Bowkerville, where the slopes of Little Mount Monadnock rose out of a vast and gorgeous dark green swathe of pine forest.

We stopped again at a little town called Troy, and I got off the bus for a cigarette. It was a very still morning, and the town seemed quiet. The weather was nondescript, neither exactly winter nor exactly spring. I strolled around the back of the bus and noticed that we were parked by a large graveyard. The graveyard looked amazing, because small Stars and Stripes had been placed on many of the graves. When I asked a young woman passenger why this was, she said that today was Veteran's Day, and that the placing of flags was 'kind of a tradition'. I don't go in for flag-waving much myself, but it was an affecting sight, I must say.

I walked down the main street for a while and saw a green sheet of ice on a pond. Blackbirds swept through the treetops. Ice frosted the roofs of the neat wooden barns. All the doors of the houses were hung with corn cobs for Thanksgiving and pumpkin heads for Hallowe'en. Here and there, holly wreaths had already been put up on the doors for Christmas. If you ever go to New England in late November, you will see far more vegetation hanging on doors than you will see attached to trees.

Everything in Troy seemed to be made of wood. There were wooden houses, with wooden roofs, wooden windowframes, wooden gates, wooden chimneys, wooden sheds attached. It occurred to me that a person could have a lot of fun with a good-size flamethrower in Troy. I hobbled back up to the bus and got on. We arrived in Keane half an hour later.

I was surprised by my first sight of the town. Country towns in Ireland usually have one main street. There might be a few pubs and shops, a church, a little hotel in a little square. But as we drove into Keane I had the impression that it was really quite big. I couldn't figure this out. Keane, which barely figured on my map, seemed to be a sprawling and lively place. But then I thought about it a bit more and I realized that Keane was probably pretty typical. The thing is, once you get out of American cities there is no shortage of building space, with the result that American country towns, like the people who live in them, tend to grow outwards, and not up.

I got off the bus and looked around for a hotel. I couldn't find one anywhere on the main street. I hobbled back down towards the bus station and wondered what to do. I stopped a pleasant-looking man who was pushing a pram and asked where I could find somewhere to stay. From the style of his directions – 'down there two miles, turn left, take the highway four and a half miles' – it was clear that he had assumed I was driving. I told him I had no car.

His eyes widened. 'You don't have a car?' he gasped. 'How'd you get here?' I told him I had got the bus from Boston and that I wanted to visit Dublin. He gaped at me as though I was some troglodytic life-form recently escaped from a travelling freakshow. 'You're gonna need a car to go to Dublin,' he said. 'Matter of fact, once you get out of the town, there's not too much you can do round here without a car.' He scratched his head for a few moments and finally he said he thought there was a cheap hotel near the motorway junction.

'Is it in walking distance?' I asked.

'Everything is in walking distance in Keane.' He grinned. 'It's maybe ten minutes.'

I set off, limping and hobbling, and about an hour later I came to the motorway junction the man had told me about. I couldn't see a hotel anywhere. My ankle now felt as though Satan himself was sawing at it with a blunt steak-knife. I looked around, feeling desperate. There was a gas station a few hundred yards down the edge of the highway, so I decided to make for there.

The guy behind the desk had crooked teeth and a greasy beard.

He was wearing a Guns N' Roses T-shirt and a John Deere baseball cap, and I am sorry to have to tell you that he smelt, overpoweringly, of stale semen.

'You don't know a hotel around here, do you?' I said, trying not to inhale through my nostrils.

'Sure do,' he said.

I waited. No further information seemed to be forthcoming.

'Could you tell me where it is?' I said.

'Sure could,' he said.

'Will you, then,' I said, 'please.'

'Sure will,' he said.

'Will you now,' I said.

He laughed so hard that a little ball of snot came shooting out of his aquiline nose with the force and velocity of a thermonuclear missile. It missed my hand by a few inches.

'Why it's just across the street there,' he said, picking up the snot and wiping it on his T-shirt.

Now, there is a funny thing about New Englanders. They don't exaggerate. They understate, pathologically. Just a ten-minute walk, to a New Englander, means just an hour's hike over rough country. And just across the street, to a New Englander, means just across that quarter-of-a-mile wide, incredibly busy, eight-line interstate highway that was never designed for pedestrians to cross it.

It took a good twenty minutes to get across the motorway and I hobbled into the motel like a man in a desert staggering into an oasis. The first thing that happened, as I put my hand down on the counter, was a really zinging stinging electric shock.

'How are you today, sir?' the girl said, as I clamped my hand into my armpit and chewed my lip.

'I've been better,' I confided.

She looked deeply surprised that I had not said 'fine'. She glared at me for some time before deciding to plunge into the labyrinthine depths of an opinion, something which had clearly not come into any branch of her training.

'I'm real sorry to hear that,' she said, and smiled.

'Don't worry about it,' I told her, and I had the distinct feeling she wouldn't.

'Would you like a room tonight?' she asked, and I sighed and said yes, I would. 'Just tonight?' she enquired, and I stopped to think. The thing is, I was in a bad mood now. I was feeling guilty. You see, I had originally planned to spend at least a night in each American Dublin – not in a hotel in a neighbouring town, but in the actual Dublin itself – but it had become obvious to me that afternoon on the bus that this would not be possible. My ankle was beginning to swell up, and I knew that soon it would be the size of a grapefruit. Having made it as far as Keane, I was in no state to begin dealing straight away with the difficult business of transporting myself to Dublin. If I didn't lie down soon, I would spontaneously combust.

I told the woman behind the counter that I would want a room for one night, but I asked her if she could do me a favour and look up the number of a hotel in Dublin for me. What she said next cheered me up enormously. There was no hotel in Dublin. She was almost sure about this. I was so relieved not to have gone hopping out to Dublin in the name of professional dedication that I practically went down on my knees and said the rosary. I asked her to check, and she very kindly looked through a list of every hotel, motel, bed and breakfast joint, inn, flophouse, dosshouse and campsite in the greater New Hampshire area. Not one premises in Dublin was listed. 'Shirley,' she called to her colleague, 'this gentleman wants a hotel in Dublin. You know one?'

Shirley laughed long and loud. 'There's no hotel out there in Dublin,' she chortled. 'There's nothing at all out there, darling. You'd be just as well off to stay here with us.'

Shirley and her colleague apologized at some length for Dublin's apparently complete failure to cater for its tourists. But they needn't have. They had released me from a terrible burden. The truth was, I could have kissed them both. And if the opportunity ever came up to do so, I resolved, I would seize it with both hands and never let it go. But, sadly, it wasn't that kind of hotel.

Next morning I woke up early, feeling much better. I ate a bowl of really cold strawberries for breakfast, and reader, if you have never done this, believe me, you should. It is without a doubt the second best way in the world to wake yourself up. Outside the hotel the taxi was already waiting for me when I emerged. We drove east from Keane on Highway 101, through Marlboro and past Chesham. All the signposts for the local towns sounded like English lords or Oscar Wilde characters. Antrim, Peterborough, Chesham, Harrisville, Walpole, Chesterfield. I noticed an amazing number of antique shops along the roadside, all full of stuffed animals, lamps made out of wine bottles, and bad paintings of violins. We bounced along the rough country road and eventually arrived in Dublin.

'This is it,' the driver said.

'This is what,' I said, 'the main street?'

'This is Dublin,' he said. 'What you see is what you get.'

I got out of the car and looked around. In the middle of the street was a dark green signboard, which announced: 'Dublin, New Hampshire: Originally Monadnock No. 3. Highest village in New England, according to United States survey – 1493 feet above sea-level. The greater part of Monadnock Mt. lies within the town, which received its charter from King George the Third, in 1771.'

I looked around again. I had travelled three and a half thousand miles to get here, and I have to confess I wasn't initially certain that it had been a good idea. Dublin, New Hampshire turned out to be an almost nauseatingly pretty little village, and looking at it for the first time I was reminded of something I had read in my motel room the night before, my aching foot sunk into an ice bucket, about how the New England landscape had been influenced almost as much by literature as it was by nature. Towns in the rest of America had more or less just happened. A gang of bedraggled farmers would show up, find a river, build a few shacks, and pick a name out of a hat. But it had always been different in New England, probably the most self-consciously designed region in the entire union. The early settlers brought with them and circulated vividly detailed descriptions of villages back home in rural England, which came to be slavishly copied by the early New England townbuilders. Thus, in no time at all, your average New England town began to look like it had come out of a self-assembly catalogue. Indeed, early literary texts from New England are full of these weirdly precise descriptions of towns, which owe far more to a nostalgic and essentially conservative fantasy of England than they do to a pragmatic American reality. Here is a particularly laughable example, from the rantings of that humourless old virago, Harriet Beecher Stowe:

Did you ever see the little village of Newbury, in New England? I dare say you never did: for it was just one of those out of the way places where nobody came unless they came on purpose: a green little hollow wedged like a bird's nest between half a dozen high hills, that kept off the wind and kept out foreigners; so that the little place was as straitly sui generis as if there were not another in the world. The inhabitants were all of that respectable old standfast family who make it a point to be born, bred, married, to die, and be buried in the selfsame spot. There were just so many houses and just so many people lived in them; and nobody seemed to be sick, or to die either, at least while I was there. The natives grew old till they could not grow any older, and then they stood still, and lasted from generation to generation. There was, too, an unchangeability about all the externals of Newbury. Here was a red house, and there was a brown house, and across the way was a yellow house; and there was a straggling rail fence or a tribe of mullein stalks between.

The minister lived here, and Squire Moses lived there, and Deacon Hart lived under the hill, and Messrs Nadab and Abihu Peters lived by the crossroad, and the old 'widder' Smith lived by the meeting house, and Ebenezer Camp kept a shoemaker's shop on one side, and Patience Mosely kept a milliner's shop in front: and there was old Comfort Scran, who kept store for the whole town, and sold axe heads, brass thimbles, licorice balls, fancy handkerchiefs, and everything else you can think of. Here, too, was the general post office, where you might see letters marvellously folded, directed wrong side upward, stamped with a thimble, and superscribed to some of the Dollys, or Pollys, or Peters, or Moseses aforenamed or not named. For the rest, as to manners, morals, arts, and sciences, the people in Newbury always went to their parties at three o'clock in the afternoon, and came home before dark; always stopped all work the minute the sun was down on Saturday night; always went to meeting on Sunday; had a school house with all the ordinary inconveniences; were in neighborly charity with each other; read in their Bibles, feared their God, and were content with such things as they had — the best philosophy, after all.

Now, one thing needs to be said about all this. That one thing is: it is not true. It is quite simply bogus. It is made up. It is a pile of steaming horseshit. There never was a town like that, anywhere in the world, ever. I mean, come on, a place so twee that people didn't die?!! But you could see that the people who had built Dublin must have been big Harriet Beecher Stowe fans. Dublin looked like a place that had sprung already formed out of Anglo-American literary imaginings of English village life. It was small. It was so small it was almost portable. The buildings were like overgrown children's toys. There was a cutesy little church and a real pretty little fire station and a miniature town hall that was just asking to be dynamited. There was a schoolhouse and a gift shop. There was an antique shop and a gas station and a white clapboard building which was the office of a magazine called *Yankee*. That was it. There was nothing else.

I went into the antique shop. Three men were packing stuffed animals and paintings of violins into crates. As I came in, they did something odd. Even though I had just walked in, and even though the shop was utterly tiny, and even though they all knew that I had just walked in, they continued the conversation as though they were alone.

'So you just keep packing that stuff up,' one man said, 'and then we'll see what happens.'

I mean, I was close enough to these three guys to smell their anti-perspirant, which was not, I noted, Irish Spring, although it may have been Argentinian Summer. They seemed amazingly shifty and nervous. For a moment, I had the impression that they thought I was going to whip out a magnum and rob them. Yes, perhaps that was it. Perhaps I looked like a really desperate stuffed-animal thief.

'Hi there,' I said.

One of them turned around, affecting surprise.

'Why hello,' he grinned. 'Can we help you today?'

I said that I was just browsing. His grin widened.

'Browse away,' he said.

I did my best to browse for a few minutes, but I knew that they were still watching me and I found this frankly disturbing. So after a time I gave up pretending, and I turned around and explained that I was from Dublin, Ireland, and that I was interested in buying something which had the words 'Dublin, New Hampshire' printed on it.

The proprietor gaped at me as though what I had just said was in some way extraordinary. 'Why?' he said.

This flummoxed me a bit. I had to think about it for a while. Why indeed? Then I remembered that I was in America. 'Because it would make me happy?' I said, hopefully.

'I guess,' he said, thoughtfully scratching his chin. 'It's just that nobody ever asked for something like that before. I don't think we have anything that has "Dublin, New Hampshire" written on it.'

I said I would take another look around anyway, and he nodded and said that would be fine, and he went back to his packing cases. The shop was full of hideous crockery and bits of rusted agricultural machinery. There was nothing there that I wanted to buy, although I did toy with the idea of a very nice combine harvester ratchet, which, I thought, would make an attractive lamp stand. After a time I turned around and caught the owner's eye again. He had clearly been staring at me for some time. He nodded and grinned.

'Happy?' he asked.

'Not yet,' I replied.

'Is that thing still going on in Ireland?' he said. 'You know, that Protestant–Catholic thing. You guys still killing each other over there?'

Now, I should have explained the situation. I know that. I should have gone through the delicate balance of political forces, and said there was a class basis to the war in Ireland, and that it wasn't to do with religion, and that it all went back to the plantations of Ulster, and that it probably went all the way back to 1169, and that what was needed was for the working class of both communities to organize to break down the sectarian divide between them and build a new community based on tolerance, consideration, mutual respect and a large amount of EU money. Instead, when he asked me, is that war still going on over there in Ireland, that Protestant–Catholic thing, I have to confess that I just said, yeah, it is.

'Bombs and stuff?' he said.

'Yeah,' I said.

He shook his head. 'That's so stupid,' he said. 'After all this time too, huh?'

'Why, yes,' I said. 'I suppose it is, now that you mention it. Gee, I never thought of it like that before.'

But I couldn't be too hard on the chap. It is important for the visitor to remember that America is a country that has never been invaded, except by the Beatles. With the sole exception of the difficult business at Pearl Harbor the United States has never once been attacked by an outside force. I mean, this was before Oklahoma City or the World Trade Center had happened. The notion of car bombs regularly exploding in the streets of Keane, New Hampshire or Jersey City as they did with some frequency until recently in London or Belfast is quite simply astonishing to an American.

One of the assistants came into the shop from a storeroom with two books he had found for me. One was a beautifully produced catalogue of the many rare birds which apparently migrate to Dublin every year, and the other was a little pamphlet about the history of the town which had been put together by the local history society. The assistant had read the second publication himself, he said, and it was kind of interesting.

The proprietor refused to take any money for the two pamphlets. I tried hard, but he kept shaking his head and waving his hands. I was touched, I have to admit it. I felt a little embarrassed by his generosity. I said thanks. He looked away. 'Just don't tell your friends back in Ireland that all Americans are greedy,' he said.

I left the shop and went across the road and into the town cemetery. The Dublin graveyard, like the one in Troy, was full of the Stars and Stripes. I thought of those first Irish emigrants who had come all this way. Many of them were buried here around me. I thought about Ireland, and I thought about what the man in the shop had said about Irish people thinking Americans were greedy. The sun came out from behind a cloud and it started to glow over Dublin Lake. The yellow light spread out through the sky. I felt bad for not talking more openly about Northern Ireland. I stood in the graveyard in Dublin, New Hampshire, thinking about what was going on over in Belfast, while all around me lay the bodies of those who had died for their patriotism. There were Irish and English names side by side. There were German and Jewish and Italian names, all buried beneath fluttering American flags.

I waited for the taxi to return and collect me, and when it did, I went back to my hotel and fell asleep.

That afternoon, after I had taken my siesta, I went downstairs to the reception desk and asked one of the women behind the counter to direct me to the town library. She not only looked it up in the telephone directory, she also called to make sure that they would be open. She smiled across the counter at me as she told the woman who worked there that I would be coming down straight away, and that I would be looking for information about Dublin, New Hampshire. 'He's from Dublin, Ireland,' she said. 'Isn't that just the wildest thing you ever heard in your life?!'

By the time I got to the library, the assistant had amassed a considerable pile of material about Dublin for me to peruse. It turned out the town had quite an exotic history, and that around the turn of the century Dublin had really been the place to hang out. The impoverished Irish presbyterian farmers who had settled the town in the mid eighteenth century had had a tough time trying to grow anything there. The soil was patchy, good for the spectacular evergreen trees which still speckle the landscape today but bad for anything a human being might actually be able to eat. The poor unfortunate bastards. It must have been a major disappointment to come all the way from grinding rural poverty in Ireland and find yourself in grinding rural poverty in New Hampshire, without having even collected some air miles in the process.

But Dubliners are nothing if not clever. One day in the last decade of the eighteenth century, a few resourceful Dublin, New Hampshire farmers found themselves reading about an epidemic of tuberculosis in Boston when they suddenly realized what they had going for them: clean air. Dublin, New Hampshire was the highest town in all New England. The air was pure. They promptly tarted up their wooden cabins, put in little luxuries like roofs and floors and began to rent them out as summer residences – at quite exorbitant charges – to spluttering and febrile and namby-pamby Bostonians.

Thanks to the efforts of local historian Elizabeth Pool and her wonderful pamphlet *Pen, Brush, Chisel and Clef; Dublin's Halcyon Days*, we know who the first few visitors were. The guest list sounds like it was penned by P.G. Wodehouse. There was a General Caspar Crowninshield and his recently widowed sister-in-law, Mrs John Singleton Copley Greene. Mrs Singleton Copley Greene's first cousin, the disappointingly named, Mary Greene, came along too, as did the Hamilton Osgoods (he was a Boston doctor, she an accomplished musician and student of Liszt).

These early visitors took to Dublin like toddlers to dogdirt. They liked it so much that they came back every year. Then, being Americans after all, they liked it so much that they decided they wanted to own it. Each of them built several houses and bought up huge tracts of land from the locals, who, funnily enough, were more than willing to sell. The redoubtable Mrs Greene purchased a whopping 1,400 acres which she then subdivided and sold on to friends.

Henry Hill, Harvard professor of science, was one early Dublin householder, as was his brother-in-law Dr Raphael Pumpelly, also a science professor. Raphael Pumpelly! Jesus Christ almighty. I mean, I used to be embarrassed in school because my second name is Victor.

By the 1890s Dublin was becoming pretty trendy. The summer houses became bigger and more opulent, and they spread across the mountain. If all this had happened a hundred years later someone would have built a helicopter pad on the main street, but thankfully, even though Dublin's fame was broadcast far and wide, the locals managed to keep things pretty quiet. It was then that a chap called Henry Vaughan entered the picture.

Mr Vaughan was an English architect, a fanatical devotee of the hideous English Gothic Revival, who came to America to follow his moll, an American woman he had met on holiday, one Mary Bradford Foote. Ms Foote was a schoolteacher, but despite this, poor old Vaughan was smitten with her charms. On his arrival in America, Vaughan promptly began designing buildings. He must have been pleasantly surprised to discover that English Gothic Revivalism was even more popular in America than it had ever been back home in Blighty. In no time at all the order books were full and Vaughan was suddenly a rising star. (He did the National Cathedral in Washington, for instance, and three chapels at St John the Divine in New York.)

Ms Foote seems to have recognized a good thing when she saw one, and she asked Vaughan to build her a house in Dublin. Sensing perhaps that a major body-fluid-swopping opportunity might be imminent, Vaughan did as requested. This was a little tricky. Vaughan was a great man for cathedrals and churches but had never designed a house in his life. Still, he managed to do the drawings for

Ms Foote's house without adding naves and transepts on to the living room, and the good teacher was apparently happy with the results. Suddenly romance was in the air. The house was built and christened – 'The Thistles' – and the two lovebirds moved in.

This seems to have given the locals some cause for gossip. Ms Foote was eighteen years older than Mr Vaughan, and back in those days polite lady schoolteachers were not supposed to act the way Joan Collins acts now. But it's all quite a sweet story. Vaughan and Ms Foote settled down to a life of clean air, nature walks and frequent non-marital rumpy-pumpy.

Shortly after this, artists, writers and other boho types from Boston began to discover Dublin. One of the first artists to build a house in the town was the eccentric landscape painter Abbott Thayer. Unlike The Thistles, Thayer's place was basically a glorified shack. His biographer, Ross Anderson, has left us a piquant impression:

> It had no central heating and only a pump in the kitchen to serve for plumbing. But the Thayers saw no reason to improve its condition, even though temperatures in the winter could fall to 40 degrees below zero. They revelled in the pristine beauty of the region, and except in mid-storm, windows were rarely closed.

It sounded, I thought, quite like the motel in which I was staying in Keane.

> To take full advantage of the salutary effects of fresh air, the Thayers made a habit of sleeping out of doors, summer and winter, in individual lean-to's surrounding the house. Every night, each member of the family would appear in strange nightwear and then disappear into the woods, leaving the help and any guests there . . . to vie for positions near a fireplace.

Vying for position. I love it. I would have been beating little old lady visitors out of the way with a shovel, myself. 'Owls and rabbits wandered freely through the house, and porcupines would eat with the utmost delicacy off plates at the dining table. Guinea pigs were in evidence . . .' You can't help wondering what the coy phrase 'in evidence' means when applied to guinea pigs. Guinea-pig shit on the living room floor, perhaps? '. . . also two prairie dogs called Napoleon and Josephine. And a tame crow would appear every spring and eat from the same dishes as the cats.'

Thayer's students, Barry Faulkner, Richard Meryman, Rockwell Kent and Alexander James (nephew of Henry), all spent a lot of time hanging about and trying to look pale and interesting in Dublin. But perhaps the most fascinating visitor of all was the important imagist poet Amy Lowell.

It is difficult to give a brief and non-academic explanation of the term 'imagist' but, basically – bear with me here, and pardon the jargon – an imagist poet is one who wrote poems around the turn of the century which were a load of laughable crap. Nevertheless, Ms Lowell sounds like a good old bird. Six foot tall and weighing in at over fifteen stone, she dressed in loose flowing multicoloured silks and fabulous head-dresses, smoked enormous cigars and openly espoused the cause of free love. My kind of gal. Well, you have to admire her for trying. She must have made quite a sight traipsing the country lanes of Dublin, looking, as she did, like a disgruntled transvestite and annoying the hell out of the locals.

One colourful account exists of a poetry reading Ms Lowell gave to a polite literary gathering in Boston. Her brother, a mild-mannered and conservative chap who was President of Harvard University, was in the audience. Amy began the gig by performing her best known work, 'I Wish for Night and You,' reading in her usual full-throated and declamatory style.

I wanted to see you in the swimming pool
White and shining in the silver-flaked water,
While the moon rode over the garden
High in the arch of night
And the scent of lilacs was heavy with stillness.
Night and the water and you in your whiteness, bathing.

Poems about Rubenesque broads salivating over skinnydippers were not quite the thing in respectable Boston society back then, and the evening broke down in disorder and mayhem. But Ms Lowell was utterly undeterred by her brother's pleas for a public apology. Good old Amy. She gave it the full welly.

Her biographer David Heymann has another good yarn concerning the swotty brother.

While motoring in the countryside near Boston one day Amy's car broke down. She managed to pull into the nearest garage and ordered the car repaired. When the mechanic presented the bill she told him to charge it and started to leave. He objected.

'My brother is president of Harvard,' she huffed, suggesting that the mechanic call the university to verify her story. To Abbott Lawrence Lowell the mechanic said, 'Some big fat dame whose engine broke down wants to charge the bill — claims she's your sister.'

'What,' asked the president, 'is the big fat dame doing now?'

'Sittin' on the stone wall smokin' a cigar.'

'In that case,' intoned Lowell, 'you may charge the bill.'

In time, spending a summer in Dublin came to be considered almost as *de rigueur* for creative people as having had an abusive childhood is now. Writers, artists, musicians and sculptors flooded into the place. Even the great Mark Twain often rented out a house in Dublin. 'Abbott Thayer said the New Hampshire highlands was a good place,' he wrote.

He was right — it is a good place. Paint, literature, science, statesmanship, history, professorship, law, morals — these are all represented here. The summer homes of these refugees are sprinkled among the forest-clad hills, with access to each other by firm smooth country roads which are so embowered in dense foliage that it is always twilight in there, and comfortable. But for the help of signboards, the stranger would not arrive anywhere. The summer houses are high-perched as a rule and have contenting outlooks. It is claimed that the atmosphere of these highlands is exceptionally bracing and stimulating and a fine aid to hard and continuous work. It is a just claim, I think. When I first came, I worked thirty-five days without a break. I think I got the disposition out of the atmosphere. I feel quite sure in fact that that is where it came from.

★   ★

American motels are really quite odd places. In other countries, hotels are proud of such highly marketable concepts as 'character', 'charm' and 'personality'. Not in America. The Holiday Inn chain used to pride itself on the contention that it didn't matter whether you were in Iowa or Alaska, your room would look exactly the same. In an American motel you could be anywhere else in the world, and perhaps for this very reason you frequently wish you were.

The hotel in Keane was pretty typical. It was a soulless and rigorously decontextualized concrete bunker which didn't even have a cheap picture of anywhere in New England on the walls. In Ireland, of course, we go to the other extreme. It is virtually impossible to find a Dublin hotel which does not have a bar named after a person from Irish history or a character in a James Joyce novel. We overdo it in Ireland. But it would have been nice, I thought, as I wandered around the hotel in Keane getting electric shocks off the door handles, not to have to keep stopping in my tracks to remind myself of where on the planet I actually was.

That night I ate in the motel dining room, which had a grotesque black marble fountain, plastic imitation cacti arranged around the floor and a mural of an empty desert scene on the wall, complete with big red sun and silhouette of a lonesome gaucho on a skinny horse. I mean, we were in New England, for Christ's sake, not Tijuana, but the joint looked like it had been designed either by Imelda Marcos's interior decorator or a person under the influence of some terrible drug. Cocktail-jazz-type muzak tinkled from a speaker somewhere. At the table next to mine, two women were having an argument.

'You resent me very deeply,' one of them hissed. 'You're being so hostel here.'

This woman was speaking so loudly and ferociously that for a moment I was sure she was addressing me. I froze in my seat as I scrutinized the plastic menu and wondered what would happen next. Would she throw something at me? Could I duck in time? Was I about to get a stiletto embedded in my ear?

'Let's not do this now,' the other woman said. 'This is inappropriate.'

'Oh, it's appropriate,' said the first. 'It's toadly appropriate. You're being so hostel with me, and I just can't see why.'

'I'm not being hostel,' snapped the second. 'I love you very much. But you have a problem accepting love. You don't see love as a valid emotion, Felice. You have no needs. You know that. We've done some work already talking about that.'

'I do too have needs,' Felice countered. 'I have to like try rully hard not to resent you invalidating my emotions like this.'

'Boy, do you have a lot of work to do with your therapist, Felice. You're slipping back to the place you were in before. You need to get parenting yourself again rully soon.'

'I am not, Shannon,' Felice said. 'I'd never go back to that place again, and I think it's like rully . . . controlling of you to say that.'

'You are too. I'm telling you. You're practically back in that place already, and you need to give yourself permission to get out of it, like, real fast.'

I wondered where or what exactly this 'place' was. Was it some awful suburb of Boston, perhaps?

'You see?' Shannon said, to nobody in particular. 'I share my feelings, I'm controlling here. You're dumping now, you know that? You're dumping on me. Dump, dump, dump, all over Shannon, whenever things are stressed for you.'

'I am not dumping on you,' Felice insisted.

'Dump, dump, dump.'

'I'm not dumping. I'm sharing.'

'Are too. It's dumporama city here.'

'Nobody knows how much growing I'm doing,' Felice growled. 'I'm really growing so much now.'

So go on a fucking diet you pox-ridden walrus, I thought, silently. Just my luck. In a country of two hundred and fifty million people, I have to end up sitting beside the only two arguing Californian plankheads in the whole of New Hampshire.

The waitress came over to my table and smiled. She was a pleasant-looking person, I thought.

'Good evening and welcome, sir,' she said. 'My name is Connie and I'll be your waitress tonight. This Super-Tuesday voucher entitles you to a cup of soup with biscuits, or any appetizer of your choice from the special menu, and not including the regular menu, or the Super Crazy Value menu, or the snack menu. Also, to your choice of entree with mash potato, roast potato, croquette potato, hash browns or French fries or salad with blue cheese, French dressing, ranch dressing, thousand island or mayonnaise. You also get a vegetable at half price, and a free second Coke, and coffee with free refill, but only if you pass on the appetizer. No substitutions are allowed.'

She snapped up her notebook, licked the tip of her pen and regarded me with questioning eyes.

'Pardon?' I said.

Connie explained again, with the aid of an abacus, a pocket calculator and wallcharts.

'Can I have the prawns?' I said, when she had finished.

'The . . .?'

'The prawns.'

It was clear that Connie did not have even the remotest idea what I was talking about. I looked down at the menu.

'I mean the shrimp,' I clarified. 'Could I have the shrimp?'

'Well, not really, sir,' she said. 'See, the shrimp is on the snack menu.'

'Yes,' I said, 'can I have it anyway, Connie?'

She looked at me as though I had just suggested I fellate her grandfather.

'I'd have to charge you for it,' she said.

'That's OK, Connie,' I said. 'I'm happy to pay.'

She shrugged. 'OK,' she said. 'I'll have to check, but I guess that'll be all right.'

Connie came back some time later with a tray and a contented look. 'I checked,' she told me, 'and you can have what you said.' I told her that this made me very happy. 'You were right to say what you wanted,' she assured me. 'We all gotta stand up and say what we want, huh?'

'Indeed we do,' I said.

'I admire you for doing that,' she said.

I didn't know what to say. I mean, I had only asked if I could have some prawns, I hadn't written the Gettysburg fucking Address or anything. 'People should do that more,' Connie said. 'They should just say what they want.'

The dish of bloated prawns was enormous when it arrived and with all those eyes and carapaces it looked like something out of a Quentin Tarantino film. There was also a bowl of watery soup.

'I don't want the soup,' I told Connie.

'It's free,' Connie said.

'No, look,' I said, 'I know it's free. It's just that I don't want it.'

'It's real nice.'

'I'm sure it is, Connie,' I said, 'but I don't actually like soup.'

She snorted. 'Oh well, if you're sure.'

She leaned across me and removed the soup.

'The chef opened the tin special too,' she said.

'I'm sorry, Connie,' I told her.

As Connie took the bowl of soup away, I noticed that flabby Felice called her over to her table.

'Excuse me, miss,' she said. 'I didn't get any soup. Is there like some reason for that?'

'Well maam, you see, you don't have a Super-Tuesday queue-pon. I can get you some soup but I'd have to charge you for it.'

'You don't have to charge him,' Shannon said, nodding at me, 'but you have to charge us?'

I coughed, loudly. 'Would you like mine?' I said.

'No, I would not like yours,' Felice barked. 'There's like a principle thing here.'

Connie began to look like she was about to have a nervous breakdown. She said she would go and talk to somebody and see what could be done about the soup.

'I'd appreciate that,' said Felice, and Connie went away, no doubt wondering whether it was too late in life to contemplate some pretty radical career changes.

'That controlling bitch,' hissed Felice. 'Did you see how she looked at me?'

'Stop dumping on her, OK,' said Shannon. 'Just stop resenting her.'

'I'm not.'

'You're obsessing now.'

'I am not.'

'You are. You're obsessing and you're dumping.'

I had not stuck my fork into my third oozing shrimp before Connie was back over to my table.

'Everything OK for you tonight, sir?'

'Yes, Connie,' I said, 'everything is fine.'

'You about ready for another Coke, sir?'

'Why not?' I said.

'Live dangerously,' she said.

'Yup,' I said.

'Let the good times roll, huh?' she said.

'Make a night of it,' I said.

Beside us, Shannon was off again. 'Dump, dump, dump,' she droned. 'It's always the same with you. One minute you're dumping on me, then you're dumping on some waitress.'

Connie leaned over the table and whispered to me. 'Doesn't dumping mean going to the bathroom, sir?'

'I think so, yes,' I said.

'So her friend thinks she was going to the bathroom on me?'

'I don't know, Connie.'

Connie shook her head and grimaced. 'You sure meet some interesting people in this line of work,' she said. 'I think they must be from New York.'

After dinner I went to the hotel bar for what I thought would be a quiet drink. But I was surprised to find that the bar was almost completely full of middle-aged people. In the corner there was a guy with one of those enormous organs, the electrical kind that play cha-cha-cha rhythms when you press the buttons. He was playing country and western music, and the people in the bar were dancing. The men had on plaid shirts and corduroy trousers. Many of the women were wearing pink or pastel-coloured tracksuits. Everybody was chainsmoking and chatting and drinking like it was going out of fashion. The scene was like something out of a Raymond Carver short story.

I sat at the bar and ordered a drink. The barman nodded and poured out a large one which he insisted on buying for me. This is a strange American tradition, the finer details of which vary quite wildly from state to state. In New York, for instance, the barman tends to buy you the fourth or fifth drink, whereas in Texas it's the seventh or eighth. Here in New Hampshire, bartenders clearly had a streak of good old New England practicality. In New England Barman School you are obviously taught the wisdom of getting in early with your spontaneous act of unprovoked generosity.

Sometimes we visitors get the wrong idea when an American barman offers to buy us drink. This does not happen anywhere in Europe. Thus, when it happens in America, we think that the barman in question has either gone stark staring mad or is expressing a keen sexual interest in us. It takes us several visits to America to come to the subtle understanding that what the barman is actually saying is, 'I will buy you this drink and then, in the fullness of time, when you are leaving the premises you will give me a very large tip indeed or I will staple your head to the counter.'

Knowing the score as I did made things easier. I was a little bored watching the dancing, so I thought I would confuse the shit out of the barman by buying him a drink every time I ordered one for myself. Thus, by the time I had my fourth drink the barman seemed to be quite drunk. He sat on a high stool behind his bar and started to tell me about his problems, which, I felt, was really getting things the wrong way around. He was getting divorced, he told me, and his wife was going to take him to the damn cleaners. I sympathized and poured him another large one, and after a time he started to snuffle and sob, and had to go to the rest room. I sat at the bar and had a few more large whiskeys, and before too long I began to feel pleasantly relaxed. Happiness, I felt, was just around the corner. Then, however, a strange thing happened.

Suddenly, without any warning whatsoever, the singer stopped singing and asked the audience to be quiet for a moment, because he had something to say. 'Folks,' he beamed, 'I wanna tell you, we got a visitor with us tonight all the way from Dublin, Ireland, over there'n Europe. So I'd like to do a little old Irish song for you folks. And specially for Joe, he's up there at the bar and I guess he's drinkin' some of that old Irish whiskey.'

Everyone turned around and looked at me. And they clapped. They cheered. They made that whooping sound. I felt myself blushing to the roots. These people were clapping, just because I was in the room!

One middle-aged woman in horn-rimmed spectacles rushed over to me and gave me a big kiss. 'You're real welcome to Keane, honey,' she said. 'Come over here, Bill. Joe, this is my husband Bill. I'm Maureen Spivey.'

'We're real glad to meet you, Joe,' Bill said.

'All the way from Ireland,' Maureen said. 'Isn't that somethin.'

The singer had started into his Irish song at this stage, so Bill and Maureen and I listened for a few moments in solemn and reverential silence.

Toora loora loora

Toora loora lie

Toora loora loora

Hush now, don't you cry.

Toora loora loora

Toora loora lie

Toora loora loora

That's an Irish lullaby.

'Oh, isn't that lovely?' said Maureen.

'I'm practically in tears here, Maureen,' I said.

The barman returned from the rest room looking a little more relaxed. Bill and Maureen bought me a drink, and they told me how they had been to Ireland in 1977. They had visited Galway, because Maureen's family had originally come from that lovely county. They had enjoyed their trip immensely. 'Real friendly people,' Bill said. 'They were just the nicest people, weren't they, honey?'

'It was real special,' Maureen said.

Maureen had got her family tree done in Ireland, and she told me proudly that she had discovered she was related to the O'Connor family. When I told her my name was O'Connor also, she was delighted. 'Maybe we're second cousins or something,' she said. I told her it was possible, but that there were lots of O'Connors in Ireland. She said she'd been told in Galway that her branch of the family had once been high kings and queens, 'in the olden days'.

'That's possible too,' I said.

'She's my queen anyway,' Bill said. 'I always tell her that.'

'Oh, you,' she said.

They smiled at each other, and she twined her fingers in his.

Bill and Maureen had been married for thirty-eight years, and had four children, 'two of each'. The girls were married themselves now. One of them lived down the road in Keane, the other in Biloxi, Mississippi. The two boys were in business together, running a restaurant in Tampa, Florida. Bill had worked all his life at a plant which made medical equipment for hospitals in the nearby town of

Troy. He had inherited a little money in the late seventies, from a cousin who had won a prize in a state lottery, and he had retired early.

Coincidentally, I had heard about the company Bill used to work for, because on the way up to Keane on the bus that day the local radio station had announced it was closing, with the loss of five hundred jobs. People on the bus had been talking worriedly about the closure, saying it would have a terrible effect on the local economy.

'Same all over,' Bill said. 'This country's not what it was, Joe. I keep reading about this recession we're supposed to be having. I mean, I don't get it. You're talkin about the richest country in the world here when you're talkin about the United States. We got oil, we got minerals, you name it. We got natural resources, I don't understand it.' He took a sip of his beer. 'You guys have a recession over there in Ireland?'

I said yes, we did. I told him the unemployment rate was still very high, and that this was the main reason why there was still steady emigration from the country. I told him most of the friends I'd had in college had been forced to leave Ireland and go to England or America in order to find work.

'Yeah,' Bill said. 'But see, Ireland is poor, you know. You take a look around over there, you see it. Man, those roads you got over there in Ireland, and all those potholes you got in the roads. You guys don't have what we have here. You're different over there. You don't have natural resources.'

'It is hard to understand,' Maureen said. 'Nobody should be poor in America.'

'Sure it is,' Bill said. 'You wanna know what gets me, Joe? We help everyone else in the world. You name it. Iraq. Europe. Those folks in Africa.'

'Somalia,' Maureen said.

'Somalia, right,' Bill nodded. 'Mexico, you name it. All over the world, we give money to every damn place in the world, and I'm not sayin it's wrong exactly. But it's like we don't wanna help our own working people right here in the United States. I don't know. This country's gotten itself on the wrong track somehow.'

'It's real hard for people now,' Maureen said.

'Hard for the working man,' Bill said. 'Not too hard for those fancy guys up in Washington.'

I asked Bill and Maureen what they thought about President Clinton. Maureen told me she had voted for him, but Bill said that he hadn't voted at all, for the first time in his life. He would never vote Republican, he said, but he couldn't bring himself to vote for Clinton. I asked why not.

Bill shook his head. 'If you'd ever told me a draft-dodger would get to be President of the United States. A draft-dodger, a dope smoker and he cheated on his wife. Any man cheats on his wife, he can't be trusted, in my way of thinking anyway.'

'I think Clinton is trying,' Maureen said. 'He's trying to get things all fixed up, but it's real hard.'

Maureen told me a little about the problematic issue of health insurance. Thirty million Americans had no health insurance at all, she said, and Clinton was setting up a commission to see what could be done about it. She knew a woman who'd had to go to hospital for a hip replacement operation and her husband had been forced to mortgage their house to pay for it. (Actually, she said 'their home', not their house. Americans, revealingly, always use the word 'home' for a house.) She said Clinton came from a poor state – Arkansas – and she felt sure he must know what a big problem health insurance was for ordinary people.

'A draft-dodger,' Bill said. 'A yellowbelly. I was in the service in Europe in World War Two. I was over there in France. Joe, I know guys who got all shot up and died. I could tell you tales would raise the damn hair on the top of your head, and here's this guy dodging the draft.'

'Stop now, Bill,' Maureen said. 'That's all in the past now.'

But Bill was getting angrier. 'The President of the United States, see, he's the Commander-in-Chief of all the armed forces. He can send American boys into action, oh yes sir, anywhere in the world, but when the time came around this guy here wouldn't do the right thing himself for Uncle Sam.' Bill shook his head again. 'Can't be right,' he said.

I asked Bill if he thought George Bush had been any better. Former President Bush had been a war hero, after all, shot down from a fighter-plane over Japan in 1943, at the age of seventeen.

Bill scoffed. His mild face twisted into such a terrible grimace that he suddenly looked like a bulldog sucking piss off a nettle. 'I'm not even gonna talk about him,' he said. 'All he did was play golf for four years. Practise his golf swing, and make money. That's all these guys are interested in, if anyone's askin me. Nice work if you can get it, huh, Joe? Get up in the morning, play a little golf, wait for the pay cheque to come in at the end of the month. We'd like a job like that, you and me both.'

'Oh now, Bill,' Maureen said. 'There was more to it than that, and you know it.'

'Not much more, honey,' Bill said. 'See, you take Jack Kennedy, Joe, now he was different. When he was President he didn't take a cent of public money. You know that? He had money already, you see. His family had money. So he just gave his pay cheque right back.'

George Bush had come from a wealthy family too, I pointed out.

'Exactly,' Bill said. 'That's my point. But he still took his pay cheque every month. And anyway, Jack Kennedy's family worked their way up too, through the Depression, same as everyone else in those days. Same as my family and Maureen's family here. Everyone except George Bush's family. Bush inherited every damn cent he had and that's not the American way of doing things. And then he's saying the ordinary middle-class guy has to pay more taxes.'

We talked a little more about President Clinton's famously fleeting relationship with the various products of the hemp plant. Bill seemed to feel that the President's contention to have 'smoked but not inhaled' dope was a little difficult to believe. 'I mean here's this guy makin big decisions, you know, and he's all stoned up on drugs maybe, for all we know. He's runnin around the White House like a crazy person and he's seein things and thinkin he's a chicken or something, and he's got his finger on the button for the atomic bomb! That just cannot be right now, I don't care what anybody says.'

After an hour or so, Maureen went to visit the powder room. As soon as she had left us, Bill winked at me. 'Glad the little lady's gone for a minute,' he smirked, 'because, hey Joe, I gotta good one for you here. You know the three little words you gotta say if you wanna get a gal into the sack?'

'No, Bill,' I said. 'What?'

He took a sip of his beer. 'Hillary is out,' he said.

His face crumpled up into laughter. 'Hillary is out,' he repeated, chuckling and slapping his thigh. 'That's a good one now, huh? God, I love that. Ha ha ha. Hillary is out!'

When Maureen came back she asked Bill what he was laughing at but he refused to tell her. 'You boys,' she smiled. 'I hope you're not tellin Joe your dirty stories.' He assured her that he wasn't, and then Maureen looked at her watch and said they had to go home.

'Yes, sir,' Bill said. 'Look at the time there. I guess it's time to hit the hay.'

'Well, Joe,' Maureen said, 'we sure wish you the best of luck and a pleasant journey.'

She kissed me on both cheeks and gave me a big hug and Bill shook me hard by the hand.

'You be sure and look us up now if you're ever back here in New Hampshire,' Bill said. He winked at me then. 'And remember now, the three little words, OK?'

Maureen threw her eyes to the ceiling. 'Not "Hillary is out",' she laughed. 'He's been telling that joke for six months now, Joe, and he still thinks I never heard it.'

When Bill and Maureen had left, I had another drink. But I was feeling pretty tired now, so I threw my drink back, went up to my room and took a long shower. Then, while I was drying myself, I switched on the television so I could have a look at the local news programme. The newsreader's face had on a 'hey, just bear with me while I plaster on a fake smile and go through this shit one more time' expression. Here was a man who was clearly not happy. I turned off the television. Then I read a little of a depressingly lifeless book I had bought about New England's literary–cultural history. It was basically a long list of all the writers who had lived in New England with their names and addresses and vital statistics. In a curiously American way, the mere fact that these writers had come from New England was enough for the writer to get enthusiastic about them. These were homegrown local authors, and he regarded them the way a British person would regard local cheeses. I kept getting the feeling that he hadn't actually read any of their books, and that he knew nothing at all about what they had written. He struck me as the kind of guy who could tell you what Herman Melville ate for breakfast, but who would have regarded *Moby Dick* as some kind of rare venereal disease. I closed the book and threw it on the floor.

The rain was falling on Interstate 41 as I fell into a fitful and flickering sleep. I could still hear the muffled sound of the guy with the organ playing and singing down in the bar. He was doing an encore. Toora loora loora. Toora loora lie. Toora loora loora. It's an Irish lullaby.

It was a pleasant enough sound, if you want to know the truth. I've certainly fallen asleep to worse.

CHAPTER 3

Who Do You Love?

My dear cousin, I am sorry that the priest put such a hard penance on you. You will have to come to the country where there's love and liberty. It agrees very well with me. You would not think I have any beaux, but I have a good many. I got half a dozen now. I have become quite a yankee, and if I was at home the boys would be all around me. I believe I have got no more to say.

Letter from Mary Brown,
Irish immigrant, late eighteenth century

. . . poeple that Cuts a great dash at home when they come here the[y] tink it strange for the humble Class of poeple to get as much respect as themselves [but] when they come here it wont do to say i had such and was such and such at home [for] strangers here the[y] must gain respect by there conduct and not by there tongue . . . i know poeple here from [Ireland] that would not speak to me [there] if they met me on the public road [but] here i can laugh in there face when i see them . . .

Letter from Patrick Dunny,
Irish immigrant, 1856

I am not a person who sleeps well in unfamiliar places. This is perhaps the main reason why I have never become a Tory Member of Parliament – the sexual peripatetics would be my undoing. Give me familiar sheets, or give me death. But I'm here to tell you, as they say in America, that I sleep particularly badly in hotel rooms and, oddly, the more expensive the hotel room, the worse I sleep.

Cheap hotels have their own unique limitations. The pink velour curtains, the suede carpet, the plastic green rose in the chipped vase on the windowsill, the drip-dry Dralon eiderdown speckled with the light brown cloudshapes of ten-year-old menstrual blood, the battered lampshade scarcely shielding the overbright lightbulb, the pages missing from the Gideon Bible in the bedside drawer – ripped out to be used as toilet paper. But expensive hotels, now they are a problem.

I once stayed in a hotel in Los Angeles where they put a box of chocolates on the pillow before you went to sleep at night. Now, I don't know about you but I don't sleep so good with half a pound of sugar coursing through my veins. I had to get up and take the toilet cistern to pieces to try and relax.

In the hotel in Keane, I did not sleep well. It was not particularly expensive, but somehow my inner child seemed to behave as though it was. I kept waking up in a frazzle of anxiety and tension, thinking that the wardrobe was going to jump across the room and stab me to death.

So I spent those few days in Keane feeling very tired. I would get up in the morning and descend to the breakfast room, which would be empty, apart from me, Connie the waitress, and maybe a couple of circumferentially challenged truck drivers. After eating a half ton of grease and cholesterol and reading half the front page of the *New York Times*, I would stride purposefully out and sniff the fresh New Hampshire air, pound my chest Tarzan style, reassure myself that it was great to be up so early, then go back to my room at about nine thirty and fall into a coma with my clothes still on.

I would then wake up about eleven to hear the maid battering the door and trying to get in to clean the room. The maid was a very pleasant woman called Eneyda from El Salvador. She loved being in America, she told me, although like Bill Spivey, she too seemed to feel that America 'spent too much money on foreign countries'.

Now, I never studied economics in school and I know nothing at all about it. You could tell me that John Maynard Keynes was a blind blues singer from the Mississippi Delta who once sat in with John Lee Hooker and Clarence 'Gatemouth' Brown on an impromptu jam version of 'I Can't Get No Grindin' Baby, What's the Matter with the Mill?' and I'd believe you. But I did wonder about this. So far, I had discovered two things about Americans. One, they all want to be happy. Two, the main reason they are not happy is the widespread and deeply held belief that their government is run by slavering junkies who give all their money to foreigners. So that morning I went down to the public library in Keane again to check this out. I ordered up a few books and newspapers and learned journals, and I found that all this stuff about foreign aid was quite simply untrue.

The fact is that America forks out about thirteen billion dollars a year on international aid. (Included in international aid is the giving of military help to 'emerging nations', chief among which would be such contemporary flowerings of pluralist democracy as East Timor, Indonesia and Cambodia.) This figure is not peanuts, by any means, but it's not that much either – a good deal less than 1 per cent of America's GNP, actually. Yet nearly all the Americans I had met so far believed that their government was giving away great barrow-loads of their tax dollars to communistic Africans and ungrateful South American losers. There must be something deeply amiss at the heart of a society which is so obsessed with believing things which are demonstrably untrue, I remember thinking. But then again, I come from Ireland, where a great many people believe that *Finnegans Wake* is a good novel.

I stayed in Keane for a few days, and I enjoyed wandering around the town, particularly at lunchtime when the place seemed to take on a peaceful and lazy ambience. There was a nice little bookshop called the Toadstool, where you could have enormous cups of coffee and sit around being deep. And in the afternoons, because there was nothing much else to do, I would go back out to Dublin and just look.

One day I walked the ten miles or so from Keane. The weather that afternoon was absolutely glorious. The air was just cool enough to make walking almost comfortable, and the lightest of caressing breezes swept in from the east. Peace! Beauty! Emotion recollected in tranquillity! The feeling was only slightly spoilt when I turned a corner in the road and saw two mangy dogs having a particularly rigorous shag under a bush.

When I got out to Dublin that day, the place was even more deserted than usual. All the stores were closed and there was nobody around. The town looked like it had just been struck by one of those bombs which kill people but leave buildings standing. I walked around and took a few photographs. I tried to imagine what Dublin must have looked like a hundred years ago, with every glorious eccentric and crazed poet on the eastern seaboard strolling its streets, chanting loud experimental sonnets and frightening the local children. Did Mark Twain sit on that park bench? Did Amy Lowell compose one of her fantastically pretentious odes sitting under that tree in her caftan? But the truth is that I couldn't do it. Try as I might, I couldn't summon up any ghosts. All that literary history I had read about in the books about Dublin suddenly seemed to be just that. Just history. I don't know what I expected. A statue of Twain, maybe, or some kind of monument to the town's literary past, or a nice bookshop, or perhaps even a contemporary poet or two, slashing his wrists on the sidewalk. But there was nothing at all to indicate that this tiny place had once contained such a delirium of wacky people within its limits. Where had they all gone? Dublin, New Hampshire was just a quiet little town halfway up a mountain, with hardly anybody around, and a cold wind sweeping in off the lake. So after a bit of incredibly pointless and gloomy pondering, I simply went into the office of *Yankee* magazine and asked the woman who worked there if she knew where Mark Twain's house was. She looked puzzled.

'Did Mark Twain have a house in Dublin?' she asked me.

I said yes, he did, and she seemed surprised. She picked up her telephone and made a few calls, and then she told me that somebody thought Twain's house had been on the far side of Dublin Lake, at a place evocatively called 'Loon Point'.

I walked all the way around the lake to Loon Point, but I got a bit lost on the way, and if the house is still there I never reached it.

So I just sat down on a rock and looked at the birds, and then I stared across the water at the miniature town nestling in the trees and looking so remarkably inoffensive that you really had to like it. OK, so it wasn't exactly Vegas. But somehow I had taken to Dublin, New Hampshire, I must say. It was peaceful and tranquil and quiet. But with the orange sun melting down over the epic blackness of Monadnock Mountain, and the breeze coaxing waves from the lake, and the rushes whispering and dancing, it was just about possible to close your eyes and hold your breath for a second and imagine the wild days that must have once been spent here. And the wild wild nights too.

I was sorry to leave Keane, but after three days there I felt it was time to move on. So it was that on a cold morning I checked out of my hotel and got a taxi over to Brattleboro, Vermont, the nearest town which boasted a train station. We took Highway 9 west through Spotford and past the outskirts of Chesterfield, and after a time we came to the vast and impressive Connecticut River which marks the New Hampshire–Vermont Border. The taxi driver seemed to feel that I would be interested in the legal intricacies of the taxi trade in New Hampshire versus those of the taxi trade in Vermont, and he spent the whole journey telling me about them. He clearly felt that the taxi drivers of Vermont were the luckiest men alive, that they lived in a paradise of free enterprise, local government support and cheap car insurance, whereas those poor unfortunate taxi-driving bastards like himself from New Hampshire had to contend with a psychopathically hostile police force, higher taxes and punters so mean that they wouldn't give you the steam off their pee. 'I sure wish I lived over here in Vermont,' he sighed, as our journey neared its end. 'Tell you that for nothin. If I was a young man now, I'd say Goddamn it all to hell and just go live in Vermont. Boy, I was a young man, you wouldn't see my heels for dust.'

Brattleboro is a charming little town that looks like it was designed by the art director on *The Waltons*, but I didn't really have the time to look around it properly. I got out of the taxi and went straight to the Amtrak station to buy a ticket for New York. 'Gosh almighty, New York,' the woman behind the counter said. 'New York. There's no train to New York from Brattleboro, dear.'

But Brattleboro and New York were connected up on my Amtrak map, I pointed out. She shook her head and said that this route was no longer in operation. There wasn't the demand any more, she said, since the local economy had gone into recession. 'People only want to go to New York when things are good,' she said. 'I don't know why, but that's the way it seems to be.' She suggested that I take the bus from Brattleboro down to Springfield, Massachusetts, where I could get a connecting train to the big smoke. 'The bus goes from right outside in ten minutes,' she said. 'This is the train station but it's the bus station too.' This seemed to be the best solution, so I told her I would take a ticket.

It turned out that practically the only place in Brattleboro where you can't buy a bus ticket is the train station which is also the bus station. The assistant directed me to a travel agent's office in the middle of the town, so I sprinted up there at double quick speed to see if they could help me.

'Take a seat,' the travel agent said, with the hopeful smile of a woman who intends selling you a six-week luxury cruise to the Caribbean. Or the Kribbean, as Americans call it.

'I just want a train ticket to New York,' I said.

She nodded and smiled and insisted I take a seat anyway. New Englanders are nothing if not friendly. She asked if I wanted 'a cup of coffee today?' and I said OK, I'd have a quick one. She poured me a coffee and then typed out — yes, typed — my name on the ticket and when I asked if she knew a newspaper store in town, she insisted that I take her own newspaper. On seeing this act of spontaneous generosity I was going to ask her if she had a daughter of marriageable age also, but in the end I decided against it.

I put my ticket in my pocket and ran back down the hill to the Amtrak station. By the time I got there the bus was waiting, and the driver's head was poking out the window with an anxious expression on it. 'Come on, come on,' the driver screeched at me, 'move it, buddy.' Impatience was not something I had come to associate with New Englanders, so I couldn't help wondering what he was getting so uptight about. I soon found out.

There was a loud clanging sound and the gates closed on the level crossing beside the station. 'Aw, shoot,' the driver said, pounding the steering wheel and groaning.

A train started to pull past. I say 'started' because this was the longest train I had ever seen in my life. Honest to God, it took a full twenty minutes to pass through the level crossing. American goods trains are long. I suddenly understood how Woody Guthrie and his rambling hobo buddies had been able to ride around on the trains without being discovered. No train driver would be able to see that far back without a telescope. Not only was this train in two different states, it was practically in two different time zones. My being thirty seconds late had delayed the bus by twenty minutes. To say the very least, this had not made anybody on the bus happy. They glared and murmured and as I clambered down the back blushing and stuttering my apologies I had the distinct and uneasy feeling that they wanted something bad to happen to me.

We drove south from Brattleboro on Highway 91, crossing into Massachusetts about fifteen miles down the road. We went on, through Bernardston, Shelburne, Greenfield, West Deerfield, Wapping, South Deerfield, Whately, North Hatfield, Bradstreet, West Hatfield, Hadley and stopped for a while in the biggish town of Northampton, where we picked up a crowd of young people. From there we continued further south. Strange and beautiful birds wheeled through the air, from the Audubon Bird Sanctuary. After two hours on the road we reached the outskirts of Springfield where the driver said there would be a rest stop for thirty minutes. 'Those of you who are going to New York,' he said, and he paused and glared at me in his rear-view mirror, 'might like to know that the train for New York will be leaving in two hours. And trains do not wait!'

I managed to alight from the bus without being assaulted and I decided to go for a walk. Springfield was an unprepossessing town, full of ugly shopping malls and dodgy-looking restaurants and single-storey office buildings. I wandered into a diner and ordered lunch from a menu which featured glossy colour photographs of the various dishes on offer. When my hamburger arrived it bore very little relation to the photograph, and it tasted like a fossilized dogturd, but still, as they say back home in Ireland, hunger is a very good sauce, and so I ate up without complaint or hesitation.

After lunch I still had some time to kill, so I doubled back into town and walked up the main street. Something deeply troubling happened then. As I was passing the little theatre in the middle of Springfield's main street I saw that George Thorogood and the Delaware Destroyers were playing that very night. *The* George Thorogood and *the* Delaware Destroyers!

Now, I should tell you that I have been a fan of George Thorogood and the Delaware Destroyers ever since I saw them supporting the Rolling Stones at Slane Castle, Ireland, in June 1984, when I was twenty years old. Mr Thorogood is a small man with a big big sound. He looks remarkably like a suburban bank clerk who still has his Holy Communion money stashed under his pillow, but he sings like Howling Wolf after a hefty night on the town and he plays his guitar like a man possessed by Beelzebub and all his unholy minions. With his three-piece band the Delaware Destroyers he has spent the last twenty years touring the world and hammering out terrifically loud, raucous, ferocious, electric blues, with the passion of a snotty teenager and the skill of a master craftsman. George Thorogood, let it be said, is the utter business.

George's presence in Springfield threw my carefully planned travel schedule into disarray. Here was God almighty in human form, about to descend and commune with his public. Heck, I thought, George was probably in town *already*! He was within a one-mile radius of me! I considered my position. A good friend was supposed to be meeting me at the train station in New York. We had planned to go for a drink, maybe something to eat. I hadn't seen him in two and a half years, and he was one of my closest friends in the whole world. Look, this man had once saved me from practically drowning. I thought of his hopeful face waiting for me at the station. I thought about how great it would be to see him, after all this time. I thought of the enjoyable evening we would have wandering around New York and getting slowly plastered together. And then I thought about George Thorogood and the Delaware Destroyers. Fuck it, I decided, I can always make more friends.

I went up to the box office and purchased a ticket. The man behind the counter seemed astounded by my request. He said that tickets had not been selling well, but he predicted that the concert would nevertheless be completely full. Springfield was a college town, he informed me, and students were well known to be lazy good-for-nothing sumbitches who were too busy taking drugs and having acrobatic sex with each other to bother buying their tickets in advance. 'If Madonna was playin here tonight,' he said, 'I woulda sold only half dozen tickets by now.' If Madonna was playing there tonight, I reflected, I could understand that very well indeed.

I asked the man where I could find a cheap hotel and he directed me to a street near the train station. The place was small and cosy and the woman who ran it made me a cup of hot chocolate and a big plate of cinnamon toast, for which she absolutely refused to charge me. What the hell was going on here?! New Englanders had been so generous that I was beginning to wonder how tourist-based business ventures in the region ever make any money at all. I went up to my cosy little room and fell into a deep and comfortable slumber.

I woke with a sudden start at seven thirty-five. The concert was due to begin at eight. I jumped out of bed and into the shower and then I dashed down the stairs still soaking wet and galloped up the street to the theatre.

The tiny hall was absolutely crammed full of people, and as I pushed my way up to the front, loud rhythm and blues music was blasting out over the PA system. I managed to get to the very edge of the stage and I stood there, practically hyperventilating with anticipation as a tape of the Irish guitarist Rory Gallagher doing 'Calling Card Blues' came on, followed by a good blast of U2 and B.B. King performing 'When Love Comes to Town'. Suddenly all the house lights went out and George shambled on to the stage. After a few brief moments the spotlights blazed on and there they were, the Delaware Destroyers! The drummer began to pound the daylights out of his drums. The bass player started to slap out a wicked bluesy rhythm. And as George plugged in his guitar and burst into the Bo Diddley number, 'Who Do You Love?', I swear to you, every single hair on my body stood up on end and began to dance the Mashed Potato. It was difficult to believe that a single-digit number of human beings could make a sound so loud.

The first number ended with an explosion of applause. There may have been some between-song patter at this stage, but I am not in a position to report it to you. I couldn't really hear what George was saying because of all the hysterical screaming and cheering, a good deal of which, I have to say, was emanating from myself. I must have looked like one of those teenage girls you see in films of early Beatles concerts, as George grinned and shimmied and duck-walked along the front of the stage.

The performance was a stunning tour de force. George took the audience on a guided tour of the whole history of the blues, wrenching emotion and raw visceral power from a music which is far too often regarded as properly belonging in a folk museum. This was the blues as the living poetry of America; the songs were about sex, drinking, work, love, death, about good times and bad and about trying your ass off to laugh at both.

After the show I bought every George Thorogood and the Delaware Destroyers CD on the merchandizing stall. I bought a George Thorogood and the Delaware Destroyers T-shirt and a George Thorogood and the Delaware Destroyers souvenir pro-gramme, and if they had been selling sealed glass jars into which George Thorogood or, indeed, any single one of the Delaware Destroyers had once breathed or even broken wind, I would have bought a crateload. I went back to my room, in a cheap hotel in

Springfield, Mass., put on my Walkman and went to sleep with the unmatchable sound of George Thorogood and the Delaware Destroyers still ringing in my ears. Bliss, bliss, bliss.

Next morning I slept late, and when I woke up it was almost time to go down to the station and get the New York train. I got up, gave myself an electric shock from the light switch and a quick squirt of Irish Spring. I was still in a state of bliss after the thoroughly Thorogood experience the night before, and I found myself grinning and waving and exclaiming 'howyadoin' or 'yo' or 'hey, I'm bad to the bone, dude' to passers-by, who must have wondered if I was some sort of recently released lunatic, or an aspiring candidate for political office, or, at very least, an elder of the Church of Jesus Christ and the Latter Day Saints. (Is that a Church, I have often wondered, or is that a 1950s doowop combo?)

My happiness was only slightly threatened by the fact that I knew I was getting a cold. My nose was runny and my chest was sore and my eyes were beginning to sting like a bastard. Perhaps, I mused, I should have dried myself after my shower last night before galloping through the freezing streets of Springfield to the George Thorogood concert. I sniffed and snuffled. I went into a pharmacy and bought a load of cold medicines and cough mixtures. I drugged myself up to the eyeballs and tottered down to the station, greatly looking forward to my journey.

American trains are just the best in the world. Big, sleek, silver and blue, lined with chrome and stainless steel, they look the way trains are supposed to look, but rarely do. British trains are measly. British trains are vaguely ashamed of themselves, and in fact do their best not to be trains at all. Intercity trains in Britain try to pretend they are airplanes, and are even referred to as 'shuttles' in the timetables. This is a gas, really, because British trains are much more like cattle trucks than Concordes. In America, however, the people who run the trains clearly think that train travel is the best darn thing in the world, which, in my own view, it is. Thus, the trains in

America are clean and bright and they whistle and hoot when they pull out of a station and the staff who work on them are dressed in neat and tidy uniforms and they look like they are happy to see you. OK, so in the last few years, Amtrak doesn't have a terrific record when it comes to safety. The small matter of getting high-speed trains which run in opposite directions not to run on the same track is something which has yet to be fully mastered. But this, surely, is a minor quibble.

America's historic love affair with the train is testament to the fundamental beauty of its idealism. Poets, novelists and songwriters have all celebrated the wonder of the great steel railroad which criss-crosses most of the continent. In America, even the architecture of the train is more enlightened than in Europe. New York's gracious and inspiring Grand Central Station is an elegant cathedral paying tribute to the essentially democratic idea of train travel. All London has to offer in that line is Charing Cross, which looks like it was designed by a myopic Nazi with a particularly poor sense of humour.

I spent the first hour of the journey through the towns of Windsor Locks, Hartford, Berlin and Meridian just watching the view and sipping a cup of coffee and feeling delighted with myself. I really was in a good mood. I started to read a copy of Arthur Miller's *All My Sons*, which I had bought in Toadstool Books in Keane. Now, I should say Arthur Miller is OK in my book. I mean, you get to write *The Crucible* and marry Marilyn Monroe, you can't be all bad. Next to the great Irish-American genius Eugene O'Neill, Miller is my favourite American playwright. (O'Neill just narrowly shades it for me, because I once had a spectacularly disastrous date with a girl named Grace Porter, where we went to see Warren Beatty's film *Reds*, about the American Communist leader John Reed and his wife Louise Bryant. Eugene O'Neill appears as a character in the film, played by Jack Nicholson. There is a scene where old Gene gets a bit of a testosterone surge and assures Louise Bryant in pretty direct terms that if she was his girlfriend she would be very happy indeed. When she turns him down for being such a possessive macho shithead he practically goes nuts and starts barking. On the way home on the bus that night, Grace informed me that Eugene O'Neill reminded her of me. She meant it as an insult, I think, but I must say, I took it as the greatest compliment anyone had ever paid me.)

Irish literature is obsessed with mothers. They are usually vicious, life-denying and alcoholic. But American literature is fixated on fathers. It is a weird thing, but America is surely the most Oedipal country in the world. In almost every important American play of this century there is a scene where the second eldest son – the smouldering angry one who didn't get his bollocks shot off in the war – stands up, strides to the front of the stage and exclaims, 'I don't care a damn what you say, Ma. I'm gonna have it out with Dad tonight, for once and for all.' The poor mother then goes, 'Oh son, (whimper) don't. You'll kill him for sure.' And the son replies, 'I don't care, I tell you. I don't. I'm tired of this town, and I'm tired of this whole damn country, and you know what Ma, I'm tired of Dad too,' at which point the audience gasps and reaches for its big box of chocolates.

While reflecting on all of this, I became aware of a disturbance in the carriage in front of me. I mean, the train is quietly humming along the way American trains do, and people are chatting quietly together or reading. There's a nice peaceful feeling in the train. It all looks like a TV advertisement for Amtrak. Then suddenly an unmercifully loud voice in the carriage in front of me shrieks, 'I SAID BACK OFF YOU MOTHER OR I'LL SLIT YOUR FUCKEN HEAD THE FUCK OPEN SO HELP ME.' Well, it is the kind of thing that shakes a person up.

'TAKE ONE MORE FUCKEN STEP AND YOU DIE,' came the roar. 'I SWEAR TO GOD MAN I'LL SLIT YOUR FUCKEN HEAD OPEN AND FEED YOUR FUCKEN BRAINS TO THE RATS.'

I wondered what could possibly have happened to provoke such an outburst. Had somebody been delivered the wrong lunch or something? The train ground to a sudden halt and the guard appeared in the doorway to our carriage looking a little pale. He was a black man, actually, but believe me, he looked pale as a piece of paper.

'We have a little problem today, ladies and gentlemen,' he said. 'We're dealing with it, but I'll have to ask for your patience.' He walked down the aisle of the carriage, repeating this.

Now, the phrase 'a little problem' on a train in England invariably means one of two things: (a) the dining car has run out of revolting cheeseburgers or (b) a light dusting of snow has fallen on the tracks, thus rendering all forward movement completely impossible. What on earth was a little problem on an American train, I wondered.

After about ten minutes of suspense, punctuated by intermittent blood-curdling yodels from the front carriage, a police car appeared on the road beside the track. Four police officers climbed out, carrying truncheons and looking mightily pleased with themselves. I guess disturbing incidents on trains do not happen just any old day of the week to a police officer in tranquil upstate New York. As the cops clambered and vaulted through the bushes I noticed that each of them was roughly the size of your average heavyweight boxer. They passed by my window, practically howling with excitement, and stalked down the track to where the engine was stopped. They climbed into the front carriage. More shrieks and roars ensued. 'YOU PIGS. YOU FUCKEN SPAZZO MOTHERFUCKERS.' The train began to rock violently from side to side. More chilling screams were heard to emanate from the front carriage. 'AAIIAEEEE.' 'YEEAAARGHHH.' There were two thumps so loud that they sounded like a couple of Volvos being dropped on to a street from the top of an office block. Some moments later, a tall slim handcuffed youth was conveyed out of the train, through the bushes and into the waiting police car without any single part of him making contact with the intervening ground. The guard appeared in the doorway again, looking a good deal more healthily black than he had earlier.

'We've taken care of our little problem, ladies and gentlemen,' he said. 'I don't think we're gonna be bothered any more today.'

The train began to move forward once more. People around me went back to their books and newspapers, but I was still wondering what had happened. A young woman emerged from the carriage in front and went to walk down towards the back of the train. I stopped her and asked what had gone on. 'Guy had a knife.' The girl shrugged. 'Guess he just flipped out.'

'Weren't you scared?' I asked her.

She shook her head. 'My friend almost dropped a log,' she said. 'But I'm from New York. I guess you get used to stuff like that.'

We sped on through Wallingsford, Newhaven, Bridgeport, Stamford, and then we stopped at New Rochelle. By now the sun was beginning to go down. The train was quiet and warm, and as we pulled out of New Rochelle station I think I must have nodded off for a few moments.

When I woke up, I yawned and stretched and peered through the window. Just at that moment the train was going around a bend in the track. I rubbed the glass to get rid of the condensation. And I remember gasping out loud then, as New York slowly loomed up in the distance.

There can be few more beautiful sights in the world than the Manhattan skyline by night, when you are approaching it by train. The multicoloured lights going on in the statuesque buildings, the peaks of the skyscrapers towering through the gloom, the lasers and neons sweeping across the clouds. Paris has the Eiffel Tower. Sydney has the Opera House. London, of course, has a large number of beautifully constructed minicab offices and attractive doner kebab shops. But in New York, the entire cityscape is an icon of possibility and magic.

Henry James never liked the skyscrapers of his home town. 'Crowned not only with no history,' he wrote, 'but with no credible possibility of time for history, and consecrated by no uses save the commercial at any cost, they are simply the most piercing notes in that concert of the expensively provisional into which your supreme sense of New York resolves itself.' That's what Henry James thought. But then, let's face it, Henry James, as they say back home in Dublin, was a bit of a miserable old shite sometimes.

When the guard came into our carriage and cried out 'New York

City, ladies and gentlemen, Pennsylvania Station, New York, yes sir, New York City,' I wanted to cheer and burst into tears.

Pennsylvania Station was packed, and as I strode through the surging crowd I suddenly realized what had been so strange about rural New England. There had been no black people and no brown people. Everyone in New Hampshire had looked the same. But here I was in New York, the original melting pot. Every skin colour in the world was represented on the faces of the people cramming the platforms. Outside on the avenue a trio of Mexican buskers were playing up a storm. Neon flashed on the tall buildings. Great clouds of steam drifted up through the subway vents. Yellow cabs inched along the streets, blaring their horns. From somewhere came the sound of Muddy Waters, bawling and hollering, 'I got my mojo working baby, but it just don't work on you.' I took a deep breath and tried to take it all in. It felt absolutely marvellous to be back in the greatest city on the face of the earth. My pleasure was only slightly diminished when one of the friendly locals lurched over brandishing a bottle in a brown paper bag, asked me for some spare change and then thanked me profusely by roaring in my face, 'Fuck off and *die* you homo, you fuckin homo, yeah, go fuck off and fuckin *die*!!'

The Chelsea Hotel, traditional home of New York bohemians, has long been greatly celebrated in song and story. Throughout its decadent history it has been frequented by a bewildering number of American artists and writers, including the ubiquitous Mark Twain, who seems to have had more dwelling places than Her Majesty The Queen of England, does now. Leonard Cohen wrote a song celebrating the place, and the heartbreakingly beautiful Bob Dylan song 'Sad Eyed Lady of the Lowlands' was actually written there.

I had never been to the Chelsea Hotel before and I was greatly looking forward to my first stay. When I got there, however, the joint seemed fairly dead. The lobby was full of horrendous lumps of modernist sculpture and large abstract paintings which looked for all the world like Jackson Pollock would have thrown them away for being a bit of a mess. There was nobody behind the desk. In the lobby a young Hispanic man was sitting in an armchair reading a Henry Miller novel.

'You know where the desk clerk is?' I asked him.

'He'll be back soon,' he said.

'Oh,' I said. 'OK.'

'He'sa sick,' he said.

'Oh,' I said, 'nothing serious, I hope.'

'No,' he said. 'He'sa sick.'

As it turned out, the desk clerk at the Chelsea Hotel was a Sikh. He was a portly and handsome man in a red turban and a well-cut tweed suit. I explained that I had called from Dublin, Ireland some time ago to book a room, and that I had been quoted a very reasonable rate of eighty-five dollars. He looked through what seemed to be quite extensive notes but he could find no record of my telephone call.

He peered at his registration book and shook his head, an expression of mournfulness on his face. 'I have only one room left,' he said. 'It is not the best room in the house but I can let you have it for two hundred dollars plus tax.'

Two hundred dollars! Let me tell you, I was not happy about this. You might think that two hundred dollars does not sound like that much, but I was on a pretty serious budget, and anyway, New York has so many local sales taxes that I knew the room would end up costing me the equivalent of the entire foreign debt of the Lebanon. The chivalrous Sikh explained that the New York marathon was on that weekend. This meant that every single hotel room in New York had been fully booked. I had no choice, he pointed out, although there was always the YMCA across the street. It wasn't too bad these days, he said, if you didn't mind fighting a bit to have your own bed. That did the trick. I forked out the two hundred bucks, which he requested in advance. I silently reflected on the fact that he should have been wearing a pair of tights on his head rather than a turban, and he smiled and handed me the key.

Good Christ in heaven above, you should have seen the room! I have wiped more attractive sights off the sole of my shoe. It was tiny and dark and everything about it was depressing. The bed was rigorously unmade, so I suppose the chances of being given head on it should have appeared considerable. (Ask a Leonard Cohen fan to explain.) Nevertheless I was not in a good mood. I knew that Sid Vicious, the former bass player with the Sex Pistols, had murdered his girlfriend Nancy Spungen in a room at the Chelsea Hotel, and to judge by the smell, this was the room he had done it in.

Apart from the ghastly odour, the room had a kind of Zen purity about it, in that it was unencumbered by such bourgeois fripperies as a television, a radio, or a clock. The wardrobe had no hangers. The bedside lamp had no bulb. To say the room had no window would not be quite true. It had a little rectangular glass pane reminiscent of those skinny arrow slits you see in the walls of medieval castles. When I finally managed to remove the collected grime of several decades from the catch with the aid of a rusty teaspoon which had helpfully been left lying on the carpet, and force the window open, I could see that it led to a fire escape, which was a relief, particularly as I was now so depressed that I intended torching the entire building and throwing myself upon the mercy of the court.

If the bedroom was bad, the bathroom was a disaster of almost biblical proportions. There was no soap or toilet paper or hot water, although one of the taps still managed to give me a particularly bracing electric shock. The sink was cracked. The shower curtains were greasy and torn. The toilet bowl was encrusted with the dried excrement of what must have been several centuries. I was sure, in fact, that if I had been a DNA scientist I could have taken a very small scraping from that toilet and managed to clone either Mark Twain or Nancy Spungen back into existence. The floor had at least two sets of large footprints on it. There was enough pubic hair in the plughole of the bath to suggest that someone had recently deloused their pet aardvark in there.

I went back into the bedroom, lay down on the bed and closed my eyes. Now, the Irish novelist John Banville writes in his interesting novel *Ghosts*, and, indeed, in one or two of his other interesting novels also, about beds looking and feeling as though a corpse has just been removed from them. I never fully knew what he meant until I stayed at the Chelsea Hotel. I wondered, indeed, whether John Banville had ever stayed here himself. The mattress sagged so violently in the middle that I was almost seasick trying to get up on to my feet again.

I paced up and down the attractively stained length of fraying tent-canvas which passed for a carpet, thinking about what to do. I love New York. I really do. I am rarely happier than when I am in New York. It is a fine and exciting and vibrant city. Opportunity does not knock in New York, it practically kicks in the door and jumps into your lap and sticks its tongue down your throat. But you have to make a good start there. And this was not a good start. I sat down again. The bedsprings rocked and rolled so frantically that I had the sensation of being in a plane that had just crashlanded. A Boeing plane. I knew that much because the springs went 'Boeing, Boeing, Boeing'.

To make things significantly worse, my cold was now beginning to take a stout hold on my battered immune system. I took another anti-cold pill and a fistful of vitamins which I washed down with a good big slug of Benylin. This was a bad idea. You know that stuff they print on packets of minor drugs about not exceeding the specified dose? They mean it. I know. I swigged back half that bottle, and after a remarkably short time the room began to throb and pulse in the manner of early Led Zeppelin videos, or the beginnings of flashbacks in cheaply made soap operas. I lay down on the bed again, feeling stoned out of my tree. Here I was, stoned in the Chelsea Hotel. Perhaps this was not such a bad thing. Perhaps in a minute I would get up and write 'Sad Eyed Lady of the Lowlands, Part II'.

Well, that didn't happen. Whether it was the drugs or not, I don't know. (The back of the pill packet did say something about an overdose leading to 'anxiety'.) But slowly, the Chelsea Hotel began really to get on my tits. It began to remind me of death. Dylan Thomas had drunk himself into a morbid stupor here on many occasions, and, as the plaque on the front door tastefully put it, 'sailed out from here to die'. That other tragic Celtic boozer, Brendan Behan, had often stayed here too. 'Oh my America, my New Found land,' he wrote, in a line quoted on the plaque which adorns the Chelsea's front door, 'He who hates you hates life.' I had seen it on my way in. The fact that somebody had added the legend 'Marcia Brady sucks cocks' to the Chelsea's front door made the Behan quote seem only slightly less poignant.

But perhaps Brendan Behan had been correct, I thought. Perhaps I should get up and make a bit of an effort. I telephoned an Irish friend who worked nearby and made him promise to come down after work and meet me for a drink. Then I went downstairs and out into the street. Straight away I felt better.

My friend turned up ten minutes late but I was glad to see him. His face was full of the excitement of being in New York, and it occurred to me that he was looking about five years younger than the last time I had seen him. We took a cab down to Christopher Street in Greenwich Village, to a great little bar called the Red Lion, where there are colourful book jackets hanging on the walls and a few well-oiled customers hanging over the counter and shouting at each other. We ordered a few Rolling Rock beers and then a few more, and before very long I started to feel almost perky. The jukebox seemed to have nothing except Irish bands on it. There were songs by U2, Paul Brady, the Boomtown Rats, Van Morrison, the Cranberries. But perhaps the most frequently played tracks of the whole night were from the soundtrack of the film of Roddy Doyle's novel of Dublin working-class life, *The Commitments*. It was a pleasant irony that Ireland's greatest living band is actually made up of fictional characters. I was sure that this meant something, but after half a gallon of Rolling Rock I was not sure what, exactly.

Dermot and I knocked back a few more Rolling Rocks, and he told me about his new flatmates. He was living with two women, one of whom was a Turkish opera singer. The other was, in his own words, 'a Finnish Nazi'. I asked him how he knew this.

'Well, she's definitely Finnish,' he said. 'I've seen her passport.

And the thing is, she hates foreigners and Jews. And she keeps talking about how great Paris was in the early forties. I mean, what the fuck was a Finn doing in Paris in the early forties if she wasn't a fucking Nazi?'

We left the bar around midnight and strolled around the Village for a while. Loud disco and Hi-NRG music pounded out from all the bars and nightclubs. On the corner of Christopher Street and Waverley Place three drag queens were sitting in a car and putting on lipstick, while their car radio blasted out Aretha Franklin singing 'Respect'. A middle-aged gay couple strolled along Fifth Avenue linking arms and carrying huge brown paper bags of food from Balducci's Delicatessen. Through the windows of a strip club we noticed an all male erotic dance troop called Hidden Talents reaching the . . . er . . . climax of their act. 'Hidden talents,' Dermot said. 'Hmmm. They're certainly not hiding them tonight, are they?'

It was late and we were both tired now. Dermot told me he intended to get the subway home, but I actually like being alive and having all my limbs, and so I decided to walk. I bade him farewell and began to stroll up the Avenue of the Americas, swinging my arms, enjoying the odd and slightly frightening pleasure of being in New York and on my own.

I turned a corner and began to walk down a quiet sidestreet. Up ahead of me on the opposite side was a typical New York Irish bar, with a neon shamrock-shaped sign in the front window and a green, white and orange flag flying over the doorway. I didn't really feel like another drink, but as I walked past, I heard music coming from inside which stopped me in my tracks.

Over the sound of the weeping police sirens and the distant thud of a disco bass, a man was singing a sad Irish song. I went into the doorway and stood there, listening for a while. I could see that the bar was absolutely packed, but there was total silence as he sang, in a quiet and faltering voice. I recognized the tune: 'Paddy's Green Shamrock Shore'. This is the kind of tune at which many Irish people would cringe if they heard it in a pub in Dublin. I certainly would myself.

But hearing the song in New York was different. Hearing it in New York, thousands of miles away from home, made it inestimably more poignant. The familiar words suddenly seemed so full of fear and loneliness.

From Derry quay we sailed away
On the twenty-third of May
We were taken on board by a pleasant crew
Bound for Amerikay
Fresh water there we did take on
Five thousand of gallons or more
In case we'd run short going to New York
Far away from the shamrock shore.

So fair thee well, sweet Lisa dear
And likewise to Derry town
And twice farewell to my comrades bold
Who still dwell on that sainted ground
If ever kind fortune does favour me
And I do have money in store
I'll come back and I'll wed that sweet girl I left
On Paddy's green shamrock shore.

We sailed three days and were all sea-sick
Not one on board was free
We were all confined unto our bunks
With no one to pity me
No fond mother dear or father kind
To comfort my head when 'twas sore
It made me think more of that sweet girl I left
On Paddy's green shamrock shore.

We safely reached the other side
In fifteen and twenty days
We were taken as passengers by a man
Who led us in six different ways

So then we all drank a parting glass
In case we would never meet more
And we drank a health to old Ireland dear
And to Paddy's green shamrock shore.

I got a taxi back to the Chelsea Hotel, where I fell asleep in my broken-down bed and dreamed of Janis Joplin and Brendan Behan, dancing a slow waltz together on the deck of a coffin ship. Well no, that's what I *should* have dreamed about. What I actually dreamed about was Melanie Griffith. But you don't want to know about that. And neither do her legal advisers, I imagine.

CHAPTER 4

The Hitch-hiker's Guide to a United Ireland

All of civilization, arts, comfort, wealth that Ireland enjoys she owes exclusively to England . . . all of her absurdities, errors, misery she owes to herself . . . this unfortunate result is mainly attributable to that confusion of ideas, that instability of purpose, and above all, that reluctance to steady work which are indubitable features of the national character.

Quarterly Review,
London, 1840

The last embraces were terrible to see; but worse were the kissings and claspings of the hands during the long minutes that we remained . . . We became aware for the first time perhaps of the full dignity of that civilization which induces control of the expression of emotions . . . All the while that this lamentation was giving me a headache . . . there could not but be a feeling that these people, thus giving vent to their instincts, were as children, and would command themselves better when they were wiser.

English journalist's description of Irish family about to be permanently
separated by migration to America.
From Harriet Martineau, *Letters from Ireland,* 1852

I did not sleep well in the Chelsea Hotel. My God, that sentence rhymes! See? There you go, only one night in the damn joint and I was already turning into a poet. I did not sleep well in the Chelsea Hotel, I was thinking of Melanie Griffith. I woke with a start and a pain in my heart, the Lord taketh away as he giveth.

Anyway, I really didn't sleep well. The taps in the bathroom seemed to drip so loudly that even with the door closed they sounded like hammers working hard on the floor of my brain.

Eventually I took the blanket off my bed and hung it over the bathroom door, and that did a good enough job of cutting out the sound of the taps. But then the room seemed to be full of even more noise. Any time I closed my eyes, loud rap music would start to play in some room far above me, and I kept waking up thinking that I had died and been put into a Spike Lee film for my sins.

I was awoken at about nine in the morning by the sound of a woman's voice coming through the thin walls. 'There,' it said. 'No, there, oh yeah, oh yeahyeahyeah, oh yess, there, no, down a bit, yeah, oh YESS baby, yes, just, yeah, ah, ah, AH, I'm, YESSS, YESS, I'M, I'M . . . AAAAGHAGHAGHOH FUCKING MARRY ME, MARRY ME YOU ANIMAL!!!' Amazing how enthusiastic folks get about room service sometimes.

After a ten-minute struggle with the mattress I managed to get out of the bed. I really was hungover, I must say, and my cold seemed to be a lot worse. I felt like my intestines had turned into spaghetti in the night. I would have liked to describe pulling back the curtains on the glorious Technicolor of a New York morning, but there weren't any curtains, and the window, like I said already, looked down over the fire escape.

I tottered into the bathroom and said good morning to the cockroaches, who were now breaststroking around the sink in the manner of the gold-medal-winning Bulgarian formation swimming team. I then attempted to have a shower, only to discover that the shower-head's inability to deliver water efficiently was in inverse proportion to the bathroom's ability to clank and hum like a pneumatic drill gone crazy. Eventually, however, the water started to trickle down. What it lacked in flow it made up for in temperature. I hopped around the bath, yelping and groaning with pain as the water threatened to remove the very hair from the top of my head and roast it.

Spruced, scrubbed and rigorously degrimed, I grasped for a towel. There wasn't one, of course, but I had forgotten this. So I dried myself on the bedspread and sprayed some Irish Spring under my arms. Next, I looked into my suitcase to find my clothes waving back at me and asking politely where we were all going for breakfast. I selected a number of the less repulsive items and got dressed.

The great historical accounts of travel are full of vivid descriptions of stunning landscapes and epic adventures. There is never any mention of laundry. Why is this? Wouldn't it be good to know what Charles Darwin did for a change of underpants? How exactly did Sir Walter Raleigh wash his socks? Did Ferdinand Magellan favour drip-dry shirts or what?

I mused on all this as I inched down the corridor towards the lift. The call-switch gave me a gentle electric shock. It was almost affectionate, actually. Down in the lobby the Sikh was sweeping the floor and a number of young Germans were sitting about in black polo-necks, ostentatiously smoking wacky baccy and trying their very hardest to look pale and bored.

Out on the street, I was feeling really unwell now. My nose was running, my eyes were watering, I was trembling, and the muscles in the backs of my legs ached and throbbed. For a moment I was tempted to go back upstairs and crash into bed again. But then, suddenly, a shaft of sunshine burst over the top of the YMCA building, bathing the whole street in a glow of golden yellow light, and I started to cheer up a little.

Some New York days really hit you between the eyes. As I strolled down Fifth Avenue, soft jazz music oozed out from all the shop doorways. Hot air came blasting up from the street grilles, and the heat washed along the sidewalk like a generous wave. I found myself trying to remember that most quintessential of all Manhattan poems, Frank O'Hara's 'A Step Away from Them'.

> First, down the sidewalk
> where laborers feed their dirty
> glistening torsos sandwiches
> and Coca-Cola, with yellow helmets
> on . . . Then onto the
> avenue where skirts are flipping
> above heels and blow up over

grates. The sun is hot, but the
cabs stir up the air. I look
at bargains in wristwatches. There
are cats playing in sawdust . . . On
to Times Square, where the sign
blows smoke over my head, and higher
the waterfall pours lightly. A
Negro stands in a doorway with a
toothpick, languorously agitating.
A blonde chorus girl clicks: he
smiles and rubs his chin. Everything
suddenly honks: it is 12:40 of
a Thursday.
       Neon in daylight is a
great pleasure, as Edwin Denby would
write, as are light bulbs in daylight.
I stop for a cheeseburger at JULIET'S CORNER . . . .
And chocolate malted. A lady in
foxes on such a day puts her poodle in a cab.
       There are several Puerto
Ricans on the avenue today, which
makes it beautiful and warm.

Good old Frank O'Hara. He must have been Irish too, with a
name like that. As a matter of fact I once knew a guy called Frank
O'Hara. He wasn't a poet though. He was the fattest boy in my
school. He was so fat, that we used to call him Lard Arse until he
would burst into tears and waddle across the playground to be by
himself. Poor old Lard Arse. I wonder whatever became of him.
Anyway, summoning up his porcine memory made me feel a bit
hungry, I don't know why. So I walked around the corner to a
diner on Twenty-third Street and ordered a turkey club sandwich.

'What kinda bread?' the waitress said.

'What have you got?' I asked.

'Let's see. We got brown, white, Russian, French, rye, plain bagel, seed bagel, pumpernickel, sesame seed loaf, Irish soda.'

'Can I have plain white and a bagel on the side?' I said.

'This is New York, honey,' she beamed. 'You can have whatever you want. You want slaw?'

'Yeah, OK.'

'Potato salad?'

'Sure.'

'Lettuce?'

'Yes, please.'

'You want I should toast it?'

'Why not.'

Ordering a turkey club sandwich in New York is a dangerous thing to do. When the plate came it was so covered with foliage that it looked like a scaled-down model of the entire Amazon rain forest. There was at least half a lettuce, along with several pounds of tomato and a slab of white meat which had clearly come from the kind of turkey you would not want to meet down an alleyway one dark night near Christmas.

'You want more cawfee?' the waitress asked.

'If I have any more coffee,' I said, 'I will burst.'

'Do me a favour, baby,' she said. 'You're gonna burst, do it in ten minutes, yes? My shift's over then, you know?'

When I had finished eating I hefted myself back to the hotel and up my room where I took another shower. I felt completely bloated with food. I ate a handful of vitamin pills, lay down and fell into a doze. I remember thinking in the clarity of half sleep that if only I had not gone to see George Thorogood and jumped around sweating like a maniac I would be feeling fine now. If I had gone home early to bed, none of this would have happened. If, if, if, I thought. But then if your aunt had balls, as my brother sometimes says, she'd be your uncle, wouldn't she?

★

That afternoon I got up and went for a long walk, down Fifth Avenue in a southerly direction, through Greenwich Village and Soho, across Broadway and into one of my very favourite New York neighbourhoods, Little Italy. I had vivid memories of the area because I had lived there for a couple of months the year before, and I wanted to see it again.

Little Italy is only Italian the way Pearly Kings are English. The whole place is utterly phoney, but in some weird way it's all the more attractive for that. In recent years the surrounding streets of Chinatown have encroached to such a degree that the area is now a minuscule version of its former self. It is perhaps a telling detail that when the great Italian-American film director Michael Scorsese was making his homage to the neighbourhood, *Mean Streets*, he actually shot it not in Little Italy, but in Queens.

I lived in an old apartment block on the corner of Grand and Mulberry, over a store that sold plaster religious statues, photographs of the Italian soccer team, and T-shirts with slogans like 'Italian and Proud of It' or 'Hey! You're breakin my balls here!' proudly emblazoned thereupon. There was an Italian delicatessen across the street, where they sold home-made fresh pasta, Italian sausage and a hot aubergine and anchovy pizza for one single slice of which I would have been happy to saw off one of my legs.

Down the street from my apartment and just around the corner was Umberto's Clam House, the restaurant where gangland leader 'Crazy' Joey Gallo got whacked by the Mob in 1972.

The manager of Umberto's will happily show you the very table where Crazy Joey's ultimate fork-lift took place. And he'll show you the bullet-holes which still speckle the plaster. Little Italy is that kind of place, you see. Friendly.

But I had mixed memories of Little Italy, mainly because I had lived in the apartment from hell. The night I had first arrived, all the fuses in the apartment had blown. I rang Sofia, my landlady. 'Ya musta used the air conditioning and the TV at the same time,' she said, accusingly. 'Yes,' I admitted. 'Jeez, ya can't do that, Joey,' she barked, 'what are ya, crazy or sumthin here?'

I did my best to burst into nonchalantly apologetic laughter. Sofia had the kind of accent you hear in Francis Ford Coppola films, and I did not want to wake up with a decapitated racehorse in the bed beside me.

Anyway, I had not been one hour in the city when I found myself prowling around in the basement gripping a candle in one hand and a close friend in the other. After a ten-hour search involving helicopters and sniffer dogs we finally found the fuseboard – eight foot off the ground, a shattered maze of twisted cables, rusting jump leads, tattered wiring. It looked, as they say in Dublin, like a madwoman's fanny.

The janitor, Tony, appeared with a torch and a bottle of beer. Tony was fond of alcohol, I later learnt. Tony would drink antiseptic off a sore leg, in fact. Either he had a terrible speech defect or he was drunk all the time, I was never sure which. The night I first met him, I couldn't make head or tail of Tony, and that was the way things were always going to stay.

'Hjksalhurghgh?' Tony said.

'Yes,' I told him, 'I'm from Ireland. I'm living in Sofia's apartment. I think I've blown my fuses.'

'Nghgharfugginghabop,' Tony said, pushing me out of the way. He shinned up the wall like a three-toed sloth, jammed the new fuse into the board and grunted in smug satisfaction.

Back upstairs that evening, I felt happy enough. The apartment was small, yes. Cat swinging would be definitely off the agenda. Still, it was nice. I would be happy in Sofia's apartment, I thought. But I was wrong.

Now, as you will have realized, I have nothing against cockroaches per se. In fact cockroaches are probably my favourite revolting vermin. But Sofia's apartment would have made my bathroom in the Chelsea Hotel look like a scrubbed-up operating theatre in which Mother Teresa's appendix is about to be removed and preserved as a relic. *Alien³*? Forget it. I saw creatures crawling around that place that would have made Sigourney Weaver wet her drawers with fear.

Then there was the noise. Italians really know how to enjoy themselves. For five solid weeks in August that year they had enjoyed themselves right under my window. The annual religious festival of St Gennaro was coming up, an occasion of great importance to the New York Italian community, an opportunity for spiritual contemplation and fervent prayer, not to mention massed urination, unbelievable drunkenness and loud public fucking. It soon got to the point where I resolved that if I ever in my life heard another chorus of 'That's Amore' I would hack somebody to death with a machete.

Other minor problems: the toilet broke. The fridge broke. The chair broke. There was no doorbell. If anyone wanted to visit my apartment – which, remarkably, very few people did – they had to ring me from the public telephone box across the road and I had to throw the keys out the window to them. And then there was the shower. I am no sylph, it must be said. But I really did have to move around in Sofia's shower to get wet. The trickle of water which would issue forth from Sofia's inadequate nozzle used to remind me of my five-year-old nephew, Vincent, peeing. The shower, in the end, was my Waterloo.

I was dancing around under the drip one hot August night when something happened. There was a crash, a ripping sound, and a bang. A two-foot-square chunk of plaster fell out of the ceiling and landed by my feet, in the plughole. I looked down, the way you would. Fat bloated maggots were scuttling over my toes like enthusiastic shoppers at the Harrod's New Year sale. I leapt out of the shower, a whine of cold terror screaming from my lips, my soapy body describing a perfect arc as it hurtled through the air with the speed of the Space Shuttle re-entering the earth's atmosphere.

I landed in a gibbering heap on the sofa, picked up the phone and rang my landlady. 'Sofia, I can't take it any more,' I told her. 'I'm leaving.'

'You're breakin my balls, Joey,' she said, disbelievingly.

'No, Sofia,' I told her, 'I'm not. I'm really leaving.'

There was an ominous silence on the line. Down in the street, I remember, the singing was starting up once again:

Strangers inna nighta, exchangin glaances
Wondrin inna nighta, wut wuz da chaances
We'd be sharin lurrve, befour anighta
Wuz throooooo.

'You friggin writers,' Sofia said, disgustedly, 'you just can't be relied on for shit.'

Ah yes, the happy memories of Sofia's apartment came flooding back like poorly digested sushi, as I stared up at the window and said a silent prayer to St Gennaro for whatever poor poor bastard was living there now.

The Brooklyn Bridge towers majestically over the Hudson River, its stancheons, statuesque pylons and glorious curves chopping the sunlight into long slim rays, its proud configuration as gracefully impressive and symbolically eloquent as that of any Gothic cathedral. It is a stunning and extraordinary sight. 'The Brooklyn Bridge,' wrote the critic Kenneth Clark, 'is where modern America began.'

It is to the fine Irish–American historian, William Shannon, already mentioned several times in this book, that I owe a true understanding of the Brooklyn Bridge. For Shannon points out, in *The American Irish*, that the greatest ever Irish mayor of New York, Alfred E. Smith, was born on the lower East Side of Manhattan in 1873, the year in which they sank the foundations for the bridge's anchorage towers on the Manhattan side of the river, and that he grew up in 174 South Street, literally in the shadow of the Brooklyn Bridge, a shadow which would never truly lift itself from his turbulent and tragic life.

'The bridge and I grew up together,' Smith told his biographer. 'I spent a lot of time superintending the job. I have never lost the memory of the admiration and envy I felt for the men swarming up, stringing the cables, putting in the roadways as the bridge took shape.'

Every last rivet, screw, beam and girder of the Brooklyn Bridge was put in by hand, mainly by the poor Irish labourers who lived in the neighbourhood. Smith grew up with these men and their families, and he knew more than most the true cost the bridge had demanded of them. He wrote, many years after its completion: 'I often heard my mother say – she having knowledge of what was going on, because we lived directly under that tower – that if the people of New York City had any idea of the number of human lives sacrificed in the sinking of the caissons for the towers of the Brooklyn Bridge, in all probability they would have halted its progress.'

For all its bloodstained history, the bridge was a potent symbol of the American ideal. Starkly beautiful but above all so unapologetically modern in its design and execution, its message was clear to all those who had eyes to read such things. This was America made real, democracy celebrated in iron and steel. The Brooklyn Bridge proclaimed that there was no gulf so wide that it could not be overcome by the combination of ingenuity and labour.

The New York in which Smith grew up was already racially mixed. William Shannon has written of the city, at the time of Smith's birth, 'It would soon be able to boast more Irish than Dublin, more Italians than Rome, more Jews than Warsaw, and more Negroes than any other city in the world.' But if the city was becoming more excitingly cosmopolitan all the time, Smith's own neighbourhood was solidly Irish, Catholic, working class.

The Smith family lived in typical poverty. Al's father was a carter who worked long gruelling days in the streets of Manhattan. When the boy was eleven years old, his father became so sick with exhaustion that he lost his job. He weakened quickly, and two years later he was dead.

By all accounts young Al was a quiet and serious kid who entertained ambitions of being an actor or a song and dance man. He often took parts in amateur productions of sentimental Irish plays and melodramas. He loved to dance and sing. The more he trod the boards the more outgoing and confident he became. In later years, he was to carry into the politics of his home town and his country many of the skills he had picked up in the little theatres of the lower East Side.

At the age of fifteen he left school and went to work in the Fulton Fish Market. He joined the Democratic Party when he was seventeen. Through his party connections he was given a clerk's job. In 1903 the party sent him to the New York state assembly, where, after three years of drudgery, he eventually got a seat on the Insurance Committee.

Slowly Smith began to rise up through the ranks of the Democratic Party. In 1911 the party won control of the governorship and both houses of the legislature. Smith was elected leader of the upper house and chairman of the powerful Ways and Means Committee. His reputation as a lively and witty speaker grew steadily all the time, but there was more to Al Smith than that. His commitment to the poor of New York was fierce and unswerving. He struggled hard and dirty for them, and unlike many of his Irish colleagues in New York politics he never sold out. He fought for widows' pensions, for progressive health and housing laws. He got child labour outlawed. And perhaps remembering his youth in the shade of the Brooklyn Bridge, he fought hardest of all for a workers' compensation scheme to safeguard the rights of navvies injured while working on construction sites.

Smith was a powerful orator with a love of the poor, but he was also an able and ambitious machine politician. In 1915, he was made Sheriff of New York. In 1918, he was elected governor. He resisted the Red scare of the early twenties and risked his entire political career to campaign for the reinstatement of five socialists who had been legally elected to the state assembly and then thrown out by the fanatics who ran it. He fought all attempts to introduce a loyalty oath for teachers, state regulation for courses of study and book censorship. In 1923, he pardoned the great Liverpool-Irish trade union leader, Jim Larkin, who had been imprisoned under New

York's 'Criminal Anarchy' laws. He built parks and swimming pools for the city's poor citizens on Long Island, and thus incurred the wrath of the rich who lived there. His over-idealistic plans, one opponent informed him, 'would do nothing except bring the rabble to Long Island'.

'Rabble?' Smith roared back. 'Understand this, friend. I am the rabble.'

Smith always had a loathing for the industrialists and bosses who kept their workers in the miserable poverty which he had endured as a child, but he reserved a particular hatred for the newspaper magnate William Randolph Hearst. Hearst's papers were 'foul, dirty, slimy . . . filthy sheets'. Hearst personally was 'the greatest living enemy of the people whose very cause he pretends to espouse'.

Speaking at a public meeting in 1919, he openly attacked the millionaire tycoon in terms which Hearst would never forget or forgive. 'Early in my remarks I said something about misleading the poor. I cannot think of a more contemptible man – my power of imagination fails me to bring into my mind's eye a more despicable man – than the man who exploits the poor . . . The man who preaches to the poor of this or of any other community discontent and dissatisfaction to help himself . . . is a man as low and as mean as I can picture him.'

Hearst went ballistic and threatened to destroy Smith for ever. The corrupt New York Democrats tried to damp down his rage by offering him the chance to go for selection as gubernatorial candidate. They pleaded with Smith to resign from the party ticket and make room for Hearst, but he refused. They offered him any party job he wanted, and he said no. 'I'm damned if I will,' he said. 'I'm damned if I will! I may be licked but I'll lick Hearst too, if I never do anything again.' He ran a campaign so blistering that Hearst was forced to back down at the last minute, his political career in tatters. From then on, Al Smith was bigger than even his own party. He was bigger than any Irish-American politician had ever been.

His strongest opponent in the Democratic Party was the conservative William G. McAdoo. At the Democratic convention of 1924,

McAdoo spoke out forcefully in favour of prohibition, a policy enthusiastically backed by the racist and anti-Catholic Ku Klux Klan. Smith was opposed to prohibition and put forward a fiery motion denouncing the Klan. But denouncing race hatred was not at all popular in America in the 1920s. The motion was voted down and Smith was roundly rejected by the conference.

In the four years that followed Al Smith tried a new approach. He toured every corner of the country, trying to appear mild-mannered, conservative and safe. He hated the Klan because he was from an immigrant family, he said, like many millions of Americans. He was also a Roman Catholic, in a country which guaranteed freedom of religion. Surely the time had come for America to rid itself of racial intolerance and religious bigotry and become the pluralist society which it had the potential to be. Surely, he said, the time had come to build bridges. Al Smith did his best to reinvent himself, but the truth was that he had already lost the fight. Defensiveness didn't suit him, and it didn't suit the electorate either.

In the election of 1928, the usually Democratic South voted against him in huge numbers. The party was wiped out. To this day, historians of Irish America are still arguing about the reasons for the decimation, but there is little doubt that Smith's religion and ethnic background were important factors. Although he garnered almost fifteen million votes, Al Smith felt correctly that he had been rejected, by his own party and by the country he loved. In the years following his humiliation, he slipped into personal dejection and political insignificance. He was never consoled by the greatness of his lasting achievements and he died a bitter and frustrated man, still refusing to accept that at least his campaign had given the first serious nationwide voice to the immigrant workers who had literally built America with their bare hands.

You can still see their work today, as you stand on the Brooklyn Bridge and remember the sacrifice of the people who put it there. The area around the bridge has changed now. The poor Irish have all moved away. The lower East Side has become home to trendy art galleries, alternative nightclubs, vegetarian restaurants. But talk to

any New York Irish person over the age of fifty and they'll still swell
with pride and affection as they tell you all about Al Smith, the man
who tried to cross the Brooklyn Bridge, only to be turned back just
as the other side finally came into view.

New York was very cold that late November Saturday afternoon as
I wandered down Spring Street and into SoHo, and just as I turned
on to West Broadway the breeze whipped up and heavy snow
started to fall. I darted into a café on Wooster Street where I ordered
a Danish pastry and a long espresso with milk on the side. I sat in
the window sipping my coffee, staring out at the falling snow and
trying to look like I had read a lot of Jean-Paul Sartre in university.
I began to wish that I had borrowed a black polo-neck from one of
the Germans in the Chelsea Hotel. The wind howled and screeched
like a member of Siouxsie and the Banshees, and in a very short
time the benches and trashcans and parked cars in the street had
been completely plastered with thick snow, so that you could see
their outlines but none of their details any more.

After a while I got bored sitting in the café, so I dashed out and
ran up West Broadway to Rizzoli's bookshop. I spent a good hour
there just wandering around and browsing through the shelves, and
then I went upstairs to the artbook department and had another cup
of coffee. The American bookshop where you may not purchase a
cup of coffee does not seem to exist. Indeed, in some American
bookshops, the quality of the coffee is greatly superior to the quality
of the books.

Even though Rizzoli's cappuccino was very palatable indeed, I
had really had enough coffee, for the moment anyway. I peered out
the window and noticed that the snow had stopped, so I went back
out into West Broadway and had a bit of a look around.

A group of intense-looking people were standing outside a gallery
handing out leaflets to passers-by about the photographer Robert
Mapplethorpe. The leaflets, which had been badly typed and cheaply
photocopied, expressed what I suppose you would call critical

dissatisfaction with Mr Mapplethorpe's work. THIS MAN IS A DANGER-
OUS AND LUNATIC PORNOGRAPHER!!! one leaflet said. HIS WORK MUST
BE BANNED!! ANY DECENT SOCIETY WOULD PUT HIM IN JAIL. OR
WORSE!!! Fuck me, I thought. Whoever had typeset the leaflet had
really gone a bit overboard on the exclamation marks.

I stopped and talked to one of the protesters, a young attractive
woman with long blonde hair and a Southern accent. Debbie and
her friends had come all the way up from that fine tolerant state of
Alabama to be here today, she told me, and they intended going on
a nationwide tour to hand out even more exclamatory leaflets as
soon as they had finished enlightening the innocent citizens of New
York about the monster in their midst.

Now, I had seen some of Mr Mapplethorpe's photographs and
while I suppose they are not exactly the kind of thing you would
want to send to an aged relative recovering from a triple bypass
operation, I certainly wouldn't see any reason at all to ban them.
Yes, yes, many of them feature well-endowed young naked men
displaying all that God gave them to the camera, but so what? Big,
swinging micky, as we would say – appropriately, perhaps – back
home in Ireland. Photographs of well-endowed young naked
women seem to be quite freely available on the open market, so
why not young men also? Why not old men too, for that matter?
And old women? And middle-aged women with one leg? And old
men with toupees? (Jesus Christ, trying to be politically correct these
days is really kind of difficult.)

I said all this to Debbie but she shook her head and fervently
disagreed with me. 'Are you married?' she asked, then.

I wasn't sure whether this was a disguised come-on or, indeed, an
out-and-out proposal. In any case, I said no, I wasn't married, not
just at the moment.

'Well you never know,' she said. 'One day, huh?'

I agreed that in a world where molecular-based time travel was
now being seriously investigated by contemporary scientists, anything was at least theoretically possible, yes.

Debbie told me she had just got engaged and intended to marry her fiancé next year some time. 'And I just think,' she said, 'for the sake of our children and our children's children that we gotta do something about all the filth in this country.'

I stared at Debbie and silently reflected on the bitter truth of the old joke that it is possible for human beings, unlike public toilets, to be both engaged and vacant at the same time. I then told her that I couldn't really see how her children – or, indeed, her children's children – could possibly be affected in any detrimental way by Robert Mapplethorpe. She shook her head again and sighed. 'That's just it,' she said. 'People don't see. And then, y'know, it's really too late.'

We talked for about half an hour and the conversation was pretty depressing. America is becoming more conservative and insular and crabby and uptight all the time. It is turning into the geographical equivalent of Nancy Reagan. Pretty soon, I thought that afternoon as I trudged back to my hotel through the snow, Americans will need a state fucking permit to read Doonesbury. Why is this? I asked myself.

And I think the answer is that there are too many people from the Deep South – and if ever there was a true oxymoron, that is it – involved in American politics. Look at them! Look at their craggy wrinkled gnarled-up faces and just imagine what their balls must look like. Look at the places they live. No wonder they're all in favour of the death penalty; so would you be if you lived in a dump like Pitsville-on-the-Hellhole, Alabama, only you would want it be compulsory for everybody including yourself. In states like Alabama the electric chair is kind of a cottage industry. The electric chair, in the southern states, is just switched on all the time. It's a little like the Olympic flame, really.

Here is a brief story which says something important about a certain side of Irish New York. One evening on a previous visit to the city I found myself in a church. I had gone there to report upon an anniversary mass for Bobby Sands and the other dead IRA hunger-strikers.

There was a good crowd in the congregation. The mass was to be celebrated by an Irish priest.

It began very nicely. There was a bit of singing, a bit of incense, there were candles and flowers and bells, the whole nine yards.

As he went on, the priest seemed to become more excited. He started sweating heavily. He leaned in closer to the microphone. 'Those puppet politicians in the so-called Free State,' he spat, 'putting on their dirty, stinking, happy smiles . . . that Portlaoise Prison, that Bastille in the heart of Ireland, should be smashed.' Well, I was astounded.

I mean, don't get me wrong now, I am all for God destroying Portlaoise Prison, once he destroys the rest of Portlaoise as well. It's just that I was a little shocked listening to this. I mean, yes, I am a lapsed Catholic myself, but it was nevertheless a little disconcerting to hear such bellicose talk coming from an altar. Furthermore – and this made me even more uneasy – I felt no emotional connection with it. The Northern Irish people I knew, including those who were republican, and especially those who actually lived in Northern Ireland, would not have spoken like this. They were weary of the war in the north, frustrated with the hollow slogans of militant nationalism and desperate for some kind of peace. I really didn't like the way this little priest went on. I felt he had used his privileged position to do something which came pretty close to being blasphemous.

After the mass there was a reception in a plush nightclub in Manhattan. I walked over there by myself, and when the doorman asked me if I had been invited I said no, but I was interested in meeting some of the people who had been at the mass. The doorman was polite, but he said the event was by invitation only. I told him I was a journalist from Ireland and asked if he would go and get one of the organizers for me. After a few minutes a man came down the stairs and smiled at me warily and shook my hand. He asked if it was true that I was an Irish journalist and I said yes, I was. He shrugged. 'Nobody will be turned away from here tonight,' he said. 'No Irishman anyway.'

He brought me upstairs to the bar and insisted on buying me a drink. The place was packed with middle-aged Irish Americans, the men chubby and prosperous-looking, red-faced and jolly, the women in glamorous dresses. I overheard one man talking about his daughter who was studying law at Harvard University. Traditional Irish music was playing on a tape recorder. There was plenty to eat and drink. There were long tables lined with plates of cold meats and chicken legs and different kinds of salads and big bowls of steaming soup. It seemed an odd way to commemorate the commitment of the ten young men who, whether you agree with their principles or not, had shown very considerable courage in being prepared to slowly starve themselves to death for them.

When the meal was finished, a young handsome man who had once been imprisoned for carrying out unspecified 'Irish republican activities' got up to speak. I knew who he was, because earlier, outside the church, people had been collecting money for his legal fund. His speech began quite gently. He spoke about the great bravery of those men who had died on hunger strike, several of whom he had known personally. As the speech, went on, he became more impassioned. He began to talk about the abuse he had received while in prison. He had been beaten up and tortured, he said. He had been incredibly lonely during that time, and the only thing that had comforted him throughout his ordeal had been the inspiring bravery of Bobby Sands and his comrades. He told us how he had once been put in a cell with a Turkish prisoner who spoke no English, but how 'even this Turk had heard the name of Bobby Sands'.

Then he talked for a time about how he had come to 'the armed struggle against England' himself. A friend of his, a young unemployed man who had joined the IRA, had been shot dead by the British army. Suddenly, he almost started to cry as he remembered his friend. He stopped speaking and he gripped hard on to the lectern, rocking back and forth, with his eyes closed and his face screwed up tightly with pain and emotion. He seemed so overcome that I could not help wondering whether he would be able to go on with his speech. But after a moment or two he did.

'Like Christ,' he said, 'the Irish people will rise again.' There were loud cheers from the audience at this point. 'Like Blessed Mary, Queen of the Gael,' he shouted, 'we will crush the serpent of British tyranny.' More cheers. 'We almost flushed that foul spawn of Satan, Margaret Hilda Thatcher out of her hotel and into the English Channel,' he roared, referring to the IRA's attempt to blow up the Grand Hotel in Brighton during the Conservative Party conference in 1985. 'And please God almighty, there will be a few more surprises for the Brits in the months to come.'

There was a tremendous roar of applause from the audience, and I noticed that the priest who had earlier celebrated mass, and who was now standing to my immediate right, was clapping hard at the sentiment that the former British Prime Minister and her democratically elected government be murdered. I turned and asked if I might speak to him for a few moments, and he nodded, and said that would be fine, when the young man's speech was over.

Like most priests, he was very polite to speak to on a one-to-one basis. His voice was gentle and soft. He laughed quite often during our conversation. He would sometimes bow his head towards me and speak gently when answering a question. At other times he would touch the back of my wrist with his hand while illustrating a point.

I asked him whether the notoriously conservative Catholic archbishop of New York, John O'Connor, had objected to the saying of the IRA hunger-strikers' memorial mass in the church that night. The priest said no, he had heard no such objection at all, and that the mass could not have taken place if any such objection had been made. I reminded the priest of the recent widely reported controversy, where the Catholic authorities had banned the radical Irish New York-based priest, Father Bernard Lynch, from holding a weekly prayer meeting for gay Catholics on church property. I asked whether he detected any irony in the fact that you could not say mass in a New York church for men who made love to other men, but you could quite openly say a mass for men who had killed other men. He smiled again and said that he did not fully understand my question, but he felt that the Catholic Church's teaching on homosexuality was broadly correct, if that was what I was asking him.

'That it is a sin?' I said.

'Joe, the Church does not teach that,' he said, almost in a whisper. 'It teaches self-control and self-discipline.'

'Homosexuality is OK once you don't practise it?' I said.

'Hate the sin, but love the sinner,' he said. 'I prefer to put it like that.'

I then asked whether he felt that anything he had said in his sermon had contradicted his Christian principles. He said no, he didn't feel that at all.

'What about "Thou shalt not kill"?' I said.

'I did not advocate anyone being killed,' he said, 'and incidentally, if you read the gospels carefully, you will see that Our Lord never once said "Thou shalt not kill".'

'I thought he said we should love our enemies,' I said.

'Yes,' he nodded. 'That is the ideal. Love your enemies, but, you know, remember who they are too.'

I asked him if he had ever been asked to denounce the IRA, in public or in private. His answer was straightforward.

'I will not denounce the IRA,' he said. 'I have not denounced the IRA for some years now.'

'Do you support them?' I asked.

'I have my opinions,' he answered. 'Like any man.'

'From your sermon,' I said, 'I had the impression that you supported them.'

'I am opposed to violence,' he said. 'I am opposed to all violence. When a young child gets its face shot off by a rubber bullet I am opposed to that. Of course I am. The everyday violence of the British state is the root cause of all the violence in Ireland, all the suffering. And if the oppressed people of my country wish to defend themselves, I certainly will not denounce them.'

He said he hoped and prayed that 'the Irish people, like Christ, will rise up from their persecution, the persecution of British imperialism, and live again in glory'.

I put it to him that the views he had expressed during his sermon earlier, not to mention the views he was expressing now, would actually be total anathema to the vast majority of the Irish people. He denied this rigorously. He had been on vacation in what he called 'the Irish Free State' a year ago, he told me, and he had spent a good deal of his time driving around the countryside and picking up hitch-hikers.

'Really?' I said.

'Yes,' he said, 'and I asked them all what they thought about a United Ireland, and, do you know what, Joe, every single one of them agreed with me.'

'Honestly?' I said.

'Do you know how many of them disagreed with my position?' he asked.

'No,' I said.

'None,' he said. 'Not a single one.'

I asked how many hitch-hikers he had picked up during his investigations. 'Over five hundred,' he said, 'five hundred and four, to be precise, and every last one of them agreed with me.'

That night when I got back to my hotel room, I took out a big road map of Ireland. I looked at it for some time. I tried to figure out how many hundreds of miles you would have to drive to pick up five hundred and four hitch-hikers of any political persuasion, never mind five hundred and four Provisional IRA supporters. I reckon if you drove up and down for a month, pausing only to eat, to say mass, and to go to the toilet once in a while, you would still have difficulty doing it. And yet a Catholic priest had told me all of this had happened to him, so I knew that it was true. I suppose it must have been some sort of miracle!

Only in America would you get the hitch-hiker's guide to a United Ireland. I had heard everything now.

CHAPTER 5

Sean

Dear Mammy, here I am in New York City. No one here shines his own shoes, but has it done every day for ten cents in a shine parlour. We eat in automatic cafés – put in a nickel or a dime and pull out your favorite dinner from a machine, or sit on a high stool at a lunch counter and have a 'hash slinger' shoot it to you. Am starting for South America tomorrow.

Letter from Tim O'Brien,
Irish immigrant, 1922

i wish i ner came to new york . . . it is a hell on erth . . . i cannot get no rest thinking of home.

Letter from Irish woman immigrant,
name unknown, 1850s

Quite early on Sunday morning I checked out of the Chelsea Hotel, somehow managing to contain my grief, and I moved to the Gramercy Park Hotel, a small but comfortable place much beloved of the Irish in New York. (The great Irish actress Siobhan McKenna used to stay there whenever she was in town, and a plaque to her gracious memory still adorns the main lobby.)

The Gramercy Park is a little more laid-back than most New York hotels, and perhaps for this reason it attracts more than its fair share of visiting Irish rock stars. It is not unusual to find Shane McGowan of the Pogues in the bar, for example. Although now that I think of it, it is probably not that unusual to find Shane McGowan of the Pogues in any bar. But anyway. You get the picture.

When I got to the Gramercy Park it was still only eight o'clock in the morning and my room had not yet been made up. So I left my bags with the bell captain and took a cab out to Kennedy Airport, where I had arranged to meet my father, Sean. For the last few months Sean had been working extremely hard back home in Dublin, and so I had invited him to come over to New York and visit me for a week. The thing is, I've always liked being away from home with my father. I don't know why that should be the case, exactly, but it is. Perhaps one important factor is that my father and mother separated when I was thirteen. So I guess the times we were on holiday, either as a family or just me and him together, are pleasant memories. Another important factor is that he is very good fun to get completely drunk with, and when he is drunk he tells a really terrible joke about a parrot, and a person who can tell really terrible jokes about parrots is always a handy scout to have about you when you are on a difficult journey through unfamiliar country.

It had long been an ambition of my father's to fly Concorde. Not to fly it personally, you understand (morning, ladies and gentlemen, Captain O'Connor here), but to fly on it. He is an engineer by profession, and so he is good at things like mathematics and physics, and thus I imagine that he might even understand what 'mach two' actually means. For my own part, I do not have the first idea of how exactly the Concorde works, and how it saves you so much time, and to be honest, I do not give a fiddler's micky. Do not ask me about nuclear physics, if you don't mind, I am the kind of person who cannot even tune in a video recorder. But anyway, my father flew over from London on the Concorde that day, arriving, I think, approximately two and half hours before he had gone to bed the previous night.

He emerged from the arrivals terminal looking happy as a clam in sand and he strode across the floor laughing out loud as he threw down his case and embraced me. I asked him how the flight had been. 'Fucking wonderful,' he said. 'My God, it really was wonderful, Joe.' I think he might have said something about quadratic equations or advanced aerodynamics at this point, and I think I might have just grinned.

A long line of limousines stood outside the terminal in the early morning sunshine, their engines purring and ticking over as they waited for the horde of besuited Daleks to emerge from the Concorde building. My father glanced at the sleek cars and laughed again.

'Hey, Joe,' he chuckled, 'you shouldn't have bothered. Let's just take a taxi.'

The drive from JFK into Manhattan is probably my favourite journey in the world, but I had never before done it so early in the morning. Devoid of traffic, Manhattan looked quite hysterically beautiful. I remember the stillness of everything, the plumes of white smoke rising up out of the subway vents, a lone jogger on Sixth Avenue. The taxi driver was Croatian, which was a good thing as it meant he didn't speak much English, and so he left us alone. I sat with my father in the back of the car and watched the sun glinting on the Hudson River, feeling the odd kind of utter happiness that descends on you sometimes in New York.

On the way to the hotel, Sean told me the news from home. There was talk of something important happening in Northern Ireland, he said. John Hume, the leader of the constitutional nationalist Social Democratic and Labour Party, had been having regular talks with Gerry Adams, the leader of Sinn Fein. The whole country was talking about peace, my dad told me. People were even saying that the IRA would give up its armed campaign and declare a ceasefire. Hopes for peace were higher than they had been for two decades, he told me, and the other big news from home was that my sister Eimear had bought a new fridge.

We left the bags in the hotel and then walked a few blocks down to Twenty-third in search of a diner in which to have breakfast. On the way, we passed by a little Pentecostal church. Through the open windows came the sound of a choir singing, with a puffing and wheezing old-fashioned organ chugging out an efficient counterpoint. Sean is very fond of singing, as I am myself, and so we stopped for a moment or two in the street and listened to the words.

Amazing grace
How sweet the sound
That saved a wretch like me.
I once was lost but now I'm found
[I] Was blind but now I see.

Twas grace that brought
My heart to fear
And grace my fear relieved.
How precious did that grace appear
That hour I first believed.

We walked on and found a little diner on Forty-third. The place was almost completely empty, except for two doleful-looking waiters who were sitting at the counter playing cards for matchbooks. They seemed delighted to see us. I ordered two eggs over easy and hash browns. Sean had bacon and an English muffin and he told me all about the flight. The food and drink had been mighty on the Concorde, he said, but the plane had been thinner than you would think, and the seats were not quite as comfortable as first-class seats on an ordinary jet. Still, though, the Concorde was an amazing technical achievement. It was the one thing, he said, for which we should all be grateful to the British.

After breakfast we went back to the hotel, where we were allowed to go up to our room. It was a very nice room, with two big double beds and an enormous television and a window that looked down over the park. It was certainly a big improvement on the Chelsea Hotel, in that the bathroom had towels. We spent a happy ten minutes switching the lights on and off and scrutinizing the room service menus and attempting to make sense of the trouser press. Sean sat on his big double bed and removed his shoes. Then he kind of bounced up and down on it for some time before ultimately pronouncing it the Rolls-Royce of beds. He was so pleased with it, in fact, that he decided there was no other option but to lie down on it and sleep off his jetlag. So I left him to do this, and went out and got the subway uptown to have a look at the New York marathon.

The subway ride up to the marathon viewing point near the southern entrance to Central Park was a truly memorable experience. Across from me, five cows were sitting in a row, snuffling with laughter and languidly fingering their udders. The carriage was full of lions and tigers, cowboys and Indians. There was an Elvis Presley and a George Bush and – just like in real life – several very different Bill Clintons. I should point out to you that I had not taken any drugs. This is simply how Americans behave on big occasions such as the New York marathon. They dress up.

New Yorkers are basically children. They will do anything for a party, a jamboree, an excuse to give each other presents. They love dressing up. They love being entertained. Witness the annual Macy's Thanksgiving Day parade. How many other of the world's great democracies would celebrate a national holiday by standing in the streets applauding inflatable Muppets the size of ten-storey buildings?

When I got to Central Park, there was a salsa band playing wonderful Latin music on the sidewalk outside the subway station. A large multicoloured banner said 'MARATHON STREET FIESTA: EVERY-BODY WELCOME!' People were dancing around and laughing. There was a woman dressed as a rattlesnake. There was a man done up like the Ayatollah Khomeini. There was an extraordinary number of priests and nuns. There were belly dancers and cavemen and Statues of Liberty. There was a young man in a black skintight body-suit, holding a cardboard tube around himself. The cardboard tube had been painted with silver stars, comets and suns. When I asked what he was dressed as, he smiled. 'The centre of the universe,' he said.

The streets near the park had been fenced into lanes by the police, and an enormous crowd was cheering, blowing whistles and throwing paper streamers as wave after wave of exhausted-looking marathon runners came staggering around the corner and faced up to the long stretch of Central Park West.

People in the crowd would read out the slogans on the runners' T-shirts and then call out in encouragement to them. 'Hey, Frank's Kosher Deli? Way to go, man.' 'Yo, Donald's Auto Repair? You're doin good, dude.' A man in a Michael Jackson mask ran past. 'Hey Michael, pull up to the bumper, baby.' Another man trotted along wearing an Al Gore mask – the mask salespeople had obviously been having a lucrative morning. Someone in the crowd said that Al Gore reminded him of Clark Kent, and everyone around him laughed. 'It's true,' he said. 'Every time I see da guy on TV I'm thinkin the buttons of his shoit are gonna pop off any second.'

Even the hefty and tough-looking policemen lining the barriers were applauding, as the runners slogged past us, grabbing and sucking on plastic bottles of water held out by the crowd, then spitting and panting, their legs wobbling and threatening to collapse. All the time, the frantic crowd kept yelling encouragmemt. 'Hey, black and white T-shirt? Do it, babe, just do it!' A young man sped past in a wheelchair. 'Yo, wheelie? Burn that son-of-a-bitch rubber, OK?'

Being a northern European, I found such an outburst of goodwill to total strangers oddly moving. In the part of the world where I live, people shake hands with their mothers. But not here in New York. 'You're almost there, Ace Car Rental. Keep it up, homeboy.' A svelte blond man galloped past me in tight Lycra shorts. I thought the young black woman beside me was going to ascend body and soul to heaven, Virgin Mary-wise, so screechingly enthusiastic did she become at this point. 'Look at those damn buns,' she said, nudging her friend. 'Imagine sinkin your teeth into those babies, huh?'

A big white policeman wandered over to us and beamed at the woman. 'You gotta great paira lungs there, miss,' he said, 'you married or whut?' She replied that she was not married. 'Yeah?' he grinned. 'Well, I dunno, you wanna go get a cawfee after the race or whut?' She took his hand between her hands and squeezed it.

'Honey,' she laughed, 'you're cute, but you just ain't got the complexion to make the connection.'

I stayed for almost an hour until the very last of the runners had tottered past and turned the corner on to the avenue leading up past the park. The crowd had kept their best words of encouragement for the stragglers. Every time an older man or woman appeared on the street, legs shaking, face contorted with effort, a torrent of applause would burst forth. 'We love you, honey,' the woman beside me kept yelling. 'We're proud of you, baby, rock on!' and the runners would grimace and smile and dig deep and find another shred of energy and just keep going.

It was mid afternoon now, but I didn't feel like going back to the hotel just yet. I decided to amble down to Greenwich Village, where I had lived for a couple of months in the summer of 1992. After throwing in the towel at Sofia's apartment, I'd packed my bags and fled and found myself a new place owned by a wonderful Puerto Rican couple right at the very back of a long thin building on the corner of Houston Street and Broadway.

I spent those two months getting to know the Village, and although people will tell you with some justification that it's phoney and twee and populated by yuppie vegan assholes, there is still nowhere quite like it in the world. Yes, it has become highly gentrified. Indeed, the Village is the only place in New York where a homeless person will stop you in the street and ask you if you can spare three dollars fifty for a decaff cappuccino. But despite being a quintessential part of Manhattan, the Village is really its own world, with its own codes, fashions and customs. I remember once reading a statistic which said that 50 per cent of the households in Greenwich Village consist of one person, and 30 per cent of all the residents are between twenty-five and thirty-four years of age. In other words, the Village is full of young single people having the time of their very lives, and any place such as this cannot possibly be all bad.

The list of former Village residents reads like a *Who's Who* of the modern American arts. Henry James, Edith Wharton, Edgar Allan Poe, Walt Whitman, Edna St Vincent Millay and Eugene O'Neill all lived here. As, of course, did Mark Twain. The painters Bierstadt, Church, Kensett, Ernest Lawson, Hopper, Robert Henri, Jackson Pollock, Larry Rivers and Franz Cline all worked in the village. Today it is still inhabited by artists of all kinds, atonal musicians, ghastly stand-up comics, crap sculptors, method actors on methadone, half-baked philosophers, lunatic opera singers, inactive action painters, crazed existentialist mimesters and, perhaps most exciting of all, clerical staff from the nearby New York University. And, of course, writers.

Everyone here seems to be 'a writer'. You cannot throw a stone over a wall in Greenwich Village without hitting a promising young poet or an experimental novelist, which, in my view, is probably the best thing to do to them. People actually buy big thick notebooks full of handmade goatskin paper and go and sit in Greenwich Village coffee bars and 'write' things. I mean, who do they think they're kidding? It is about as easy to write something good in a Greenwich Village coffee bar as it is to get a cut-price electrician at the weekend. But that's the way the village is. You are nothing if you are not 'a writer'. The first time I was in New York, I went to get my fortune told in the village. Having relieved me of a half-inch-thick wad of notes, the frighteningly authentic Romany woman peered at my palm and said in a frighteningly authentic Romany-cum-New Jersey accent, 'You're a rider and you're just tryna finish some kinda book now.' I was incredibly impressed. But that was my first trip to New York. It was only in later years that I realized something. In Greenwich Village, the number of people who are writers, and the subsection of that number comprised of people who are 'just trying to finish a book now', is roughly the same as the number of stars in the sky.

I lived just around the corner from the Bitter End bar on Bleeker Street, where the young Bob Dylan had sobered up long enough to play some of his earliest New York gigs, and where he had met up with a group of Irish folk singers called the Clancy Brothers, whom he was often to claim as a major influence. OK, yes, as the sixties progressed he would often claim that little yellow slimy two-headed men from the planet Uranus were a major influence also. And perhaps most profoundly, he would go on to claim that 'the answer my friends is blowin in the wind, the answer is blowin in the wind'. Roll over Beethoven, huh? Nevertheless, we are proud of Bob in Ireland, because secretly we feel he is one of us.

One night I had gone to see Bob's old girlfriend Joan Baez playing a concert at the Bitter End. She had sung the slow and plaintive traditional Irish song 'Carrickfergus' so beautifully that the audience seemed stunned into silence and actually put down their pens and their big thick notebooks full of handmade goatskin paper just long enough to allow themselves to applaud. It was amazing! She sang unaccompanied, her eyes closed:

And in Kilkenny it is reported
On marble stone, as black as ink
'With gold and silver I did support her'
And I'll sing no more now, till I've had a drink.

And I'm drunk today, and I'm rarely sober
As I rove on from town to town
Ah but I'm sick now, and my days are numbered
Come all ye young lads and lay me down.

Good old Joan Baez. I reckon Bob missed his chance there.

When I returned to the hotel, Sean was lying on his back, fast asleep with his hands folded across his chest. He is the only person I have ever known who can sleep in a polite manner. I crept over to my bed and lay down, feeling pleasantly tired now. The curtains were open, and through the window in the distance I could see the domes of the Empire State and the Chrysler Building. The planes were tracking across the sky. The room was warm. The sheets were clean. There were no cockroaches. Understandably, I think, I fell asleep.

I woke up perhaps an hour later to find my father sitting on the edge of his bed and watching the television and making a low gurgling angry sound in the very back of his throat. On the TV screen a Christian broadcaster with a frightful Southern accent was giving his public the great benefits and consolations of the gospel message. New York was doomed, he said, and its citizens were in pretty deep doo-doo.

'Finished,' he said. 'Noo Yawk is practically burnin in hellfire and misery already. Ah have seen a vision of Noo Yawk in the vilest pit of damnation, oh yea, a vision that would have you jumpin back in the alley, brothers and sisters, if'n you saw it, you sinful, evil, wicked fornicators. I know what goes on in Noo Yawk. Drinkin goes on, and whorin and lyin and drugtakin and gluttony and slimy pleasures and unrestrained gratificashun of the flesh.'

'Hmmm,' my father said. 'So where are we going tonight?'

In search of some unrestrained gratification of the flesh, Sean and I went out to dinner that night in the Union Square Café, and I am pleased to report that the flesh was well and truly gratified, at least, the stomach part of it. Sean was in great mood. He was glad to be here in America, he said, because it was a place that had some happy memories for him.

He told me about a trip he had once made with my stepmother, Viola, not long after they had got married. They had flown to New York and hired a car and driven south; they had driven the whole length of the Blue Ridge Mountains, just the two of them together. 'The little towns were like something out of the Wild West,' he told me. 'You'd get into a town and there'd be a little saloon, with the swing doors and everything. I'd never seen anything like it in my life. Just the sheer desolation of the place.'

America had always been a source of fascination, he told me, when he was a kid growing up in the working-class Dublin area of the Liberties. Many of the poor families on the street had relations who had gone to New York or Boston. I reminded him of how, one day when I was a child, he and I had walked up and down the street where he had lived and he had pointed out to me which houses had a family member who had been forced to go away to America. After two or three minutes we had lost count, the number was so high. The whole street, it seemed to me as a child, had just upped and crossed the Atlantic en masse.

'That's the way it was in those days,' Sean said. 'America or England or Australia. But people always thought America was really the place to go.' America had always held a grip on Irish people's imagination, he felt. By way of illustration, he told me a story about an old schoolfriend of his: 'He was the kid in the class who was always getting asked to tell stories,' Sean said. 'He was a sensitive little kid, from a poor family, but he was very bright, you know, he was a bit of a dreamer. You could ask him to tell a story about anything at all, and he'd be able to. He was always great gas for the stories. The Christian Brother would give him the subject for the story, and he'd stand up in front of the class with this big look of concentration on his face, you should have seen it now, he'd be all serious, you know, and then he'd take a big deep breath.' My father stopped and laughed softly at the recollection. 'And then he would always say, "The story starts a long time ago, in a house in America."' Sean laughed again and sipped his wine. 'All the stories used to begin and end in America. No matter what the story was about. I mean, if you asked him to tell a story about going to the moon, or going to Africa, it would have all started in a house in America. The poor kid. I suppose it was his way of escaping, you know.'

We sat in the Union Square Café just talking about America, until somebody switched on the lights and the staff started to put the chairs up on the tables. I suppose you can get a bit lonely when you're travelling, and so it was great to have my father here with me now, and to be able to talk to him. And maybe because I had had a few drinks, on the way back to the hotel in the taxi, my mind started to drift back to the days when we used to go to Connemara together.

Those days had been so important to me as a child, the days and weekends we would spend in Connemara. I remembered one particular night in the Bridge House Hotel in Spiddal, when I would have been about seven years old. For some reason, it was just my father and myself; my mother and my sisters and brother were back home in Dublin. My father and I were in a small room in the hotel, trying to get some sleep. We couldn't really do this, because outside on the street there were drunk men singing. They sang all night long, ribald and raucous Irish songs, and every so often, my father got up out of bed and went to the window and shouted at the men to shut up. They would be quiet for a few minutes, but then they would start the singing again. They must have sung for hours, and no matter how much my father bawled at them, they ignored him and just kept on singing. And then, at some point in the middle of the night, my father gave up shouting at them and he sat down on his bed and just started to laugh. That was all that happened. He simply put his hands to his sides and began to laugh out loud. I am sure I had seen my father laugh before, but perhaps not in such an uncontrolled and joyous way. He sat there rocking with laughter, the tears spilling down his face. 'They're terrible men,' my father laughed, 'aren't they terrible?' and I laughed back, and we sat on our beds in the dark room laughing like a couple of maniacs. We couldn't stop ourselves. The louder and ruder the singing got, the more we laughed. And on the way back to Dublin in the car the following night, I remember feeling the most amazing thrill every time I thought about the sheer abandonment of my father's laughter, and the fact that I had been there to see it and share it.

There was another night I remembered. It was a time when things had not been good at home. My father and mother had quarrelled, and my father had packed the four of us children into his car and driven away from our house. Back then I thought what we were doing was exciting. Imagine, I thought, driving through Ireland in the middle of the night. It seemed exotic, magical. I felt like a desperado in a cowboy movie.

But now, when I think of that night, I see it more clearly. I see a man still in his twenties, wondering where to go, with four young frightened children huddled on the back seat of his car. It is a picture which haunts me. My father must have had little or no idea what was the right thing to do that night. We drove and drove for what seemed like hours and after a time I must have fallen asleep.

When I woke up, the car had stopped. We must have been somewhere in the middle of Ireland, because I remember looking out the window and seeing nothing but flat gloomy fields all around us. It was a very clear night, I remember, although it must have been very late. Everything was quiet and the moon was bright and low in the sky. My two sisters and my brother were asleep beside me in the back of the car. For a few moments, my dad said nothing to me. He sat looking out at the road, his hands gripping the steering wheel. I asked him if we were going to Connemara, and he smiled and said, yes, we were. But he didn't drive on. He just sat there for what seemed like a long time, clutching the wheel and looking out at the road.

He asked me, then, if I did not think we should go home.

I remember that I told him, no, I thought we should go to Connemara. He didn't speak for a while. But then he said that my mother would miss us all if we didn't go home, and that she would be worried about us, that we should go home now, and that the next weekend we would all go down to Connemara together. I said that I wanted to go to Connemara now, but he smiled and said we really had to go home, that if I thought about it, it really wasn't fair to my mother to leave her at home by herself, missing all the fun. I think I must have got into a sulk then, because I remember him asking me if I wanted to sit in the front seat, and I remember that the prospect of this cheered me up. I said, yes, I did, and I clambered through the space into the passenger seat and put on the safety belt. My father started up the car again, and we turned around and drove home through the darkness to Dublin. And just as the yellow lights of the city came into view I remember that he reached over and held my hand and squeezed it hard, without saying anything at all to me.

It is the oddest thing about travelling, really. It always takes you home in the end.

CHAPTER 6

Rebel Music

'Get up here, son, and face me in a step, for likely it will be the last step we'll ever dance.'

Words of west of Ireland father to his son, about to emigrate.
From contemporary account of nineteenth-century 'American Wake',
MS 1411, folklore department, University College Dublin

One Irishman stood up and sang the shamrock so green and the decay of the rose the steward is an English man and when he heard England cut down he rushed and said he would not allow no more of this so the Irish persevered in singing . . . the brave man sang national songs until he made us sleep with them.

From diary of Irish immigrant, name unknown,
covering sea voyage to America, late nineteenth century

Yesterday morning I was spectator of a strange, weird, painful scene. Certain houses are to be erected on . . . this street and Fourth Avenue and deep excavations therefore are in progress. Seeing a crowd on the corner I stopped and made my way to a front place. The earth had caved in . . . and crushed the breath out of a pair of ill-starred Celtic laborers . . . Around them were a few men who had got them out . . . and fifteen or twenty Irish women . . . I suppose they were 'keening'; all together were raising a wild, unearthly cry, half shriek and half song, wailing as a score of daylight banshees, clapping their hands and gesticulating passionately . . . It was an uncanny sound to hear, quite new to me . . . Our Celtic fellow citizens are almost as remote from us in temperament and constitution as the Chinese!

From diary of George Templeton Strong,
American journalist, 1857

On my fourth night in New York something really disgusting happened to me. I had been out for dinner with my father and he had gone home early to bed and I had just gone out for a walk to sober up and take the air. I found myself outside a nightclub called Denim and Diamonds. Something about the place intrigued me, so I took a deep breath and strolled in.

The place was the size of a small airplane hangar and it was completely full of punters. There must have been several hundred of them, and they were doing something so ineffably strange, so truly horrifying, that if I had not seen it myself, and if I had not somehow summoned up the presence of mind to capture it all on several rolls of high-grade Kodak film so that I could examine it later, in the cold light of day, and rub my eyes in numb and gaping horror, I would not have believed it was possible. I would have thought I had been slipped some potent hallucinogenic drug. Two hundred check-shirted and chubby New Yorkers all twisting and grinding and swivelling their hips and swinging their arses and smacking their corpulent thighs and yee-hawing, and doing it all with military precision, standing in lines, each in his or her own little defined space, not one of them ever touching another. This, I was told, was called line dancing; this was the latest craze. I remember thinking, as I gazed in abject dread upon this terrifying scene, that if the Nazis had succeeded in conquering the world, this is how everyone would dance.

Now, reader, as you will have gathered, I am not a religious person. But when I got back to the Gramercy Park Hotel that night I do not mind confessing that I went down on my knees and thanked God and His Holy Mother and all the Saints that I lived in a country where this ghastly madness would never catch on. John O'Hara once wrote that America was a society which had passed from barbarism to decadence without ever going through civilization on the way. I thought line dancing, like Little Jimmy Osmond, the Waco massacre and the foreign policy of the Reagan administration, was just another poignant illustration of the remarkable perceptiveness of John O'Hara.

It is two years now since I stood in that nightclub in New York City, and if you have been to Ireland at any stage recently you can imagine how bad I feel these days. Line dancing has caught on in 1990s Ireland the way leather trousers caught on in 1930s Germany. It is practically the new national sport. We kicked out the English, we kept out bovine spongiform encephalitis and rabies, but we let line dancing in. I don't know how it ever got here. I don't know how this happened. I suppose we must have just looked the other way for a moment, and now, here it is, in every corner of our little country, working its wickedness, destroying the minds of our young people and attacking that specific part of the human brain that manufactures and develops good taste.

Dancing is probably the greatest and most universal form of creative human expression. It exists in every culture on the planet. The Bible, the Greek myths, the *Iliad* and the *Odyssey* all refer to dancing. Unlike almost every other art form, it is impossible to point to an example of dancing that is genuinely ugly. Except line dancing. Indeed, the very idea of dancing is predicated on the notion that individual physical movement is a thing of beauty. Whether you are Rudolf Nureyev sashaying across the stage of the Royal Ballet or a pogoing punk in a malodorous basement, dancing says the same thing: it says that being alive is somehow worth celebrating. 'My soul is fastened to a dying animal,' wrote Yeats. Well, one of Yeats's problems was that he obviously didn't dance too much. If only he'd asked Maud Gonne to accompany him to the local hop, instead of bombarding her with doleful sonnets about fishermen and scarecrows, things could have been so different, and she definitely would have ended up snogging him. Dancing proclaims that the very physicality which seems to weigh us down can be used to transcend its own limitations. But this obnoxious line dancing business is a different bucket of sick altogether. Next to *Little House on the Prairie*, this is the worst thing Ireland ever imported from America. This is dancing invented by a committee of semi-comatose turds. It is dancing imagined as an act of negation. Just try watching it for more than five minutes. It is the dance of the living death.

Quite apart from its irredeemable ghastliness, there is something truly Orwellian about line dancing. In some important sense, it represents the choreography of the Cold War. It is about isolation, about submerging the self in the essentially fascist whole. The logic implies that once you stay literally in your own place, once you don't stray from the script, once you don't get out of step, once you don't do anything at all that you haven't been told to do, everything will be fine and the dance can continue. You can tell it was invented in Texas, George Bush's adopted state, the world capital of sheep-shagging, racism and big hair. But I don't know, maybe that's taking it all a bit too seriously. Maybe that's reading too much into it. Maybe line dancing is quite simply a load of embarrassing old shite and nothing very much more.

In which case, how in the name of God has it happened to us? We Irish are a proud and independent people, with a noble tradition of rebellion and anti-authoritarianism. Where did we go so wrong? In an effort to clarify my thoughts, I spoke to one victim recently, a young woman from Dublin who did not want to be named. 'Mary' is an attractive woman in her late twenties, has a good job in the media, a steady boyfriend, a beautiful home. Hers is a tragic but typical story. She thought she could handle it, she says, her lip trembling. 'At first I just went to the beginners' class in this bar called Break for the Border on a Friday night,' she weeps. 'I knew it was wrong, so very wrong, but I suppose I was just looking for kicks.' Soon, though, things went downhill for Mary. One night she fell in with a party of hardened Randy Travis fans, visiting Dublin from Nashville. Before long she was wearing cowboy boots and shoelace ties and lurid belt buckles shaped like prize bullocks' heads. When she began addressing her widowed mother as 'pardner', she realized she had to take control. She is now in intensive therapy, which involves regular listening to the Clash's back catalogue and compulsory supervised trips to the only two remaining Dublin nightspots where line dancing is absolutely banned on pain of death. But she has to take things 'one day at a time'. She still has her bad moments, she says. Indeed, even while we were speaking, a Dwight

Yoakam song came on the radio, and what happened next was truly pitiful. 'Mary' stood up, put her hands on her hips, wiggled her backside and cried out loudly, 'Take me to the hoedown, Tex, guess I'm fixin for a ride.'

Our politicians and religious leaders have stood by and let this menace take root. Indeed, some sources indicate that many of them are secret line dancers themselves. It is hard to confirm these allegations, but it seems to be generally accepted that former Prime Minister Charles J. Haughey is 'a bit of a hoor on the floor', that second-in-command Mr Dick Spring is a paid-up member of a shadowy organization called the Turkey Trot Society and that even Her Excellency President Mary Robinson was overheard mumbling, 'With a hey and a hoe and a dosey-eye-doe,' at a late stage of an official function in Dublin recently.

What is to be done about this scourge? It is said that even Bono of U2 'regularly wears spurs' and has installed swing doors in his south Dublin home. Already Irish toddlers, particularly in the midlands of my poor unfortunate country, are being dressed up in frilly-fronted shirts and taught to kick their little legs in the air to the corrupt and demoniacal outpourings of Clint Black and Travis Tritt. (A friend who lives in County Offaly telephoned me recently in a state of terrible distress. His new baby had just come home from the creche and spoken its first words. 'Garth Brooks!' My own little nephew who lives in Youghal, County Cork, was asked by his teacher to write down the name of his home town. The poor little mite spelt it 'Y'all'!!)

If only I could have been more perceptive that night in New York. If only I could have stopped my stomach churning for long enough to see what a potential threat to Ireland I was witnessing. There they were, the youth of the greatest city on the face of the earth, prancing about in ruthless lobotomized formation like so many denim-clad Stepford Wives. As I stood at the bar a young female victim approached and greeted the barman with a brisk 'howdy', to which he responded with an equally brisk 'howdy my ass'. She displayed what I now know to be all the usual diabolical symptoms, the wide-eyed vacuous stare, the Stetson hat, the jeans so tight you could read the dates on the coins in her pockets.

We chatted for a while. She pointed out her fiancé, there in the middle of the floor, lurching about like a zombie in trousers which reminded me of the town of Kinnegad, County Westmeath (no ballroom). They were getting married in the summer, she told me, and she showed me her diamond ring. I offered heartiest congratulations. It was going to be 'a line-dancing wedding', she said. I should have told her that it wasn't too late. I should have offered to help her kick the habit. Even if she couldn't give it up completely, I should have said, couldn't she at least cut it down to the occasional square dance or country polka? Jesus Christ almighty, *for the sake of her unborn children?!!*

Instead, I did nothing but feebly ask if she really enjoyed this horrific pursuit or if she was here for a bet. She gazed at me and emitted a hollow chilling laugh as she threw back her Jack Daniel's and burped like a common cowpuncher. 'Would you take me back to Tennessee and lassoo my lovely lariat,' she said. 'This here's the most fun you can have with your boots on, pardner.' She weaved back through the crowd and took up her place in the line. She beamed at her future husband as she teetered about without touching him, an invisible force field of spectacular tastelessness coming between their love. In that awful moment I should have feared for the future of Ireland. I should have known. I could have saved my country then and there, but I didn't. All I did was look at these two bozos and wonder whether for them it was already too late. Mind you, they probably had amazing sex when they went home that night. Whereas I went back to the hotel, put a Clash tape on my Walkman and sat up late and alone thinking about how awful line dancing is. Perhaps we are all victims in the end.

Although it is a deeply horrifying development, it is perhaps not much of a surprise that line dancing has caught on in Ireland. The truth is that throughout the history of Irish migration to the new world, Irish and American folk musics have always travelled backwards and forwards across the Atlantic, to the extent that the distinctions between them have often become so blurred as to be practically meaningless.

Nuala O'Connor's book *Bringing It All Back Home* points out that, like American country music, Irish traditional music is in essence mainly a dance music which mostly dates from the eighteenth century. At that time it was part of a vibrant tradition of dancing which was then reaching its peak of popularity. It would extend that appeal for almost another century, despite the devastation of the famine and the condemnation of the Catholic Church.

This last point is important. Dancing always had a secret redolence of sexuality in Ireland. One hard-hitting priest, as far back as the seventeenth century, had lectured his congregation: 'Dancing is a thing which leads to bad thoughts and evil actions . . . It is dancing which excites the desire of the body. In the dance are seen frenzy and woe, and with dancing thousands go to the black hell.' Another holy man, as recently as the 1930s, opined that 'Young people would be better off attuning themselves to the quiet rhythms of nature instead of the epileptic lurchings of the negroid races.' It is perhaps significant that the Irish language, which contains several dozen words for seaweed, offers no truly Irish word for dancing. (The two Gaelic words *damhsa* and *rince* are actually English loanwords.) Dancing was so taboo, and therefore so pleasurable, that it didn't even exist in the language.

To some modern observers, it is hard to see what the clergy was getting uptight about. They will tell you that most traditional Irish dances involve very little physical contact, and, indeed, if they are in the mood to risk getting a good slap in the head, they might even tell you that Irish dancing and the dreaded line dancing are similar. This is, of course, complete bullshit. Real Irish set dancing, influenced by the European traditions of courtly dance, is very physical indeed. Furthermore, in a repressive and priest-ridden society, the crossroads dance was one of the few places where young men and women could meet, and the Irish folk tradition is full of tall tales about the sexual athletics that would go on at these events. In any case, the popularity of dancing gave rise to a peculiar view of the purpose of music in Ireland. Although the countryside was full of spectacularly talented musicians, their musicianship as such was not what was admired so much as their ability to get your feet tapping and your sap rising.

The early Irish migrants to America brought their tunes, their instruments and their approach to the music with them, and as they spread across the continent, they began to influence the home-grown American brand of country. Thus, musicologically, Irish dance music and many forms of modern American country are clearly related. Jigs, reels, slides, hornpipes and polkas appear in both traditions and not simultaneously in any other. Guitar and fiddle fingerings are almost identical; indeed, it is almost certain that the use of the violin as a folk instrument hardly existed in America before the first Irish immigrants arrived. Another important common element is that neither Irish music nor American country use the scales on which European classical music is based. Irish and American traditional musics are modal, a trait they share with some – but only some – kinds of English folk music. But where Irish folk and American country music differ radically from the English tradition is in their frequent use of improvisation. Again, because the main purpose of this music was to accompany dancing, a traditional Irish player might have to play for hours at a time. As much to avoid boredom as anything else, the musicians would change and rearrange tunes, turning them on their heads to keep themselves interested while they watched everyone else having a good time.

As the Irish became assimilated into American culture, they absorbed and reinvented their own music, and, in the modern post-recording technology era, often sent it back home to Ireland in the guise of American country. Back in Ireland, where country music has a vast and fanatical audience, American singers like Emmylou Harris and Dolly Parton would have had a huge influence on Irish traditional singers like Mary Black. Who went on to record with

Tammy Wynette. Who has admired the songwriting of Irishman Paul Brady. Whose songs have been recorded by Bob Dylan. And so on. But this constant historical movement of music from Ireland to America and back again is perhaps best illustrated by tracing the journey of one particular song.

In 1811, the Irish collector Edward Bunting noted down a song called 'Rosey Connolly' from a singer in Coleraine, County Derry. It is a chilling tale about a man who murders his lover beneath a salley tree – the local name for a willow – for no stated reason, but probably because she is pregnant outside of marriage. Perhaps understandably, given its morally dubious sexual undertones and bloodthirsty subject matter, the song did not become widely popular in Ireland.

A few years later Yeats wrote his famous poem 'An Old Song Resung', better known as 'Down by the Salley Gardens':

Down by the salley gardens my love and I did meet;
She passed the salley gardens with little snow-white feet.
She bid me take love easy, as the leaves grow on the tree;
But I, being young and foolish, with her would not agree.

Yeats tells us that the poem (dated 1888/89) is an attempt 'to reconstruct an old song from three lines imperfectly remembered by an old peasant woman in the village of Ballysodare, Sligo', in the west of Ireland. It has lyrical elements very similar to 'Rosey Connolly' although the unfortunate Rosey herself does not make an appearance. Indeed, whether consciously or not, Yeats actually turns a song about an appalling murder into a song about romantic love, which perhaps tells us a good deal about Yeats.

Moving on again, the National Library of Ireland collection contains the text of an untitled Irish folk poem from the mid-nineteenth century, which goes as follows:

Down by the Sally Gardens my own true love and I did meet
She passed the Sally Gardens, a tripping with her snow white feet.

She bid me take life easy just as leaves fall from each tree;
But I being young and foolish with my true love would not agree.

In a field by the river my lovely girl and I did stand.
And leaning on her shoulder I pressed her burning hand.
She bid me take life easy, just as the stream flows o'er the weirs
But I being young and foolish I parted her that day in tears.

Perhaps this is the song that Yeats heard. In any case, some years after he wrote 'Down by the Salley Gardens' a musical version of the Yeats poem itself – and not the original song once heard by the poet – was composed. It became immediately popular and was recorded by many Irish tenors and sopranos in the twenties, including the famous Margaret Burke Sheridan. The new song was particularly admired in the United States, where its Yeatsian provenance was gradually forgotten. It passed into the Irish tradition in America as a true folk song of unknown origin, not a poem.

Some scholars of Irish folk music maintain that Yeats's poem is based on 'Rosey Connolly', or on the untitled poem in the National Library. But others argue much more convincingly that what Yeats is recalling is not 'Rosey Connolly' or the National Library poem, but a much later song, 'The Rambling Boys of Pleasure', the second verse of which runs:

Down by yon flowery garden where me and my true love do meet
I took her in my arms and to her I give kisses sweet
She bad me take life easy just as the leaves fall from yon tree
But I being young and foolish with my true love would not agree.

This song has been recorded by a number of well-respected Irish artists, including Paddy Tunney and Planxty. Its melody is totally different to the well-known tune to which the Yeats poem has been set, and it retains the asymmetrical rhythms of an Irish language poetic form. But the similarity to the words of the Yeats poem is surely too much to be pure coincidence. We can thus deduce that what Yeats heard in Sligo and thought an ancient folk song was actually a relatively recent version of something which was in essence much older.

Moving to America: around the same time as 'The Rambling Boys of Pleasure' appeared in Ireland, across the Atlantic in rural New Hampshire the important song collectors Flanders and Olley wrote down a strange 'New England Ballad' which they had never heard before. It was called 'Sally's Garden', and the first verse went as follows:

It's down in Sally's garden, oh there hang rosies three
And there I met a fair maid who told me her mind so free
She bids me take love easy as leaves they do fall from the tree
But I being young and foolish could not with her agree.

The words of this 'traditional New England' song differ from those of 'Rosey Connolly', 'Down by the Salley Gardens' and 'The Rambling Boys of Pleasure'. 'Sally's Garden' has a different melody and shorter lines. The word 'salley' – that is, an Irish description of a willow tree – has become 'Sally', a woman's name. But it is quite obviously another distant cousin of the song first written down by Bunting, then embellished by an unknown folk musician and later tarted up by Yeats.

The years passed. In 1929, a collector heard yet another version of the song in Galway City. And then in 1992, almost two hundred years after Bunting first noted down 'Rosey Connolly', RTE (the Irish television channel) made an important documentary series about Irish traditional music called *Bringing It All Back Home*. The accompanying soundtrack album, which featured members of U2 and the Hothouse Flowers, became a massive hit in Ireland. Specially for the show and the album, the Everly Brothers were asked to contribute some material. One of the numbers they selected to record was an old American folk song about which they knew very little. It was a country waltz. Their father had taught it to them. It was called 'Rose Connolly'.

Down in the willow garden
Where me and my love did meet
She passed the willow garden
With little snow white feet.
I had a bottle of burgundy wine;
My love she did not know,
And I did murder that dear girl
All on the banks below.

I drew a sabre through her
It was a bloody sight;
I threw her in the river
It was a dreadful night.
My father he often had told me
That money would set me free
If I did murder that dear girl
Whose name was Rose Connolly.

This was a new version of the same song, somehow returned to its roots. No longer the delicate love song it had been for a hundred years, it was once again what it had originally been, a tragic ballad about a terrible crime. Amazingly, somehow the song had reverted to type.

The song had started as an oral folk piece. It had been picked up by Bunting, then by someone else, who turned it into 'The Rambling Boys of Pleasure'. A snatch of it had then been remembered by Yeats, whose own rewriting of it was moved across the Atlantic by Margaret Burke Sheridan and the other early Irish recording artists. It was brought back to Ireland again, then re-exported over to America as 'Sally's Garden', and finally transported home to Ireland once more, not by an Irish folk singer, but by the Everly Brothers, two former American country and western singers who went on to become fifties rock and roll stars, and who had no Irish connection whatsoever. The bottom line is that this song is more widely travelled than the Pope.

Happily, the song has been welcomed home, and is now widely known again in Ireland. You hear it being sung in pubs and at parties, from Donegal to Kerry. It's kind of touching really. The unfortunate Rose Connolly, lost in death for two long centuries, come back after all these years to claim the lament once intended to bear her name and mourn her tragedy. All of which shows you two things. Which are: a) Irish and American music are very frequently the same thing, and b) you can't keep a good woman down for ever.

Next to the advances in recording technology, perhaps the most important factor in the development of Irish traditional music in the modern era was the existence of the ceilidh bands. These were groups of musicians – sometimes very large groups – who played a simplified, radically scaled-down version of Irish traditional music which stressed rhythm and verve at the expense of delicacy, individual experimentation or improvisation. The ceilidh bands were frowned upon by purists of Irish traditional music, who saw them as some sort of vulgar aberration. Indeed, the greatest Irish musician of the present century, Sean O'Riada, wrote of the ceilidh experience, 'Everyone takes hold of a tune and belts away at it with as much relation to music as the buzzing of a bluebottle in an upturned jam jar.' But among ordinary consumers of the music in Ireland, and particularly in America, the ceilidh bands came to be widely seen as representing the wild and true and ultimately accessible spirit of Irish dance music. As ceilidh musicians experimented with new forms and particularly with country and bluegrass musicians, early American country began to take on something of the anarchic character of the Irish ceilidh.

In time, American country came to be influenced by gospel, jazz, rockabilly and blues, as well as by Irish ceilidh music. Indeed, the true inheritors of the ceilidh band approach to the Irish tradition were not the early American country stars, but the sentimental Irish bands which sprang up in the Irish-American cities in the 1920s and 1930s. These were performers like Dan Sullivan's Shamrock Band, the

Flanagan Brothers, Michael Hanafin, John McGettigan, Murty Rabbet and His Gaelic Band, Hugh Gillespie. They tended to be either first- or second-generation Irish, based in Boston, Chicago or New York. They began their careers by playing at weddings, wakes, christenings, family events, as they had in Ireland. Sometimes they played at 'rent parties', spontaneous boozing sessions held in private houses, to which a small admission price was charged to help a poor family. But the sheer size of the American Irish population made it possible for the best of these musicians to become professional, a scenario which would have been quite unknown for a traditional musician in Ireland. Constantly improving recording, distribution and marketing techniques opened up possibilities which had never been available back home in the old country. The music began to borrow elements from other immigrant American musics, Jewish klezmer, German bierkeller ballad, barber shop quartet. Sometimes the lyrics, now influenced by New York vaudeville and music-hall styles, became saccharine, self-parodying and kitschy. The Flanagan Brothers' song 'My Irish Molly-O' is a good example. Recorded with a backing track of blasting trumpets, a tinkling bar-room piano, oom-pah-pahing tuba bass and Inkspots-style four-part vocal harmonies, it is about as far from traditional Irish music as it is possible to get without mutating into Guns N' Roses. In yet another example of the constant back-and-forth traffic of Irish-American music across the Atlantic, in 1981 the frighteningly talented Irish band De Dannan recorded an entire album of this sentimental Irish dance music, making 'My Irish Molly-O' a huge tongue-in-cheek number one single in the Irish pop charts that summer.

Later albums by De Dannan attempted to explore even more interesting links between the Irish and American traditions. The 1992 collection 'Half Set in Harlem' experimented boldly with jazz forms, Jewish klezmer music and southern black gospel singing, with spectacular success. Listeners to this album sometimes thought they detected a strange high-pitched whirring sound, somewhere in the background of the mix. But it wasn't the record. It was poor old Sean O'Riada spinning around in his grave.

CHAPTER 7

Woollybacks!

... the Irish in America are particularly well recvd. and looked upon as Patriotic republicans, and if you were to tell an American you had flyd your country or you would have been hung for treason against the Government, they would think ten times more of you and it would be the highest trumpet sounded in your praise.

Letter from James Richey,
Irish immigrant, c. 1830

The raw Irishman in America is a nuisance, his son a curse. They never assimilate, the second generation shows an intensification of all the bad qualities of the first ... they are a burden and a misery to this country.

Boston newspaper editorial, 1850

It was early on a Tuesday morning in that late November when my father Sean and I got up and ate breakfast and went out to walk the streets of New York in search of a car-hire place. In a moment of staggering generosity the night before, Sean had offered to drive me down to Dublin, Maryland, a distance of several hundreds of miles. I had tried hard to dissuade him, but he had assured me fervently that he would enjoy it. To be honest, I did not initially think that he *would* enjoy it, but then my father's idea of enjoyment is perhaps not quite the same as my own. Here, after all, is a man who seems to enjoy both mathematics and parenthood, and really, there is no arguing with a person like that. So we agreed that we would hire a car next morning and just do it. It didn't take long to find a hire establishment.

America really is a great country. Where else in the world could you stroll into an office at eight in the morning with a credit card and have a free cup of coffee and a cream cheese bagel and stroll out again at ten past eight to find a long slim white Thunderbird gleaming on the sidewalk, just waiting for you to get into it and drive away.

The doors closed with a softly satisfying 'click'. The interior of the car looked and felt like the cockpit of a small airplane. There were dials and gadgets and buzzers of all kinds. For God's sake, there was an automatic device to prevent you having to swivel your shoulders when putting on your seat-belt. This car was like something out of a science fiction movie. It was so computerized that I thought if we accidentally pressed the wrong sequence of buttons we could launch a thermonuclear attack on the White House.

My father started up the engine, which purred like a sleeping kitten until he put his foot down on the accelerator. At this point it began to roar like a bastard. We eased out into the street, already feeling like Thelma and Louise with a surfeit of testosterone. Immediately, however, there was a problem. New York rushhour crosstown traffic is quite something. The drivers of that fair city must surely be the rudest in the whole world. They honked and blared, they wound down their windows and yelled abuse. OK, OK, so they drive on the right-hand side of the road in America. Big deal. Anyone's entitled to one little mistake, aren't they? Anyway, the drive through downtown New York to get to the Holland Tunnel was completely nerve-racking and I was glad that I was wearing my brown trousers.

'Fuck them all bar Nelson,' Sean exclaimed, as we swerved across Third Avenue and into Broome Street. ('Fuck them all bar Nelson' is one of my father's favourite expressions.)

'Why not Nelson too?' I asked him.

'Because he's fucked already, son,' my father said.

Just then, a ten-ton truck rocketed into the lane in front of us, belching out thick clouds of noxious gas. 'Get outta me way and bury me decent,' Sean said. We sped out into the passing lane. There was a high-pitched screeching sound at this point, which was either me or the tyres of the Thunderbird, I'm not sure which, and

then we sped back into the downtown lane and we put the radio
on.

As a structural engineer, my father was interested in having a look
at the Holland Tunnel. This was handy, as we would be going
through it just as soon as the massive queue declined enough to
allow us to do so. Me, I'm not sure if it was worth the wait. I do
not like tunnels. If God had meant us to tunnel, the voles would
now be running the world. But I really didn't like the Holland one
little bit. The Holland was the world's first underwater tunnel for
vehicles and it is really beginning to show its age. Knowing you are
a hundred feet below the Hudson River without a life-belt is a
disconcerting enough sensation without seeing the long patches of
leaking dampness which adorn the tunnel's ceiling. The walls were
damp too, and there were puddles on the roadway. Now, I'm sorry,
but you should not see puddles in a damn tunnel, OK? Parts of the
thing were like driving through a car wash, there was so much water
spraying down from the tiles. I have never felt so glad to see daylight
in my entire life.

We crossed the Pulaski Skyway and turned on to Highway 95
South, the New Jersey Turnpike. We took the turnpike south for
maybe fifty miles, parallel all the time to the modern Interstate 295.
Small towns sped past us in a blur. Willingboro went by, then
Moorestown and Ramblewood. A few miles past Cherry Hill we
saw the smog of Philadelphia beginning to loom up on the right.
We were going to turn off and go take a look at Philadelphia, but
then, just for the hell of it, we decided not to. We would go and
look at it tomorrow, we thought, on the way back to New York.

We drove on through the early darkness. Our headlamps carved a
thirty-foot swath through the rain, and the orange lights from the
instrument panel on the dashboard bathed the inside of the car in a
ghostly glow. Lightning flickered in the distance, making the sky
appear to flutter like a tablecloth hung on a clothesline. It was a cold
and dirty morning. Sometimes we would hit a patch of road which
hadn't been salted or sanded and the car would slide around on the
ice. The approaching car beams made the raindrops shine brightly

on the windscreen. Little piles of grey slush lay crumpled up under trees, under porches, where the sun's light couldn't get to it. The culverts and ditches at the roadside overflowed with gurgling fast-flowing water. Two young boys were playing on a rope hung from the bough of a thick oak tree. The road twisted and weaved so much that you would have prayed for God to pick it up and stretch it straight.

We went through Barrington and Runnemede, and soon after-wards we crossed the border into Delaware, through Wilmington. One strange thing was that after a while there seemed to be no towns any more. We were driving through one long suburb. On either side of the motorway sat enormous barn-like single-storey buildings that looked like they had been put up overnight, and could be taken down in half an hour if the owners of La-Z-Boy furniture, K Mart, John Deere, Wendy Hamburgers, Taco Bell, Shoneys or McDonald's decided on a whim to locate somewhere else.

We drove on through the spectacular Keatsian beauty of suburban Delaware and just after Newark we crossed into Maryland, heading west now on Highway 95, the John F. Kennedy Memorial Highway. And it was at this point that the roadside signs started to appear: 'NO NAFTA. NAFTA OUT. CLINTON OUT. COME BACK BUSH. BUSH–QUAYLE FOR 92. WE WANT GEORGE BUSH!'.

NAFTA stood for the North American Free Trade Agreement, a programme of economic cooperation which was then being negoti-ated between the United States and its neighbours Canada and Mexico. There was a lot of opposition to NAFTA, from the trade unions and from some conservative political groups. I wasn't sure where I stood myself, but one thing I was sure about was that Maryland was pretty weird. Any state whose citizens could actually erect roadsigns appealing for George Bush to come back and run the country was not entirely to be trusted. Maryland was quite obviously world capital of the stupid roadsign.

Though, having said that, I guess you have to hand it to George

Bush, really. I mean, the guy lied again and again, quite blatantly, to the American people. He twisted and weaved like a plainclothes bishop in a dubious Dublin discotheque. George said he would not put up taxes. He did. He said it wasn't a recession. It was. He said he wouldn't allow F-16 fighter planes to be sold to Japan. He did. He said Bill Clinton was a high-spending liberal. The week before the presidential election, George gave $1 billion in subsidies to American wheat farmers and $2 billion to retrain unemployed workers. Old Mister Financial Rectitude sure could spend like a bastard when there was an election coming up.

In *King Lear*, Shakespeare speaks famously of 'the glib and oily art to speak and purpose not'. George Bush had this ability, king size, big time, with fries to go. Purposing not was bad enough. But the way he spoke was a nightmare. Those rambling sentences, weird non sequiturs, frazzled syntactical somersaults. Some people wanted to know what George was on about. Other people simply wanted to know what George was on. The potent tranquillizer Halcion, it seemed. What else could explain the breathtaking verbal incontinence which became his hallmark?

'Fluency in English,' George said, in 1989, 'is something I'm frequently not accused of.'

False this most certainly was not. *New Republic* magazine once published George's views on abortion:

Well, it appear to a double standard to some, but I . . . that's my position and it's . . . we don't have the time to philosophically discuss it here, but . . . we're going to opt on the side of life. And that is . . . that is the . . . that really is the underlying part of this for me. You know, I mentioned . . . and with really from the heart . . . this concept of going across the river to this little church and watching one of our children – adopted kid – be baptized. And that made for me . . . it was very emotional for me. It helped me in reaching a very personal view of this question. A very definite view. And I just don't know.

The political philosophy of his speeches made Ronald Reagan's drooling lunatic fantasies seem like the more elegant and stirring passages of the Gettysburg Address. Here's George on the collapse of Communism: 'So,' he explained, 'it's trying to find this common ground that's moving through Eastern Europe and indeed the world, of freedom and democracy and . . . er . . . things of that nature.' And here he is, the most powerful man in the world, pondering the ethics of that democracy: 'I think in politics there are certain moral values. I'm one who . . . we believe strongly in pluralism . . . but when you get into some questions there are some moral overtones. Murder. That kind of thing.'

Jean-Jacques Rousseau, roll over.

Maybe it plays well in Maryland. But for me, George Bush was a fifty-dollar haircut on a fifty-cent head. Beside his boss, asinine Vice-President Dan Quayle was an intellectual colossus. George Herbert Walker Bush the third. The man who put the er back into America. And yet here we were in lovely Maryland, my father and I, glancing up at the signs as they flashed past us in the early morning rain: COME BACK BUSH. WE LOVE YOU GEORGE BUSH! BUSH AND QUAYLE PUT CLINTON IN JAIL! What a very strange country America is.

I had done some reading on the Irish in Maryland, and very interesting it was too. It was to this state that many of the earliest Irish immigrants to America had come as indentured servants. We are not taught about this in school in Ireland. We are taught that the Irish only went to America in great numbers during the famine, and that they were met with open arms in the land of the free. But this is not the case. The first federal census in 1790 already listed 44,000 people of Irish birth; many of them resident in Maryland. In addition, there were almost 150,000 who had Irish ancestry. Most of these earliest settlers were poor Irish Protestants. Irish Catholics did not come to the colonies in large numbers, except as servants, because many of the anti-Catholic laws which then operated in

Ireland were on the statues in America also. Indeed, when the Maryland legislature in 1704 levied a head tax on indentured servants, the act was pretty upfront about its purpose. 'To prevent the importing of too great a number of Irish Papists'. Charming, huh?

Anyway, forty miles after Newark, Delaware Sean and I and our Thunderbird came to the banks of the Susquehanna River, which was so impressive that I had to get out of the car immediately and take a photograph. I don't know why I bothered doing this, because even as I was pressing the shutter I knew I would fail. You simply cannot photograph something like a waterfall or a large river and hope to capture anything at all of its power. I have stood by the Atlantic ocean photographing majestic fifty-foot waves battering the rocks, and when I've got the pictures back from the chemist's shop they have looked for all the world like they were taken in my bath.

We crossed into the town of Havre de Grace, and at Aberdeen we turned off Highway 40. The morning started to brighten up although the rain was still falling hard. We drove on for a while, and then suddenly saw a sign for Route 136 North for Dublin. We turned off the highway and started up the side road.

The radio was playing a wonderful country gospel song as we surged on through the driving rain.

It's G–L–O–R–Y to know I'm S–A–V–E–D
I'm H–A–P–P–Y because I'm F–R double E
I once was B–O–U–N–D in the chains of S–I–N
But it's V–I–C–T–O–R–Y to know I've Christ within.

Sean and I stopped for coffee in a tiny town which had a nice little café that sold pie and sandwiches. The coffee was free and the sandwiches were cheap. The other interesting thing about the place was how clean it was. Roadside cafés are not known for their hygienic standards, after all. You would find things in the fridges of most roadside cafés that could be successfully entered in a rodeo. But not this one. The guy and his wife were scuttling around the café in a cleaning frenzy. Listen, the guy was cleaning the ceiling, for Christ's sake, with a long-handled mop. His wife was cleaning the cash register. When she had done the outside of it, she pressed a few buttons and made the drawer open, then took all the money out and started dusting the inside of the drawer! Then – I swear to God that this is true – she began going through the banknotes and straightening them. Removing the dog ears from their corners. For one awful moment I thought she was going to start Mister Sheening the coins, in which case I know I would have cantered screaming and dribbling from the establishment and into the path of an oncoming truck.

The guy was no slouch either. While his wife gave a new meaning to the phrase 'money-laundering', he crawled around on all fours, working a nailfile into the cracks between the floortiles and removing bits of dirt so infinitesimally minute that he couldn't have possibly been able to see them. When he had finished, he went over to the magazine rack, took down the magazines and started dusting the covers. 'That's nice,' Sean said, 'the way they take care of the place. You wouldn't see that in other countries. Not out in the sticks like we are here.'

I mean, it's not as if the reading material sold in American roadside cafeterias is usually very edifying anyway. I watched, enthralled, as this man continued lightly polishing the covers of *Swedish Sluts from Hell*, *Spank* and *Beaver Monthly* (which was not, incidentally, a wildlife magazine).

'They really understand service in this country,' observed Sean.

'They sure do,' I agreed.

We got back into the car and drove onwards, looking for Dublin. The land was lush and green and it looked very fertile. There were tall trees and well-ordered fields. There was a timeless quality to the landscape. Apart from the occasional car or truck, it was possible to imagine you were in a world that had actually disappeared centuries ago.

One good thing you notice when you are in rural Maryland is

that Americans take an admirably free-market view of religion. This, it seems to me, is a wonderful thing. If you don't like a particular religion in America, you don't get upset about it and blow somebody's head off, as we used to do until quite recently in Ireland. You simply set up your own.

As we sped along the quiet country roads, there were churches galore. First Lutheran. Second Methodist Reformed. Third Christ Jesus. The list of churches sounded like the Atlantic City horse-racing results. There were great big glamorous-looking buildings with tall crosses, and there were small clapboard huts with just the name of the preacher, and a quotation or two from the Bible. 'Jesus Came Forth,' for instance. 'And Moses came fifth,' Sean snickered. 'Jesus Saves' was another. 'But Schillachi hammers in the rebound with a power header,' I said. One church advertised the sabbath services of the splendidly named Reverend Thrasher.

We drove past another sign that said 'Dublin Maryland' and thus – I think reasonably – we began to entertain serious expectations of finding ourselves in a town before too long. But no matter where we went, we seemed to keep missing it. We drove up and down the highway and kept seeing more signs that said Dublin and following them. Each sign seemed to lead to another sign, and after a while I began to get the uneasy feeling that Dublin, Maryland was a place that did not really exist.

After about an hour and a half of this we pulled up in a gravel car park on a country lane. A guy in a tartan shirt was shovelling muck into the back of a little dumper truck. I got out of the Thunderbird and approached him cautiously.

'Afternoon,' I said.

He stood up slowly, like a gunman in a Western movie, and turned to face me.

'Hep yew?' he said.

'I'm from out of town,' I said.

'You don't say,' he grinned.

'I was looking for Dublin,' I said.

'Well,' he said, pointing. 'Yew just go down that way and follow the signs.' He got down on his hunkers and started doing something to the wheel of his truck.

'I suppose it's a small place,' I said.

'I suppose you could be right there,' he said, without turning.

This was clearly not going well. 'I was wondering,' I said, 'what's there to see around here?'

He shrugged. 'What'd you have in mind?'

'I don't know,' I said. 'What do people do for fun?'

He stood up. 'Fun,' he said. 'Oh yeah. Fun.'

He turned to me again and grinned so disturbingly that I suddenly began to fear that the local idea of fun might be giving a naive tourist a ten minute headstart into the woods before getting a posse of hayseeds together, tracking him down and bludgeoning him to death with farming implements.

'You mean like sights?' he said.

'Exactly,' I said.

He scratched his head and jammed his finger up his nose with such force that I thought he might do himself a mischief. 'Thur's a air fawce base just south of here,' he said. 'They gotta whole lotta tanks and shit there. From the Gulf War, y'know? Planes and shit. Gut 'em all in a lawng line down there, y'should see it, it's about as long as mah dick.' He scratched his head again. 'I dunno what else I'm gonna say,' he beamed. 'S'kinda quiet around here.'

'You must have a bit of fun sometimes,' I said.

He considered this for a moment or two. 'Not rully,' he said, then.

I took this as my signal to go back to the car. I got into it, feeling heavy of heart. Sean asked me what this guy had said. I told him. He looked out at our new friend. 'Bogtrotter,' he said, with contempt in his voice. As we started up and pulled away, I noticed that your man had got into his dumper truck, and pulled on a lever and started dumping the dirt which he had just been shovelling into the truck back out on to the ground. I wanted to stop the car and ask him why he had done this, but Sean said he didn't think this was a good idea. 'The guy's a fucking woollyback,' he said. 'He'd ate us for dinner if we let him. It's best not to get involved.'

We drove around for another hour, desperately trying to find Dublin. This was really not going well. I kept getting out the map and trying to come up with a better route, but every single turn we took seemed to keep bringing us back to where we had been before. Finally, we came to a tiny little building in the middle of nowhere. It had a glass front and it looked like a store of some kind, so I got out with the intention of asking the shopkeeper for directions. The place was not a shop, as it turned out. It was a bail office. I asked the guy behind the desk how the place worked. He explained that the state was inundated with requests from criminals for bail. If you waited for your request to be processed through the official channels, it could take ages. But if you were prepared to go private and pay a little more, a bail office could speed things up for you. In other words, if you or one of your loved ones ever get locked in a Maryland jail, there are people who will be only too happy to make a fast buck out of getting you out again. I don't know. Call me a bleeding heart liberal, but is that not the weirdest and most unfair thing you've ever heard in your life?

Anyway, the guy in the bail office gave us directions and even drew us a little map – I guess there weren't too many serious crimes being committed in Maryland that afternoon – and after a while we did manage to find Dublin.

At least, I think we did. Because Dublin, Maryland is small. Indeed, it is so small that you would need a hell of a nerve to describe it as a town at all. It is more of a crossroads, really. In fact, there is absolutely nothing in Dublin, Maryland except a church, a lot of trees, and a very large high school. That's it. My father, who had driven several hundred miles to get me to this epicentre of total nothingness, was in a remarkably philosophical mood, all things considered.

'Bit of a one-horse town,' he said. 'And the horse is fucking well dying.'

Sean and I got out of the car. He wandered off with his camera, no doubt pondering the fact that a mere seventy-two hours ago he had been on the Concorde, sipping champagne and nibbling canapes, whereas now he was in Dublin, Maryland, at least a hundred miles away from the nearest hamburger stand. I walked around the school playground taking photographs of the building. After a few minutes, the school librarian came out and asked me rather shortly what I was doing.

'I'm from Dublin, Ireland,' I said.

Her face brightened up considerably.

'Dublin, Ireland,' she said. 'Oh imagine. Dublin, Ireland. Gee whillakers.'

I had never in my life met anyone who would actually say something like 'Gee whillakers', but I was delighted to do so now. She brought me in and showed me around the school.

High schools in certain parts of New York are like something out of Dante's *Inferno*. To get in you have to be searched by security guards, and then pass through an airport-style X-ray gate. Then, when you have finally proved that you do not have any weapons with you, the security guards kick the shit out of you. Here in Dublin, Maryland, however, things were a lot more relaxed. There were cute little drawings of spacemen and animals on the walls. There were photographs of basketball and baseball teams. It looked like the kind of American high school you would see in *The Wonder Years*.

'You got a really pruddy accent,' the librarian said.

'Thank you,' I replied, blushing. 'So do you.' There was an awkward silence at this stage. 'And you have a very nice school too,' I added.

'We try to concentrate on educating the whole person,' she beamed. 'We like to think we raise decent people here.'

Much as I liked the school, I told her, I was also interested in learning a little more about other aspects of life in Dublin. Her face went a little blank at this stage. 'Like what?' she asked me. 'I don't know,' I said, 'what about the history of the town?' She smiled again, so extremely that her eyebrows almost disappeared into her hairline. 'Oh,' she said. 'If you want history, you just hold on there one second.' She went into her office and telephoned the woman who ran the local history society.

'You're really going to too much trouble,' I said. 'I'm just passing through, you know.'

'It's no trouble, dear,' the librarian said. 'You just hold on there, and we'll give you all the history you can handle.'

A few minutes later a car pulled up outside the school. Out stepped Mrs Smith, the history society's head honcho, and also a lady called Ruby, who was the oldest resident of the town. I was incredibly touched that they had made the effort to come and see me. I was also terrified, because now I would have to ask them some intelligent questions. Through the window of the school I saw my father wandering around the car park absent-mindedly taking photographs of the trees, with a plastic K Mart bag on his head to ward off the rain. How in the name of God would he ever forgive me for this?

'Now, Ruby,' the librarian said, 'wait till you hear this feller's voice.' She turned to me, smiling.

'Say somethin, honey.'

'Like what?' I said, feeling myself blush.

'I dunno. Say the Lord's prayer or somethin.'

'Seriously?'

'Yeh. Why not?'

'Our Father who art in heaven, Hallowed be thy name, Thy kingdom come, Thy will be done . . .'

'Ain't he got a pruddy voice, Ruby?' the librarian said.

'He sure does,' Ruby confirmed. 'Why, it's jest softer than a new dishcloth.'

Ruby was in her late eighties. She had attended Dublin High School as a girl. Indeed, she had met her husband there. Apart from this highly interesting fact, she seemed to know nothing else about the town at all. Was it settled by Irish immigrants, I asked Ruby and the lady from the history society. They looked at each other vaguely, as though what I had just asked was the most ridiculous question anybody could imagine. 'Why do you think that, dear?' Ruby asked. 'Well,' I said, 'it's just a small thing, but Dublin is the capital of Ireland, you see, and this town is called Dublin, and so, I just thought, maybe . . .'

The lady from the history society shook her head. 'I never heard of anybody Irish around here,' she said, 'did you, Ruby?'

'No,' said Ruby, 'I don't really know how it came to be called Dublin, do you, dear?'

'No, I don't,' said the history society lady. 'I guess that just never occurred to me.'

I was beginning to sense that this had all been a terrible mistake. Desperate, I decided to kick for touch. Was there anything of interest in the locality that I should see?

The lady from the history society pursed her lips and began to think. 'I'm sure there is,' she said, 'it's just that at the moment I can't really . . .' Her voice trailed off.

'There's a big nuclear shelter here,' Ruby said, so suddenly that it made me jump. 'If there's ever an attack we gotta go over there and get in that shelter. That's what it said in the paper. They have cans of food in there, and toilets, and, you know, mineral water and everything. They have everything a person would need in there.'

'Really, Ruby?' I said.

'Oh yes,' she said. 'It's beautiful, but of course it's closed up right now.'

I had the distinct impression Ruby would have quite liked Saddam Hussein to bomb Dublin, Maryland right that minute so she could show me the nuclear shelter.

'Apart from that,' she said, 'it's pretty quiet around here.'

We stood in the school corridor simpering at each other for some time while everybody thought of something to say. Finally it got too much for me. I said I really had to go.

Ruby looked delighted at this news. She didn't mean to be rude, she said, but she had to go too. She was on her way home to start preparing the Thanksgiving dinner for herself, her children, her grandchildren and her seven great-grandchildren. She was cooking everything herself, and she hadn't even started on the pumpkin pie.

'I've never had pumpkin pie,' I said.

'Oh Jeekers, you're joking,' Ruby said.

'We don't have Thanksgiving in Ireland,' I said.

'You don't have Thanksgiving in Ireland. Good Lord. You don't have pecan pie?'

'No.'

'Pumpkin pie?'

'No.'

I told Ruby that not only did we not have pecan pie in Ireland, but that I had never actually seen a pecan in my life. I would not know a pecan, I confided, if it walked up to me in the street singing 'God Bless America'.

'What a shame,' Ruby said.

We agreed that Ireland was a barbaric and completely uncivilized kip of a country, not to have pecan pie, and I left them still standing in the corridor and discussing this gastronomical atrocity while I made my excuses and ran. As I stepped out into the rain, I reminded myself to write away and become an honorary member of the Dublin, Maryland History Society some time. I'm sure the meetings are really wild affairs.

Out in the yard, two teenage boys were playing basketball. One was very tall and gangly. He had on a baseball cap and a tracksuit with the words 'Brooklyn Dodgers' on the back. The other was short and pudgy. He was wearing a T-shirt which announced 'My Baby Left Me', and a pair of lurid luminous green shorts which went all the way down to his knobbly knees.

'Hi,' said the fat one.

'Hi,' I said.

'What you doin?'

'Nothing,' I said.

'S'whut I thought,' he said, and tittered.

I asked if these two fine fellows went to school here, and they

nodded. What was it like, I enquired. They said something unprint-
able. And what was living in Dublin like? They said something
unthinkable.

'And what are you going to do when you leave school?' I asked.

'I'm goin in the army,' the tall one said.

'Why?' I wondered.

'Cos you don't have to work too hard,' he said, 'and you get to
blow seven kinds of shit out of Ay-rabs.'

Fatso snuffled with laughter.

I said I had heard, on the contrary, that hard work was very much
an essential part of army life. And that blowing the shit out of Ayrabs
was not. At least, not very often.

'Well see, I'm real good at sports,' he said. 'If you're good at
sports you don't have to work so hard in the army.'

I asked what kind of sport he was good at.

'Football, basketball, baseball.'

'Anything with balls,' Fatso said.

'Shut your mouth, Retardo,' said the elongated one.

'Do you have a good football team in Maryland?' I said.

'In my dick we do,' said Fatso.

I took this to be something of a negative.

'So who do you support?' I said.

'Miami Dolphins,' he said. 'Best deefence in the NFL.'

'I like the Dallas Cowboys,' his lanky friend said.

'You like my dick,' he said.

'No, I don't.'

'That your car?' said the aspiring soldier, nodding in the direction
of the Thunderbird.

'Yeah,' I said.

'Nice,' he said. 'That a rental?'

'Yes,' I said.

'Where you from anyway?' he said.

'Ireland,' I said.

'Where?'

'Ireland.'

'In Europe, right?'

'Yeah.'

'Near Germany, right? And Poland?'

'Not really, no.'

'Not near Germany?'

'No.'

'It ain't near Germany, you dork,' said Chubby. ''Snear Scotland.'

'That right? Is it near Scotland?'

'Well, it's quite near there.'

'Like how near. Like Maryland–New York near or what?'

'Do you know U2?' I said.

'Sure,' they said.

'They're from Ireland,' I said.

'No way,' they said.

'Way,' I said. 'They're from Dublin, Ireland. That's where I'm from. The same town.'

'You live in Dublin, Ireland,' said Fatso.

'Yes.'

'The same town as U2?'

'Yes.'

'You know U2, right?' he said.

'I don't know them,' I said. 'I've met them once.'

'Yeah, right,' they both said. 'In my dick, you have.'

'I have,' I said.

'Bullshit.'

'Have you?'

'Yes,' I said. 'But only once.'

Another young fellow appeared at the entrance to the car park, riding an expensive-looking bicycle. He was doing wheelies.

'Hey, Jimmy,' he bawled. 'There's a guy here says he knows U2.'

Jimmy leaned down low to his handlebars and pedalled hard. When he got off the bike he threw back his head, made a hawking sound with his throat, snuffled hard and spat on the ground.

'Oyster for lunch,' he said.

'Oh God you're so gross.'

'Shut up, pussy.'

He looked up at me, his round teenage face a veritable symphony of florid acne and semi-healed scars.

'So anyways. You know U2?'

'Look, I didn't say that. I just—'

'You know U2?'

'Well, no. I—'

'You know 'em or not?'

'I met them once.'

'In my big fat juicy dick you did. Where?'

'In New York. I only met them once. Very briefly.'

'Really?'

'Truly.'

His mouth opened and closed a few times in the manner of a goldfish.

'Fuck me backways with a chainsaw,' he said. 'You met them.'

'Well, I—'

'What were they like?'

'I don't know,' I said. 'They seemed very nice.'

'Nice? Nice? You met U2 and they were nice? What kind of a fucken word is nice?'

'I mean they seemed very friendly, but, I mean, I didn't talk to them for very long or anything.'

'You ever met any other celebrities?'

'No,' I said. (I had, actually. I just didn't feel like going into it right now.)

'Me neither,' said Jimmy. 'But my brother met Oprah Winfrey once.'

There was silence for a few moments. I could hear the birds croaking in the fields. I could see my father, enthusiastically photographing a fence-post.

'He wants to meet Madonna,' said Fatso.

'I do not,' Jimmy scoffed.

'You do too.'

'Do not.'

'Tell him what you said, you know, about what you wanted to do to Madonna.'

'No.'

'Tell him.'

'No way.'

'I'll tell him if you don't.'

'You do that and I'll rip your arms off and beat you to death with the wet end.'

Sadly, Jimmy didn't ever tell me what he wanted to do with Madonna. Give her singing lessons, I was hoping.

'You never met anyone else famous?' asked Lanky.

'No.'

'My dad met Joe Namath once,' Jimmy said.

'Oh yeah,' tittered Fatso. 'Well your dad met my big fat dick once too. OK?'

'Fuck you.'

'And you.'

'And your mother.'

'And your dog.'

'Retardo.'

'I know you are.'

'Thalidomide.'

'I know you are.'

'Pussy.'

'I know you are.'

'Homo.'

'Douchebag.'

'Pizzafeatures.'

At this point, I decided I'd leave the lads to their merry banter. And so I departed, to a final fanfare of fucks.

Desperate for inspiration, I went off to look around the Dublin graveyard. There was a John Connor buried there, and there was a woman whose surname was Ward. These were the only two Irish names I could find. I took photographs of the two tombstones. I took photographs of the grass. And then I walked around for a while looking for something else to photograph. But there really wasn't anything else. I had the sinking sensation that I done Dublin, Maryland.

On the way back to the Thunderbird, I passed the three lads still hard at it in the playground.

'Scumbag.'

'Shitstabber.'

'Your grandmother sucks cocks in hell.'

'You know the difference between your grandmother and the bus to Philadelphia?'

'No, Spazzo. What?'

'Not everyone's been on top of the bus to Philadelphia.'

'Toilet-head.'

'Testicle-face.'

'Worm-dick.'

'Shrimpfucker.'

Shrimpfucker? I thought.

I got into the car. Sean was dripping all over the driver's seat, shivering and looking at the map.

'Well, where'll we go now?' he asked.

'Anywhere,' I said. 'Just let's burn rubber.'

'Anywhere like where?' he asked, reasonably.

I took the map from him and looked at it. 'Baltimore?' I said.

He started up the engine and pushed the accelerator to the floor. 'Outta me way,' he said, 'and bury me fucking decent.'

As Sean and I sped along the highway we saw a signpost for Carrolton, the townland named after the most important Irish Catholic family in colonial America, the Carrolls, the first of whom came to Maryland in 1688 under the patronage of the Catholic King James II. The Carrolls survived and became large landowners in Maryland, in fact a descendant of the first immigrant Carrolls, Charles, born in 1737, must have pissed off a great number of people when he became the only Catholic to sign the Declaration of

Independence. He added insult to injury by becoming extraordinarily rich, and dying only when he was ninety-five.

Readers who entertain ambitions to keep kicking on until they are ninety-five themselves will be interested in the Charles Carroll workout system, as described by the great American diarist, Philip Hone.

I paid this morning a visit which I have long been wishing for to the venerable Charles Carroll, the only surviving signer of the Declaration of Independence. He will be ninety-four years of age next September. His faculties are very little impaired, except his sight, which within the last few months has failed him a little, and deprived him of the pleasure of reading at all times, which he has sometimes enjoyed. He is gay, cheerful, polite and talkative. He described to me his manner of living. He takes a cold bath every morning in the summer, plunging headlong into it; rides on horseback from eight to twelve miles; drinks water at dinner; has never drunk spirituous liquors at any period of his life, but drinks a glass or two of madeira wine every day, and sometimes champagne and claret; takes as much exercise as possible; goes to bed at nine o'clock, and rises before day.

I read all this out to Sean as we drove the narrow roads in search of the turn-off to Baltimore. He said it sounded a lot better than playing squash and having liposuction.

Maryland was founded as the sole Catholic colony in America. It was also the northernmost slave state. Its main city, Baltimore – named after the town of Baltimore in west County Cork – has never had a very good press.

Baltimore is actually a pleasant enough town, with a nice little gallery, the Walters on Charles Street, and a colourful Little Italy section which is more fun than the one in New York. And any city that gave to the world Billie Holiday, Edgar Allan Poe and profoundly sick exploitation film-maker John 'Pink Flamingo'

Waters cannot be all bad. 'You can look far and wide,' Mr Waters once fondly insisted, 'but you'll never discover a stranger city. It's as if every eccentric in the South decided to move north, ran out of gas in Baltimore and decided to stay.'

The best thing that ever happened to Baltimore was a terrible fire which, in 1904, burnt almost the entire ugly city to the ground. It was rebuilt over the next two decades, and while it is not exactly pre-Socratic Athens, it does at least have something like a human scale. The people of Baltimore, perhaps unused to the idea of tourists, are extremely – not to say weirdly – friendly. For those with a taste for all things odd, the Peale Museum near City Hall is well worth a visit. The excellent Charles Willson Peale built this exotic junkshop which does its heroic best to masquerade as an educational establishment for young people. It is unlikely that young people will find this fabulous cornucopia of voodoo artefacts, severed limbs, shrunken heads and wax models of carnival ghouls particularly educational, unless, of course, they happen to be Bart Simpson, but it is a very fine place nevertheless. Poe's grave is underneath Westminster Church. The great scarifier actually only lived in Baltimore for three years, during which time he managed to get married to his teenage cousin, but many moons later he completed a nostalgic vacation to the city by keeling over and dying in it. I liked Baltimore, I seriously did. After Dublin, Maryland it seemed like Vegas. I couldn't really see what Randy Newman was on about.

After a little stroll around, I suggested that we find a motel and check in for the night. But Sean had had enough by now. He wanted to get back into the Thunderbird and drive back to New York. I wondered whether the stress of the day had been too much for him, and whether he had actually lost his mind. But no, he said, he simply fancied driving back to New York, just for the hell of it. So just for the hell of it, I said OK. And we did, arriving into Manhattan as the lights were coming on in the skyscapers and a gentle fall of snow began to rain down over Broadway like so much gorgeous confetti. I have to tell you, it felt very good to be home.

CHAPTER 8

Pennsylvania Über Alles

My dear Father and Mother, I remit to you in this letter twenty dollars, that is, four pounds, thinking it might be some acquisition to you until you might be clearing away from that place altogether – and the sooner the better, for believe me I could not express how great would be my joy at our seeing you all here together where you would never want or be at a loss for a good breakfast and dinner.

Letter from Margaret M'Carthy,
Irish immigrant, 1850

Sucking up the coal dust into your lungs
Underneath the hills where there is no sun
Try to make a living on a dollar a day
Digging bloody coal in Pennsylvania.

Traditional Irish song,
nineteenth century

The next morning Sean and I found ourselves once again on the New Jersey Turnpike and heading south from New York. It was a nice bright sunny morning, which was only very slightly spoilt for me by the lambent horror of realizing, after perhaps a whole hour of driving, that we were on Interstate 280 West, whereas in point of fact we should have been on Interstate 90 South.

I wondered what to do about this. At first, I thought I would do absolutely nothing and try to just gently steer us back on to the correct road without acknowledging my error. But as time went on and southern California became an ever increasing possibility, I decided I better come clean. I broke the news gently to my dear father, whose patience I really did think had to be reaching its end. He had come to New York for a few quiet days of rest and had ended up driving halfway around the south-eastern states being navigated by a person who never even succeeded in getting his Boy Scouts' orienteering badge. If he had started to roar and bawl abuse at me I could have taken it. Instead, he just sighed and smiled and assured me that these things happen, and this, of course, made me feel even worse.

We drove on through Harrison, under the Garden State Parkway, through Orange, Bloomfield, Livingstone and Parsippany, managing to miss the turn off for the motorway at every single one of these small towns. Finally, just outside Parsippany, with the Pacific practically coming into ocean view over the hills, we managed to turn around and get on to Interstate 287 South.

So here we were in rural Pennsylvania, the state which was named after its original proprietor, the famous William Penn. Mr Penn was an interesting chappie, and like just about everyone else in American history, he has an Irish connection if you are prepared to go trawling back far enough.

Penn was a Quaker who was expelled from Oxford University for holding religious meetings. Those were the days, huh? These days students get expelled from that fine rustic university for quaffing Benylin/champagne cocktails and molesting their scouts, but back in the olden days things were different.

Penn's family did not like his religion and pursued a variety of approaches towards getting him to chuck it in. One early and admirably objective biographer tells us:

> He was turned out of doors at the age of eighteen, soon to be recalled and, in hope of ruining his religion, sent to gay and profligate Paris and continental Europe. On his return two years later he was placed in charge of his father's affairs in Ireland where his religion caused his imprisonment ... This youthful choice to obey God and conscience rather than man and custom and to follow duty ... moulded his whole future life, influenced the history of Pennsylvania and helped to make the United States the world's grandest, richest and most influential republic.

Anyway, Penn's family managed to get him home from Ireland, but in time they appear to have become sick and tired of having the holy little git around the house. So when, in an attempt to secure payment of debts due to his father, Penn asked the King to give him a tract of land in America, and the King said yes, they were more than happy to see him go.

Off he went to set up Pennsylvania as a land of religious liberty, or, as he put it himself, 'a free colony for all mankind'. Unless you happened to be a black member of mankind from Africa, of course, or an Irish Catholic indentured servant, in which case you were shipped over to enjoy the phenomenal benefits of Pennsylvanian freedom whether you actually wanted them or not.

Still, all such bitter and negative thoughts were banished from our heads that morning as we passed through the splendidly named towns of Cedar Knolls, Basking Ridge, Liberty Corner and Pluckemin. At Martinsville we managed to turn on to Interstate 282 South. We drove through Bridgewater, Raritan, South Branch, Centerville, Flemington, Larison's Corner and Ringoes, and just after Mount Airy we came to the Delaware River, which we crossed at New Hope Creek.

The landscape became even more rural now. There were fields full of scarecrows, there were broken-down picket fences, rugged stone walls, decorated mailboxes. We drove on, through Lahasca, Buckingham and Furlong. Just past Furlong we turned on to Route 113 North. Irish place names started to appear on the roadsigns. There were signs for Shannonville and Limerick. We drove through Doylestown, home of the Delaware Valley College, through Fountainville, and came to Dublin.

Dublin, Pennsylvania looked a little more promising than Dublin, Maryland, in that it at least seemed to be a real town, with real shops and restaurants and bars. At the crossroads in the centre of the town there was a large store selling kitchen equipment and we swept into the car park and pulled up to make a plan. I noticed that the sign on the wall said the car park was strictly for customers only. This might be a problem, I pointed out to my father as we got out of the car.

Sean glanced at the sign, ran into the shop and emerged thirty seconds later having purchased a box of matches. This, he said, made him a customer and gave him full and legal parking rights. 'But I looked at some really nice stoves too, though,' he told me. 'I think the poor eejit thought I was going to actually buy one and stick it in the back of the Thunderbird.'

We wandered down the main street and found a bookshop. I thought this might be a good place to begin my research so I went in, leaving Sean out on the street with his camera. The very pleasant woman behind the counter greeted me warmly. I told her I was from Dublin, Ireland, and she smiled. 'You know, the most highly interesting thing about Dublin, Pennsylvania,' she said, 'is that it is definitely not named after Dublin, Ireland.' Well, you can imagine how highly fucking interested I was to hear this. I wondered whether I should go outside and tell my father this, or should I just skip out the back door and hang myself?

In 1762, the woman explained, the first log tavern in the area was erected at the main crossroads by a man called Robert Robinson. Soon after this a sharp-eyed competitor built a second log tavern alongside the first, similar in design and size. At a later date the two taverns came under one ownership and the two buildings were joined together. As other business were formed nearby, and more and more settlers arrived, the area began to be called Double Inn, which in time became Dublin.

'So,' I gasped, 'this place has nothing to do with Dublin, Ireland.'

'Nothing,' she smiled. 'Isn't that just the funniest thing?'

'Hahahahahaha,' I said.

Pennsylvania generally and Bucks County (the county in which Dublin lies) in particular are very much in love with a constructed and cutesy version of their pasts. Down in the Dublin library that afternoon, I found myself leafing through a copy of the local magazine *Bucks County Town and Country Living*. This is the kind of magazine that calls its recipe section 'Grandmom's Pies'. Another magazine, *Old Bucks County*, had an advertisement for turkeys. 'We're still raising them on our Bucks County farm the way Old Grandpop did in 1940.' The fact that in between raising turkeys Old Grandpop was probably cantering around the countryside burning crucifixes and wearing sheets was not mentioned. You might think I'm joking about all this. I'm not. Another local magazine featured a mock interview with a seventeenth-century slave. The slave is asked how he feels about Bucks County. 'All our work would be pleasant,' he replies, 'if we had but the happy faculty of singing at our toil.'

This self-mythologizing of Bucks County is pretty puke-making, when you consider some sources estimate that at one point perhaps as many as a quarter of the entire population were slaves, and as many as 40 per cent were indentured servants. Lowest on the social scale, of course, were the blacks, who were treated in Pennsylvania every bit as badly as they ever were in the South. Next up were the indentured white servants – very many of them Irish men and women – who were bought and sold like chattels by their Christian masters.

This loathsome system of indentured servitude was one of the most important arrangements England used for populating her far-flung colonies. Thousands of servants were promised land, money and freedom in America. Fifty shillings and fifty acres of land in exchange for a period of four to eight years of unpaid service would have been a relatively common agreement. But even this had absolutely no standing in law. Once you found yourself in Pennsylvania you could be treated pretty much the way your master wanted to treat you.

Penn, to his credit, did his best at least to define the conditions of these miserably poor people's servitude. In April 1782 it was ordered that 'There shall be a register for all servants, where their names, time, wages and days of payment shall be registered.' They were still to be treated as slaves, however, and could be openly sold, with no compunction even to keep families together. The same law gave masters sweeping powers of punishment against slaves or servants who tried to escape. To induce a servant to run away was considered as serious an offence as to actually abscond.

The number of indentured servants in Pennsylvania was so large that at one stage, early state records note, there was a plan to set up a 'town allotted for servants' called, with an irony so cruel that it anticipates Orwell, 'Freetown'.

In 1729 an act was passed placing a duty on 'Irish servants imported into this province,' and it remained in place for almost a hundred years. It established that Irish servants could be legally sold by merchants and sea captains. (Ten pounds would buy a freedom-loving Pennsylvanian an Irish slave for five years.) A later law defined these indentured servants as 'a legal property' and stated that an owner could 'sell or bequeath them: and like other chattels, they are liable to be seized for debts'.

There is an optimistic and chirpy Irish emigration song about the state of Pennsylvania, the opening lines of which go as follows:

With my bundle on my shoulder
Faith, there's no man could be bolder
I am leaving dear old Ireland without warning.
For I lately took the notion
For to cross the briny ocean
And I'm bound for Philadelphia in the morning.

The poor old songwriter must have got a heck of a shock when he found himself in the real Pennyslvania rather than one that had existed in his imagination. Perhaps he might even have been one of the unfortunates I read about in the Dublin Public Library that morning. (This announcement is from the *Pennsylvania Gazette* of 12 September, 1765.)

SERVANTS. Now remaining on board the Ship Neptune, near Willing and Morris's Wharff, and to be sold very cheap, for cash or short credit, by John Hart. A few Irish servants, Men, Women and Boys, amongst which are . . . Plaisterers, Farmers, Labourers &c.

I read this passage several times over and tried to imagine the true depth of the human misery which lay behind the words. Grand-mom's pies, indeed. There was something about Pennsylvania which really made me want to chuck my cookies.

The afternoon was getting cold now. I went into a little store just off Main Street which sold antiques and bits of broken furniture. There was a small carved wooden swastika sitting on a shelf. The man behind the counter came over and explained that this was a 'hexafoo' or 'witchfoot'. I said I found it a little disturbing and he laughed. He said that the swastika was actually part of Pennsylvania's more humane history. He rooted through the shelves and found an old dust-covered book, in which he showed me this extract: 'If by a swastika sign on a door or a forebay, the power of a witch on the building concerned could be averted, there was no need of hanging the witch, and the danger of hanging some excellent old lady under wrong apprehensions was avoided.'

He then tried to sell me the book. When I said that I didn't want to buy it he looked a bit miffed. He went off to search his shelves again and came back ten minutes later with another dusty tome. He showed me the following passage:

Pennsylvania is richer in the best racial elements than is any other state. The Swedes and the Dutch were the first settlers. The Germans of various religious organizations like the Moravians, and the French Huguenots followed. Then, of course, there was the very large element of English people who came with Penn or on his invitation. We have here, therefore, the five finest racial elements, both as regards character in general and the aesthetic arts in particular, if we omit the Italian.

It was nice of the man to have gone to all this trouble, but I must admit that I felt just a tad uncomfortable reading blithe accounts of racial superiority in a town where my countrymen and women had been sold into slavery and the swastika was considered a desirable item of interior decor. And anyway, I thought, let me get this straight here. The Swedes, masters of the aesthetic arts? Was this perhaps a reference to Abba?

I left the shop and strolled back into the town. At the main crossroads there was a plaque commemorating men from the area who had fought in the world wars. I noticed that there was not one Irish name on the list, although, funnily enough, there were quite a lot of German names. I couldn't figure this out for a while. What had happened to all those thousands and thousands of Irish slaves? Had even their names been taken away from them?

I went into the town hall, where Assistant Borough Manager Robert H. Edwards and his assistant Joanna were hard at work on their typewriters. I asked if they had any information about Dublin. They looked at each other and smiled. Mr Edwards took a deep breath and started to recite:

'The borough of Dublin, Pennsylvania, is six miles northwest of Doylestown, the county seat of Bucks County. The earliest settlers were mixed, English and Scotch-Irish, but the name of the town has nothing to do with the capital of Ireland. The main industries of the town are . . .'

'I know all that, Robert,' I said. 'I was really looking for an impression, you know, of what it's like, living in a place like this.'

'How do you mean, an impression?'

'Well is there any crime, for instance?' I asked.

'You're not lookin at much crime in a place like this,' Joanna said. 'I think we had a murder mebbe six years ago. But apart from that, nuthin much.'

'But we got all the records of the council from day one,' Robert told me proudly. 'You wanna take a look at 'em?'

'Sure,' I said. To tell you the truth, I didn't really. But I was so amazed that a place as small as this would actually have official council records that I kind of had to see them.

A glance at the original petition for the charter for the incorporation of the Borough of Dublin reveals how thoroughly the Irish assimilated in this corner of Pennsylvania. There are no Irish or Scottish names. Dublin was established by Buckners, Yoders, Strohms, Albrights, with a sprinkling of Gruvers, Steinhauers, Rosenbergers and Worthingtons. And the town records reveal very clearly that as soon as they set the place up they did what all great pioneers do in the end, that is, they broke up into sub-committees and started having arguments so exciting as to be practically orgasm-inducing. You might be interested in some of the highlights:

6 January 1913: On motion made by Mr Albright and seconded it was agreed to pay 17½ cents per hour for labor; the laborer to furnish his own tools. On motion made by Mr Schuler and seconded it was agreed to pay 2½ cents per horse per hour and 3½ cents per hour for 2 horses.

5 May 1913: On motion of Mr Albright and seconded a fee of $2.00 is charged for all circuses and medicine shows coming into our borough.

2 February 1914: The street commississioner's pay was raised to $1.90 per day, Joseph Tyson being appointed.

4 June 1914: On motion of Mr Musselman and seconded the president was authorized to appoint a committee to buy chairs and cuspidor for use of council during their meetings.

8 August 1916: It was ordered that Frank D. Arnold be instructed to paint the signs or finger boards within the town limits.

Dublin grew pretty slowly. By 1962, the entire borough only contained one and a half miles of road, and less than $800,000 worth of property. The council report for that year proudly proclaims that the 'Biggest Building Boom' of the year has been the issuing of '21 building permits including 10 chicken houses (Eggs to be sold at $1.00 per dozen)'.

Phew, democracy in action, huh? I must have spent several hours looking through the written history of the town of Dublin, Pennsylvania and I found only one reference to anything Irish. This was the following:

Mass was first read at Saint Patrick's mission, Dublin, on Christmas Day 1944. The announcement book for that occasion reads 'The first mass will be said at the mission in Dublin today at 11 a.m. The building was formerly a garage and we are now using it for mass. Our Lord first came to a stable and today we will have Him come down to our new mission which was a stable since the auto replaced the horse. It is quite appropriate then that we should have the first Mass on Christmas Day.'

Here in Dublin, where the sons of Erin are the exception, many hands from many lands are contracting to build a monument of the greater honor and glory of God and the Holy Mother Church, wherein they will adore him with a single tongue of Roman Catholic Unity. There is a Cead Mile Failte to all at Hilltown and Dublin. [Cead Mile Failte is an Irish phrase, meaning 'a hundred thousand welcomes'.]

That was it. One single written reference to Ireland in a town called Dublin, part of a county that had once contained tens of thousands of Irish slaves. The sons of Erin are the exception all right. Whether by accident or design, the Irish had simply been removed from the area's history.

When I had finished in the town hall I went down the street to the restaurant where I had arranged to meet my father. He was sitting at a table with his head in his hands.

'Did you find anything interesting?' he asked me.

I told him I didn't know.

'Well this is certainly the fucking sticks,' Sean said. 'You'd end up writing poetry if you lived around here too long.'

We ordered some food and I began to go through my notes. The waitress came over to give us glasses of water.

'Pardon me, gentlemen,' she said, 'but are you gentlemen from Ireland?'

We said yes, we were indeed.

The waitress smiled and said she had been to Ireland herself some years ago. She had gone to Belfast for the wedding of a friend. After the wedding she had taken a trip to Donegal and Sligo. We told her that we were from Dublin, Ireland. She frowned.

'I never went to Dublin,' she said. 'People said it was too dangerous.'

'Dublin was too dangerous?' I said. 'And Belfast wasn't?'

'Oh no,' she shrugged. 'Belfast was fine. People all said there was a lot of crime in Dublin. But Belfast was neat.'

Perhaps only a Pennsylvanian would regard a city being busily ripped asunder by all-out sectarian guerrilla war as 'neat'.

After lunch we took another walk around the town, but there really wasn't anything else to see. Sean delicately suggested we go back to New York. I was in a bad mood, I suppose. The day had been a bit of a disappointment. I had tried hard to find out what had happened to all the Irish who had once lived in this area, and I couldn't help feeling there was something I hadn't been told. I still felt guilty too, for dragging Sean on this wild-goose chase with me.

Back in the car my father told me to cheer up. He was enjoying himself anyway, he said. Earlier that day in Dublin he had seen a cowboy. A guy in all the old-fashioned cowboy gear. He had been wearing spurs and everything. He laughed when he told me this and I asked him what was so funny.

'Ah, nothing,' he said. 'But it made me think. When I was your age I worked for a fellow in Dublin called Sir Hugh Moloney. His father was the last English viceroy in Ireland. Sir Huge Baloney, we called him. He was a decent fellow. But he was the meanest man in all Ireland. He wouldn't spend Christmas.

'And anyway, there was a fellow worked there in the office, he was a terrible messer. He used to make spurs out of pieces of paper and he'd attach them to the shoes of whoever would come in. I'd have to engage them in conversation, you know, and the door behind them would slowly open. Then Mike would come shuffling in on all fours, and attach these spurs to the back of their shoes, and they'd go off out into the street not knowing they were wearing spurs.'

He laughed again. 'So the world is full of fucking cowboys, son,' he said. 'You don't have to come over here to see them, but I'm glad I did all the same.'

It was great that the world was so small now, he told me. It was great that a person could just hop on a plane and be in America in a few hours. How awful it must have seemed for the poor emigrants, he said, knowing that when you went to America you'd probably never come home again in your life. It must have seemed like going to the moon, he said, or to Mars. I asked him whether it was like that when he was a kid. When his own brothers and sisters had to emigrate, did he think he was saying goodbye to them for ever? He laughed. When he was a child, he said, even the rest of Ireland had seemed like a vast and terrifying place. Anywhere outside of Dublin was foreign, he said.

He told me a story then, about the first time he left Dublin by himself. He was thirteen or fourteen and he wanted to go to Dundalk, a town near the border with Northern Ireland, to run in a race. His mother hadn't wanted to let him go, but he had insisted and in the end she had backed down. He had set off early in the morning of the day before the race on his bike, with a paper bag full of sandwiches and a few shillings. Along the way, all sorts of disasters had befallen him. He had lost his money and got a puncture. He had slept in a barn somewhere and eaten all of his sandwiches because he was so hungry. But the next day he had turned up in Dundalk to run in the race.

'I came second in it,' he said. 'I was wrecked with the tirdeness now, I really was. But I got straight back up on the bike and rode all the way back to Dublin, and I showed my mother my medal. And that's what foreign travel was to me.'

'You must have been thrilled with your medal,' I said.

Sean paused for a minute. He stared out at the road unrolling ahead of us. He shook his head and laughed softly. 'I'll tell you what, son,' he said. 'That was the first time in my life I was ever away from home. And the night I got back, there was no happier boy in all of Ireland.'

I spent most of the rest of that week in the New York City Public Library, taking notes and frantically photocopying large chunks of utterly useless information on the history of the Irish in America, and on Thursday night Sean and I took a cab uptown to the Metropolitan Opera House to see *La Bohème*.

It was my first time at the Met and I must say the place was looking well. *La Bohème*, for the benefit of unoperatic readers, is about a number of creative types eking out an existence in a Parisian slum in the middle of the nineteenth century. Whoever designed the Met production, however, had clearly never lived in poverty themselves. The impoverished artists' garret in Act I looked like a particularly expensive SoHo loft.

Early on in the opera there is a moment where the evil landlord comes in demanding his rent money from our heroes. The audience, being American, practically stood up on their seats and began to boo at this point. 'Jesus, everyone's against the poor old landlord,' Sean whispered to me. 'But he's the only one of the whole lot who isn't a complete fucking eejit.' I did think my father had a point, I must say. I was further convinced when towards the end of Act III Rodolfo says he will not take Mimi back because she is so ill from consumption and he loves her so deeply that he simply cannot bear to see her suffer any more.

'Why doesn't he go out and get a fucking job?' Sean said. 'And get her a fucking doctor for God's sake?'

The next night we had another musical treat. We went to the Music Box Theater on Broadway to see *Blood Brothers* by Willy Russell. David Cassidy and his brother Shaun played Eddie and Micky, the eponymous siblings, separated at birth by ill fortune. It was extremely enjoyable, I must say, particularly because the audience was full of thirty-year-old women whose febrile adolescent fantasies had clearly been fuelled by either David or Shaun Cassidy, or, who knows, perhaps both. Thus, every time either one of the brothers bounded on to the stage and grinned at the crowd, the theatre echoed with hysterical screams, loud foot-stamping and the sound of a large number of body clocks ominously ticking in unison. I imagine they had to hose down the seats at the interval.

At the end of the show there was a standing ovation. David Cassidy came back out on to the stage alone and held up his hands to appeal for silence. At this stage women were being passed over the heads of the crowd, salivating and having multiple orgasms. When the screaming finally died down, David said: 'Hey, thank you, and I just wanna say, we all gotta stick together and do somethin about this AIDS thing, OK? Thank you. We love you. G'night, New York. You're beautiful.'

People with AIDS can relax now. David Cassidy is on the case.

Next morning Sean and I woke up early and had breakfast in the hotel dining room. Afterwards we went for a short walk in Gramercy Park. It was a beautiful autumn New York morning, with a crisp silver frost on the trunks of the trees. We didn't have very long, because my father had to pack. He was going back to Ireland today. I was going to Virginia.

'Well it was a great break, Joe,' he said, outside the hotel. 'Thanks for asking me.'

He gave me a hug, then clambered into the taxi and roared away down the street. I went back upstairs to the room and put on a sweater and a coat. Then I came out again and walked all the way up to Central Park by myself.

It was still early enough when I got to the park. There were only a few people around, a couple of joggers, a solitary roller-blade skater. I thought about my dad. I felt suddenly very lonely. I was really going to miss having him around.

CHAPTER 9

Duke and Alison

Oh, there's brandy in Quebec at nine cents a quart, boys
The ale in New Brunswick is a penny a glass
And there's wine in that sweet town they call Montreal, boys
At inn after inn we shall drink as we pass.
And we'll call for a bumper of ale, wine and brandy
And we'll drink to the health of those far far away
And our hearts will be warm at the thought of old Ireland
When we're in the green fields of Amerikay.

From 'The Green Fields of Amerikay',
traditional Ulster song, nineteenth century

Come all you loyal Irishmen and listen for a while
All you that wants to emigrate and leave the Emerald Isle
A kind advice I'll give to you for you to bear in mind
How you will be forsaken when you leave your land behind.

From 'Edward Connors',
traditional Ulster song, nineteenth century

That Monday afternoon I took a taxi out to La Guardia airport to catch the flight down to Roanoke, West Virginia. The plane was absolutely tiny; it held about twenty passengers including myself, my English neighbour, who insisted on telling me that he was an aspiring actor, and his ego. I was sitting in the front seat, and the stewardess was opposite me. Every time I tried to engage her in conversation old Prince Hamlet beside me would butt in and ask something really intelligent like 'So, is Ireland still part of Britain or what?'

When we got to Roanoke airport the terminal was almost empty. I wandered up to a security man and asked if there was a bank around, or some other place to change travellers' cheques. He laughed uproariously, as though having such a facility in an airport would be like having a condom machine in a convent. He then directed me to a shop where, he said, the assistant might be able to help me.

The shop was one of those places you only see in airports, where they sell individual tampons and packs of anti-travel sickness pills and big fat books which tell you how to become a millionaire without ever having to work for it. I asked the girl behind the counter if she could change my cheque for me. An anxious look invaded her face. She looked over her shoulder even though there was nobody there. 'If you could buy somethin,' she said, 'it'd make things a whole lot easier, sugar.'

I told her I really didn't want to buy anything very expensive, but she said that would be all right, as long as I bought something. So I bought a postcard of the sun setting over a lake and handed her a hundred-dollar travellers' cheque. She handed me back ninety-nine dollars and seventy-five cents.

'You come back now,' she beamed, and I assured her that I would.

The airport lobby featured a large plastic display unit divided into panels. Each panel featured a faded colour photograph of a local hotel with a telephone number underneath. This was great, I thought, as I stepped up to it full of eager anticipation. Sadly, however, most of the numbers seemed to have been disconnected. The few hotels with functioning phone numbers were all full. I wondered what to do.

Outside on the rank there were no taxis, and the place seemed pretty dead. I went back into the lobby and asked a man on crutches if he knew where I could find a hotel. He didn't. I hung around for almost an hour waiting for a taxi but none showed up. It was getting late and dark now and I didn't fancy a night in Roanoke airport. So I wondered back into the building again, determined to sort myself out. The lobby was full of car-hire stalls, none of which had any staff working behind them. The only counter which was staffed offered a limousine service. It was a bit pricey, but I figured I had no choice. The woman on duty said one of their drivers would find me a hotel if he had to drive a hundred miles to do so. I nodded and signed the agreement form. She put her fingers in her mouth and let out a piercing whistle. 'Driver,' she yelled. 'Over here.'

The man I had seen hobbling along on crutches turned out to be the only limo driver on duty. I was a little nervous at the prospect of him conveying me around the back lanes of Virginia but he grinned and winked and waved one of his crutches at me and assured me that everything would be 'just fine'. He hobbled out to his car and manoeuvred himself into it. I followed, still feeling apprehensive as I slithered into the back seat. He insisted on calling me 'sir', I noticed, even though he was old enough to be my grandfather.

'You ever bin dayun sayouth bufaw, suh?' he said, as we pulled out of the airport.

'Sorry?' I asked.

'Dahn sayouth, suh? Yevah bin in Vurjinny beefowuh?'

What the fuck was he saying to me? Had I ever been in a virgin before?

We drove down the airport approach road and west on Interstate 81. The view of the Blue Ridge Mountains at dusk was simply stunning. If you've never seen them, all I can tell you is that they really are blue and they really have ridges and they look the way mountains do on ornamental place-mats but never do in real life. You would have to be made of stone not to gasp at the Blue Ridge Mountains. Not even the fact that John Denver once wrote a song about them can diminish their phenomenal majesty or greatness. We drove on through downtown Roanoke, Salem, Lafayette, Ironto and Christiansburg, where we turned off for the road to Blacksburg and found a motel on the outskirts of the town.

The woman behind the desk was short and friendly. She said she could let me have a room for eighty dollars, and I said OK, that would be fine. She asked whether I wanted smoking or non, so I said smoking, and she nodded. She handed me the key and took my money and told me she hoped I had a real pleasant evening.

I got the elevator to the first floor feeling mighty. Virginia was going to work out well, I felt. But then, as soon as I started feeling good, things started going bad. I walked into the room and almost keeled over, so awful was the stink of stale cigarette smoke. Now, I smoke myself, as I believe I may have mentioned. I smoke rather too much, in fact. But being in this room was like sucking on an exhaust pipe. I opened both windows as wide as I could and switched on the air conditioner. The stench was still appalling. I changed my shirt and went down to the dining room.

There was nobody there. No staff. No diners. Nobody. I selected a table and sat down at it, waiting for something to happen. After about fifteen minutes a waiter came in with a Walkman on his head. He was humming and singing along with the tune, which was, to judge from his high-pitched squeaks and guttural grunts and extreme pelvic thrusts, something in the heavy metal genre. I waved my arms in the air and managed to attract his attention. He took off the Walkman and peered at me as though he had just woken up from an intense dream and was surprised to find me there.

'Any chance of some food?' I asked.

'Weze abayut closed, suh,' he said. 'We done closed fav meenutes ago.'

'I've been sitting here for fifteen minutes,' I said.

He shook his head bitterly and said he would see what he could do. I told him a hamburger and French fries would be fine, with a large glass of Coke, if that wasn't too much trouble. He disappeared into the kitchen and ten minutes later reappeared with a burger the size of a watermelon and a basket of bread rolls.

I asked if I could have some butter and he didn't seem to understand me. I repeated the word several times – butter, butter – but he still just grinned and stared at his feet. I then realized that he understood my accent about as much as I understood his. This called for something desperate.

'Could I have some budder?' I said.

His eyes lit up. 'Why dedden ya jes say thayut, suh,' he said.

I congratulated myself for my bravery, but when the butter dish arrived I was kind of sorry I had bothered. There was more hair in the butter dish than there was in the waiter's nostrils and believe me, that means a lot.

After dinner I retired to my room, full of hope that the hideous ashy odour would have abated somewhat. It hadn't. Even though I had left the windows open, and even though there was a gale-force wind howling through the curtains, the room still smelt like a cancerous lung. I took off my clothes and got into bed. The very sheets and pillowcases smelt of tobacco. It was so disgusting that I couldn't sleep. I got out and tried the other bed. The smell was even worse. I really was tired now. I crawled around the room on all fours, trying to find the one spot in the entire place where the smell wasn't so bad that it would make a skunk's fart seem like Chanel Number 5. I ended up curled on the floor by the wide open window with two pieces of toilet paper jammed into my ears to drown out the noise of the howling wind. Eighty shagging bucks. There's a sucker born every minute.

Next morning I woke up with a pounding headache. Usually I feel like a cigarette first thing in the morning, but today I just buried my face in my pillow and breathed in deeply. Outside, the morning was absolutely beautiful. The sun was glinting over the Blue Ridge Mountains. I decided to walk the few short miles out to Dublin, Virginia.

Close to Blacksburg the land seemed green and lush, but as I walked along the landscape slowly seemed to change. There were still rich pastures and vast meadows in the distance. But now the fields became smaller, and the land looked poorer. There were very few businesses, a couple of ancient sawmills, a few beaten-up stores with dusty advertisements for John Deere agricultural equipment in the windows. The houses got smaller too, their window frames warped and cracked, their paint flaking and blistering.

After a while I got bored with the road, so I walked off the edge and into the woods. What a transformation! The forest was electric with life and colour. Strange purple and reddish flowers grew on the mulchy floor, thick ferns climbed up the trunks of the trees. The smell of the pines was sweet and heavy, like some kind of drug.

Some bird with a high-pitched gorgeous song was whistling somewhere far above me where I couldn't see. A spring gurgled beside
my feet, turning the earth to rich red mud. I stood very still
breathing the sweet straw-scented air deep into my lungs and I have
to tell you, I felt happy.

Roanoke is very close to the point where Sir Walter Raleigh first
landed in America, and if the accounts of those who sailed with him
are to be believed it was as beautiful back then as it is now. Here are
the words of one Arthur Barlowe, who sailed on the first ship:

> After thankes giuen to God for our safe arriual thither, we manned
> our boates and went to viewe the lande next adioning, and to take
> possession of the same, in the right of the Queenes most excellent
> Maiestie ... Which being performed ... wee viewed the lande
> about vs, being whereas we first landed, very sandie, and lowe
> towards the water side, but so full of grapes, as the very beating and
> surge of the Sea ouerflowed them, of which we founde such plentie,
> as well there, as in all places else, both on the sande, and on the
> greene soile on the hils, as in the plaines, as well on euery little
> shrubbe, as also climbing towards the toppes of the high Cedars,
> that I thinke in all the world the like aboundance is not to be founde:
> and my self hauing seene those partes of Europe that most abound,
> finde such difference, as were incredible to be written ... This land
> had many goodly woods, full of Deere, Conies, hares and Fowle,
> euen in the middest of Summer, in incredible aboundance ... diuers
> kindes of fruites, Melons, Walnuts, Cucumbers, Gourdes, Pease, and
> diuers rootes and fruites very excellent good, and ... corne, which is
> very white, faire and well tasted ... our selues prooued the soile, and
> put some of our Pease into the ground, and in tenne daies they were
> of foureteene ynches high ... The soile is the most plentifull, sweete,
> fruitfull, and wholsome of all the world.

Barlowe had a sharp eye for the most extraordinary detail of flora
and fauna and he wrote with a keen journalistic edge. He was not

totally taken in by the charms of the new world either, as the following warning demonstrates:

> The Sharke . . . is the most revenous Fish knowne in the Sea; for he swalloweth all that he findeth . . . It hath chanced that a yonker casting himselfe into the Sea to swimme, hath had his legge bitten off aboue the knee by one of them. And I haue been enformed, that in the Tyger, when Sir Richard Greenfild went to people Virginia, a Sharke cut off the legge of one of the companie, sitting in the Chaines and washing himselfe.

I clambered out of the forest and back on to the road and headed off again in the direction of Dublin. Time was getting on now. I was keen to get my first look at Dublin, Virginia. I walked faster, as fast as I could now. At one point I passed an enormous second-hand car sales yard on the edge of the road. Although the place was vast I couldn't see any people anywhere. The only evidence of humanity was a huge loudspeaker which had been mounted on the back of a jeep. 'Special bargains today folks,' it bawled. 'Come right ahead in. Real special bargains today.'

I must have taken a wrong turning somewhere because I ended up not in Dublin, but in a nearby town called Radford. You can imagine, I am sure, how happy I was about this. Around a tall elm tree, birds wheeled and scrapped in the air. I stopped a young man on the sidewalk and asked him how I could get to Dublin. He grinned. He was going there now, he said, if I wanted a ride.

Duke was driving a pretty beaten-up 1985 Ford car but it seemed to me like the shiniest of brand-new convertibles, so happy was I not to have to walk any more. On the way out to Dublin I told him how I had managed to get myself lost. He grinned and laughed at my story and as we arrived in Dublin, Virginia and swept up the wide main street in his battered old car he invited me to come for a cup of coffee with him.

We parked the car outside a cowboy boots shop and went to a

café he knew. Outside, the streets of Dublin were full of young people loading large black sacks into cars. They were all students, Duke explained, and they were getting ready to go home for Thanksgiving. Radford – where we had just been – was a big college town. His own girlfriend, Alison, was a student there, in the veterinary college, but she was living here in Dublin because it was cheaper than Radford. He had driven down to Virginia that morning in his brother's car to collect her and bring her home to New York.

Meeting a New Yorker in this rural neck of the woods was absolutely great. I told Duke I had just spent a week in New York with my dad and we chatted about how wonderful his home town was, swopping favourite haunts as though I too was a native. He was everything you would expect a New Yorker in the countryside to be. Funny, cynical, slightly lost. He was terrific. After a while he got up and went off in search of the rest room. While he was gone I amused myself by eavesdropping on the two waitresses. They were talking about their boss.

'So he looks me in the eye and he says, Myrna, how come every week you take your pay cheque straight to the bank soon as you get it. You know what I said to him, Alice?'

'No, what?'

'I said, cos it's too damn small to go by itself, Henry. It's too damn small to go by itself.'

The two women laughed and Duke came back from the bathroom and we ordered more coffees and two slices of pie. Just then, one of the waitresses came over and asked us if we minded if she put on some music. We said no, we'd like it. She slipped a coin into the juke box and the glorious sound of Little Richard burst through the café. And then, a wonderful thing happened. Alice and Myrna began to jive, in the skilled fluid effortless way that only middle-aged women can jive. They simply stepped into each other's arms and began swaying to and fro, rocking backwards and forwards to the rhythm of the music, pushing and pulling each other and snapping their fingers and sending each other into spins and singing along laughingly with the words.

It was at this point that the door of the café opened and Duke's girlfriend Alison came in carrying a suitcase and a rucksack. She was tall and thin with long strawberry blonde hair and when I tell you that there was something of the startled deer about her, I do not mean that she had antlers or anything. No, I mean she was absolutely stunning. She had the kind of perfect teeth you only ever see in middle-class American mouths. The air around her smelt like a new copy of *Cosmopolitan*. She kissed Duke and said hi to me and then she ordered a cup of lemon tea and went off to the ladies' room. The music stopped and me and Duke sat at the table sharing my last cigarette.

'So that's her,' he said. 'That's Alison.'

I asked him how long they had been together.

'Two years now,' he said. 'Man, she's one hard-headed woman. I know she looks like an angel, but she's gotta head like a fuckin rock, man. You don't wanna argue with her.'

I said she seemed very nice to me.

He laughed. 'How'd you like to fuck somebody spends most of her time with her right hand up a cow's ass?' he said.

I took a deep drag on my cigarette. I asked him if he had any good telephone numbers.

Duke and Alison were lovely people. When they heard that I was staying in Virginia for a few days, and that I knew nobody there, they insisted that they would stay for the night and drive me around to see the sights.

Outside in the street, however, there was a problem. Duke's car refused to start. He cursed and swore and kicked it and lifted the hood and gazed underneath but nothing he could do seemed to be any use. After half an hour or so, Duke said he would have to find a mechanic. Alison said she would take me down to the library and help me find some books about Dublin. We all arranged to meet up later in the afternoon.

On our way down to the library Alison was very quiet. I tried my best to make conversation with her, and it wasn't that she wasn't friendly exactly, she just seemed to have something on her mind. When we got to the library she introduced me to the woman who was working behind the counter and told her I was interested in books about the connections between Dublin, Ireland and Dublin, Virginia. The librarian smiled dolefully and said there wasn't much of a visible Irish influence on the town any more, but the history was pretty interesting. She went off and came back ten minutes later with two wonderful volumes. One was a history of a local family, the Darsts. The other was called *The Land That Is Pulaski County*. The books were full of the most fascinating stuff.

At last, here was an American Dublin which really and truly and demonstrably had been set up by Irish immigrants. There were a number of independent sources for this, but perhaps the most intriguing was an account written by a visitor to the area in 1797. A Frenchman travelling under the name of 'Mr Orleans', he was actually none other than Prince Louis Philippe, who thirty-three years later became King of France. I found this astonishing, but there it was in black and white in front of me, an extract from His late Majesty's memoir, *Diary of My Travels in America*, dated 21 April 1797:

> The countryside was about the same as far as the valley of the Big Kanhaway, which around here they call New River. The settlements here are few and squalid. From all I heard, they exist only along the road ... There is no inn at English's Ferry [a local town, actually called Ingles' Ferry]. We dined two miles on the other side with some Irishmen who have given the name New Dublin to a shanty they've been living in for six years.

Another book by a local historian contained an extract from a diary written by one of Dublin, Virginia's earliest settlers, one Samuel Caddle from Downpatrick in Ulster, who arrived in Virginia in 1774. By 1800 Caddle was in his mid-thirties and owned a farm and a forge near Dublin. His journal records his business accounts in meticulous detail. Unlike most local traders at the time, Caddle would accept payment in American dollars, British pounds, whiskey, brandy, animal skins, meat, vegetables or labour. That's the Irish for you. Nothing if not versatile.

But Caddle's journal is much more than an account book. There are notes about the birthdates of himself and his friends, long lists of the products made in his forge, there is a scribbled entry about a runaway slave, there are drinking songs and snatches of doggerel composed by Caddle and his buddies. The whole thing adds up to an amazing piece of living folk history, and I could see the document's incredible importance. But in some odd way that I couldn't understand, I actually found the personal stuff – the jokes and put-downs and stupid little rhymes which Caddle and his friends had scrawled to each other – most moving of all.

> I thank you Caddall; for you gave me my fill
> Of Brandy that's wholesome and strong
> But the time it may come that I'll prime you with rum
> And I hope it may be before long.

Imagine being far away from your home in Ireland and being with your friends here in America and scribbling a rhyme on one of their books just for the laugh after a good hard night on the beer, and other people being able to read it all these years later. I just found that extraordinary. When I closed my eyes in the library, I could almost hear their laughter. Later on in the journal what seems to be a song written by Caddle himself appears:

> I have Lawns and fine bowers
> I have shade and fine flowers
> The Lark is my morning alarmor
> You jolly boys now who follow the plow
> Drink long life and success to the farmer.

All you jolley fellows who loves to be mellow
Attend to my song and sit easy
I'm here like a king, let's laugh, drink and sing
Dull thinking will make a man crasey.

Perhaps the most touching note was a warning scribbled to Caddle by a friend: 'Samuel Caddall when you go home take due care and hike yourself sober . . . from drink remember well this advice as it is from a frend this 5th day of April 1804.'

Back outside in the street, Samuel Caddall's words were still replaying in my head as Alison and I strolled around in the sun. I wondered what he would make of the town now. I wondered too where all that Irishness had gone. I don't know what I was expecting, but Dublin, Virginia looked just like any other small American town, and I found that vaguely disappointing. Sentimental and crummy, I know, but I would have actually liked to see a shamrock or a tricolour somewhere, and I didn't. Like Dublin, Pennsylvania, this town seemed to have forgotten its own past. Still, I was very grateful to Alison for taking me down to the library and helping me find all this terrific stuff. It had really made the history of the place come alive for me.

'Listen,' I said. 'Thanks very much for taking all this trouble. I'm really touched, you know?'

'No, it's OK,' she beamed. 'I mean, you seem like a real nice person, so it's fine.'

'So do you,' I said.

She laughed lightly and looked away. 'Do you have a girlfriend back home?'

'Yeah,' I said.

'Are you faithful to her?'

I told her yes, I was, and she smiled. 'That's good. I'm faithful to Duke too, and I get horny as hell sometimes. But I don't know if he's always faithful to me though.'

I wasn't exactly sure what I was supposed to say here. 'I'm sure he is' was the best I could manage. We walked a little further down the street in silence. She lit a cigarette and tossed it into the gutter after only a few drags. I kept sensing that there was something on Alison's mind, and so when she finally spoke again I suppose I was glad.

'Can I tell you something, Joe?' she said.

I shrugged. 'Sure.'

She looked away from me and into the middle distance, gnawing her lip. She stared hard at the street as though some interesting sound was coming from it and she was trying to locate its source. What the hell was she going to say to me? She sighed and shook her head.

'I'm pregnant,' she said suddenly. 'And he doesn't know.'

I think I might have actually laughed. I couldn't believe this was happening. I had only met this woman two and a half hours ago and she was telling me something like this, and something her own boyfriend didn't know! This was not good.

'Look, Alison,' I said. 'I don't know you. Maybe you should be discussing this with Duke or something?'

She shook her head again. 'I need to discuss it with someone I don't know,' she told me. 'I need an objective point of view. I'm really in trouble here. I wouldn't ask otherwise.'

Alison asked me to come for a walk by the river with her and she seemed so upset that I felt I had no choice. It was a lovely fresh afternoon but I felt really uneasy. This was not supposed to happen. I was supposed to go back to the library and photocopy pages from dusty old long-forgotten books and make notes about things that had happened two hundred years ago to people who were long dead and buried. But she kept asking me what she should do now. Should she have the kid without telling Duke, should she quietly have an abortion and not tell him. Really, she felt she should have an abortion. She couldn't have a kid now, it would wreck her life and her studies. But her own mother – an Irish Catholic – had got pregnant before being married to her father, and she had always told her daughter that abortion was wrong, and that every child deserved the world. It was a phrase she had never been able to get out of her mind. Every child deserves the world. What should she do?

We stood by the river staring out at the swirling water, and very suddenly she put her hands to her face and started to cry bitterly. Her whole body shook with tears. She opened her mouth wide and sobbed and her face crumpled up with pain and emotion. 'I don't know what to do, Joe,' she wept. 'I really don't know what to do.' And the truth was, I didn't know either. I think I mumbled some platitude about trying to discuss it with Duke and I gave her a cigarette and I held her hand just for a moment and then I walked her back slowly to meet him on the street by his broken-down car. He didn't notice that anything was wrong. He hardly even looked up at her. He was too busy trying to fix the car.

Back in the hotel that night I was restless. I sat in my room and tried to read some of the stuff I had photocopied down at the library but I couldn't concentrate. I couldn't stop thinking about Alison and what she had told me. It wasn't that I wanted to be involved. I didn't. But just the fact of her telling me had involved me somehow, and now I didn't know what to do. I thought about calling her at the hotel she was staying at with Duke. I thought about just going down there and manufacturing a way of bumping into her. After a while I threw the book in a corner and just went out for a walk. I had read in the local paper that there would be a gospel service in one of the nearby churches that evening, and I thought I would go along and just take a look. And OK, OK, I'm a bloody Catholic, all right? I thought I might hear something that would help me put what Alison had told me into some kind of perspective. There. I've said it. You get a bit funny about stuff like that when you're far away from home, OK?

Outside the church was a large sign which announced: THE BIBLE BELT HOLDS UP AMERICA'S PANTS! Inside, the congregation was almost exclusively white. The atmosphere was quiet and gloomy. The preacher, when he arrived, looked a little like Jerry Lee Lewis, only whiter. We all stood and sang a few morbid and decidedly non-

Catholic hymns and then it was time for the sermon. The pallid reverend began quietly enough.

'Dear brothers and sisters, tonight our text is from the Psalms. "I am thy exceeding great reward, sayeth the Lord." What does this text mean, brothers and sisters? "I am thy exceeding great reward".'

There was a bit of a silence at this stage, punctuated only by the wind howling outside in the night. The reverend suddenly opened his mouth wide and appeared to yell up at the roof rafters.

'"I can't get no saddisfackshun!"' he hollered. 'That's the cry of the young people now.'

We all sat up straight and took a deep breath.

'You think my Lord Jesus said that, as he agonized on the cross for the sins of the world? As the very life's blood spilled from his side? You think he said, "I can't get no saddisfackshun," like that Mick Jagger?'

'No,' said a few people in the congregation.

'PEOPLE, I CAN'T HEAR YOU,' he shrieked. 'You think he said that?'

'NOOOO,' everyone said.

'That's right. No is right.' He paused. 'You got these hippies now and you got your anteye-authoritarianism and your subversion, and you got yer young people all a pokin and a snufflin and a dancin and a prancin in the stinkin manure heap of sin and filth.'

I perked up a lot at this point. The prospect of spending the later part of the evening a dancin and a prancin in a stinkin manure heap of sin and filth was pretty enticing, I must say. It was just what I needed to take my mind off things. Show me the dotted line, Rev, I thought, albeit silently.

'You got your drugs,' he snarled.

'Praise God,' moaned the faithful.

'Alcohawl.'

'Oh Jesus.'

'Seckshell innercaws.'

'Yes my Lord.'

'Homaseckshaliddy and mastabayshun.'

'Yess. Yess. Yess.'

'Pawnography and vice.'

'Bless you, Jesus.'

He began to scream and hammer the pulpit. 'But the good book sayeth, "I am thy exceeding great reward." I. Yes, I. Not the cheap approval of man. Not the saddisfackshun of the world. I. I. I.'

'Praise you, Jesus.'

'And AIDS,' he bawled. 'Yew got these liberals in the media and the government and even in the *Yew*nited States supreme court all a wonderin where AIDS comes from. Like we don't know! Like it's some mystery. You know where it comes from?'

'Where?'

'FROM SIN! FROM SIN I SAID! Man shall not lie down with man. That's what the book says, isn't it?! Man shall not spill his seed upon the ground. AIDS comes from sin and vice and filth, brothers and sisters, and anyone tells you anything else, you just tell that man to stop mocking God's holy word. STOP MOCKING THE DIVINE WORD OF MY LORD JESUS FOR HE SHALL CUT MY ENEMIES DOWN LIKE THE VERY GRASS, OH YES!!!'

He stopped roaring and let the echo of his voice ring around the tiny church. 'Now,' he hissed, like a sadistic little schoolteacher announcing detention, 'we shall praise the Lord with music.' I stood up and went to leave, just as the organ started up and the people began singing:

I was tired and I was weary
I was troubled in mind.
I was sick in heart and body
And no peace could I find.
But then I stopped and I prayed
Until the sweet healing came.
Yes, I found a new doctor;
And Jesus is his name.

Outside in the night, lightning was flickering over the mountains. I walked back to my hotel by myself in the rain.

Next morning Duke and Alison were supposed to come over to the motel early and meet me for breakfast. They never did. I waited for almost an hour and then I went out and walked down the street to the motel where they were staying. They had checked out very early, the manager told me, and he didn't have a forwarding address. No, they hadn't left any message. And no, they didn't say where they were headed. I never heard from either of them again.

CHAPTER 10

Sharing a Taxi
with Randy Newman

Dear friends, if you were to see old Denis Danihy, he never was in as good health and looks better than ever he did at home. And you may be sure he can have plenty of tobacco and told me to mention it to Tim Murphy. If you were to see Denis Reen ... dressed ... with clothes suitable for this country, you would think him to be a boss or a steward, so that we have scarcely words to state to you how happy we felt at present. And as to the girls that used to be trotting on the bogs at home, to hear them talk English would be of great astonishment to you.

Letter from Daniel Guiney,
Irish immigrant, 1850

Most of the Irish come out poor, unable to purchase farms ... They are despised and kicked about. Many write home that they are happy and wealthy, when they are of that class above mentioned. I heard friends of a young man in this city enquiring if John (Mr Such a One) was not a banker here, as he wrote home that he was so ... But what was he, think you? He was sweeper of the office of the bank. They were astonished when they were told so. And thousands are just like him.

Letter from William Dever,
Irish immigrant, 1848

There are two important things which the aspiring visitor to the state of Indiana should probably know. One is that in 1991, the last year for which full figures are available, it experienced a 64 per cent increase in murders. The other is that in roughly the same period it experienced a 16.4 per cent decrease in population. I'm not saying these two statistics are related. I'm just saying, if you're thinking of going to Indiana for any reason, bear them in mind. On the up side, you might also like to know that the great city of South Bend, Indiana, is the second cheapest metropolitan area in which to buy a house in the entire United States. Come to think of it, maybe that's not a surprise.

Indiana has never had a very good press. People do tend to tell you that Indiana is in some way boring, lacking in character or excitement. This is really a shame. Indiana is, of course, a fine and exciting state, with a colourful history and a cosmopolitan atmosphere and a vibrant sense of contemporary culture. And if you believe that for even one short moment, I've got some really nice real estate for sale in downtown South Bend.

Indianapolis (or, as it is sometimes cruelly described, 'India No Place') was founded in 1821, when, with truly American enthusiasm, a miserable slice of pest-infested and scarcely habitable swampland was fenced off and designated the state capital. To be fair just for a moment or two, the city's location in the exact geographical centre of Indiana's verdant farmland bore significant commercial advantages, but the absence of other factors usually considered vital for the establishing of a major city – small things like having a river – made the development of serious industry pretty difficult, not to say almost laughably impossible. Modern Indianapolis is thus the biggest city in the world that cannot be reached by water, and it is the kind of place where the locals will tell you this fact in voices fairly quivering with pride.

The city's other main recent claim to greatness is that it is the home and political base of former Vice-President J. Danforth Quayle, the man who once so famously assured the American public that 'space is almost infinite'.

When I lived in America in 1992 I became something of a Dan fan. And I really do miss him, now that he has been swept from office. I am saying fervent rosaries that he will change his mind and run for president next time around, because the world political scene was just so greatly enriched by Dan's bovine presence. Who can forget that famous occasion in Hawaii, when he was asked why the whole country could not adopt that state's policy of universal health care? 'Well, Hawaii is a unique state,' he explained. 'It is a small state. It is a state that is by itself. It is a – well, it is different to the other forty-nine states. Well, all states are different, but it's got a particularly unique situation.' Good old Dan. He really was a particularly unique guy:

Who can forget his elegant explanation of President Bush's plans for new medical-malpractice laws? 'I, I can't tell you what exactly we do on that pain and suffering in the— Well, it doesn't address it specifically. The states – the states could in fact – what we basically do is – try to do – is try to get the states to come up with medical malpractice legislation. We have, I think it's five criteria. But once we meet the five criteria, then they get a favourable distribution from us if they meet – basically forcing the states to adopt this medical malpractice legislation, and that's the way that you do it.'

There is a famous painting by Edvard Munch called *The Cry*. It shows a hideous open-mouthed figure, demented, screeching in abject horror. When I lived in America in the summer of 1992, this image was put on a T-shirt, with the slogan 'OH NO! NOT PRESIDENT QUAYLE!' stamped underneath. You would see a lot of people wearing that T-shirt that summer. Some of them were Republican canvassers. Even they thought that Dan Quayle was laughable. It was very unfair.

Me, I was overjoyed to be here at last, in the city of my greatest hero's birth. It was almost like a pilgrimage to me. I mean, yes, as I strolled around feeling light-headed with the raw emotion of it all, it was admittedly a little difficult to imagine what I would actually do here. Downtown Indianapolis does have a lot of utterly soulless glass and steel office blocks, unbelievably boring supermarkets and quite astoundingly ghastly apartment blocks. But still, Dan had strolled these very streets dreaming his dreams of greatness and that was good enough for me.

In addition, I had an old friend from Ireland who actually lived here in Indianapolis – lucky bitch – and I was looking forward to seeing her for the first time in several years.

Shirley turned up ten minutes late to find me merrily watching paint dry on a nearby wall. 'Welcome to Naptown,' she said. We went out to dinner that night and got merrily plastered and afterwards Shirley suggested we go to a nightclub. I asked her if she thought we would have any problem getting in. She laughed like a bastard and said no. When we got there, I saw what she meant. It was the kind of place where they would have let in a pack of wild dogs, once they had the price of admission.

Deep down in the very bowels of Indianapolis the young people of the city were having fun. Boy, were they wild. Some of them were actually dancing with their shoes off! The DJ played several tracks by Irish-American rap group The House of Pain, who, for me, are the aesthetic equivalent of being repeatedly slapped in the face with a rotting mackerel. But Shirley seemed to be enjoying herself, so that was OK by me. I knew she was enjoying herself because she kept catching sight of her reflection in the attractively mirrored walls and then laughing out loud for no apparent reason. I'm very perceptive like that.

I wasn't overwhelmingly sad to leave Indianapolis the next morning, I must say. You can have too much of a good thing, after all. So at about ten thirty, off I set on the long road east to Dublin, Indiana, in the back of a nice big taxi driven by a nice big man named Randy Newman. (I promise you that I am not making this up, by the way. He really was called Randy Newman.) From there we would keep going eastwards, across the state border, to Dublin, Ohio.

I had met Randy the day before when I had hailed his cab in downtown Indianapolis and we had got chatting. He was a typical Hoosier, full of laughter and curiosity. I had been concerned about how to get to Ohio. There was no train or bus, and I had unfortunately misplaced my driving licence, so I wasn't in a position to hire a car. I really was at a bit of a loss, but Randy came to my rescue. He had never been to Ohio in his life, he told me – Indiana contains the highest number of American citizens who never leave their own state – but he would be more than willing to go.

Indeed, he would be happy to let me have the use of himself and his taxi for the entire day, for which pleasure he would charge me a laughably low one hundred and fifty dollars. This, I thought, was a bargain.

As we sped out of Indianapolis and on to the road for Columbus, Ohio, Randy was in a very good mood. He told me all about his wife, who, he said, was 'a real Irish-lookin red-headed beauty'. He took a photograph of her from the glove compartment and showed it to me, and she was indeed a bit of a stunner. 'She sure is,' he said, and he kissed the photograph several times before putting it back in the glove-box. I asked Randy what it was like being called after one of the world's most respected songwriters and he chuckled expansively and said it could have been worse, he could have been called Burt Bacharach. But he wasn't actually a fan of the other Randy Newman, he said, he didn't really listen to the radio that much any more. He didn't understand modern music.

I sat in the back of Randy's cab feeling very cosy and reading a few pages of information about Dublin, Indiana, which my friend Shirley had kindly found and photocopied for me. The first page was from a magazine, and it featured a poem written in tribute to that lovely town:

There's a road that leads to Dublin,
Out towards the setting sun
And I hope some day to take it
When perchance my work is done.

For no matter where I linger
On the way I choose to roam
Memory points with steadfast finger
To the road that takes me home.

And in all my earthly roaming
Over land and on the sea
The homing road to Dublin
Is the road that's calling me.

Hmmm. I tried to imagine this poem recorded by The House of
Pain. They would have done a lot with 'steadfast finger', I felt. The
next page of Shirley's notes pointed out that the poem was written
by a man called Will Shrawder, who actually lived not in Dublin,
Indiana but in Pittsburg. That kind of figured, I thought.

From south-east Indianapolis Randy and I drove east, shunning
the attractions of the modern smooth Interstate 70, and opting
instead for the potholed glamour of the old Interstate 40. We passed
through Cumberland, Gem, Spring Lake, Greenfield, Charlottes-
ville, Ogden, Dunreith, Lewisville, Straughn, and one hundred short
miles after leaving Indianapolis we finally drove into Dublin, Indiana.

Grey misty light lay folded over the fields and farm buildings. An
enormous tripod water tower with the word DUBLIN painted on it
loomed above the grey flat land looking like something out of a
science-fiction movie. I got out of Randy's cab and wandered over
to take a few snaps of it. I stopped then to look behind myself and
saw a trail of my own black footprints leading all the way through
the frost-covered grass and back to the car.

The city hall – a building the size of your average public toilet –
was open to the public, and so Randy and I went in and introduced
ourselves to the staff and shook hands. A couple of the local farmers
were standing at the counter paying their taxes. They stared at me
like I had walked into the office stark naked except for a pair of
stilletoes. Randy began to explain in a booming stertorous voice that
I was a really succesful young writer from Ireland and I had come all
the way to Indiana to write a book about Dublin. To judge from
their fixed and steely grins, the staff were not quite as excited about
this as Randy was, but still, they said they would be delighted to
give me all the information about Dublin, Indiana that I could
possibly handle. And hey, you know something really wild about
Dublin, Indiana? Yup. You guessed it. Dublin, Indiana has no
connection whatsoever with Dublin, Ireland.

With a sinking heart and a sense of frustration so intense that it
was now becoming almost pleasant, I wearily took out my well-
worn biro and began to make notes. Dublin was founded on 29

January 1830, by a fellow called Harmon Davis, a Quaker from Guilford County, North Carolina, and how the town got its name remains a complete mystery. It was originally thought that Davis had been born in Dublin, Maryland, which really exciting place you will recall I had visited with my poor father, but there is actually no evidence at all for this. The 'Double-Inn' elision theory – as in the origins of the name of Dublin, Philadelphia – also seems unlikely in this case, as there were no buildings at all in Dublin, Indiana when it was originally named.

I went outside with Randy and we walked up and down the main street for a while wondering what to do. I really was getting fed up of this. At home in Ireland, finding out how a place got its name is a relatively straightforward business. Here in America it seemed to be a lot more difficult. Randy was getting annoyed too, I could see it. He kept taking off his baseball cap and peering at it and then putting it back on his head and saying 'shoot'.

We sat on the bench outside the public library and Randy offered me a swig from his Big Slurp extra-large plastic container of Coke. I was touched, but I declined his generosity. After a while, an old man in faded blue denim dungarees came ambling down the main street with a mangy looking dog on a piece of string. Randy's eyes lit up. 'I bet he knows how Dublin got its name,' he said. 'No, Randy,' I said, 'it's OK, really.' But it was too late. Randy stood up, loudly cleared his throat, spat on the sidewalk and strode over to the old man with his enormous hand outstretched.

I watched, enthralled, as they began to talk and laugh and slap each other on the back as though they were old friends. Randy's instincts had been correct, it seemed. The old man shuffled over and sat down beside me and asked me if it was true that I wanted to know why Dublin was called Dublin. I said it certainly was. He coughed and spluttered a few times, and then he began to explain that the name came from the old practice of 'doubling in' teams of horses to haul heavy equipment over the appallingly muddy local roads.

'Not from Dublin, Ireland?' I said.

'Where?' he asked.

'Dublin, Ireland,' I said.

'Gee,' said the old man, 'I never heard of Dublin, Ireland. Say, is that named after Dublin, Indiana?'

I went back into the city hall and asked them to verify the doubling-in theory. The staff said it was possible, but unlikely, because there were no roads at all in the area at the time Dublin was named. Then an interesting thing happened. One of the old farmers who was queuing up to pay his taxes told me that he had been born in Dublin, Indiana and had lived there for his whole life, as had his family before him. His grandfather had once told him that Dublin had after all been named by an Irishman, the man who had first surveyed the town. 'The way it worked back then,' the farmer said, 'if the local people couldn't think of a name for their town, the surveyor was given the honour of naming it. And my grandfather always said to us kids that his grandfather told him that's what happened here. The feller who surveyed the place and drew the first map, he was an Irish feller, from Dublin.'

It was an attractive theory, I thought. I kind of liked the idea of this irresponsible Dubliner wandering around the country in the early years of the nineteenth century merrily naming new towns after the town of his birth. But the staff in the city hall said they had never heard this explanation before and couldn't be sure that it was true.

However, once again, as in the case of Dublin, Pennsylvania, the town's early records had been lovingly preserved by the present authorities, and I was invited into a back room to have a look at some of them. At this stage I was getting just a tad bored with poring through thick sheaves of yellowed old papers, but, basically, I'm a sucker for this kind of stuff, and the Dublin, Indiana records did at least give a lively picture of the town forming itself. Here's a few of the more interesting bits:

12 April 1836: Ordinance controlling Isaac and Michael Harvey shall pay a license of twelve dollars per annum on their grocery.

Resolved that the present Tavern keepers shall pay a license of three dollars per annum. Ordinance passed that every person who shall be convicted of intoxication within the corporation as to be unable to provide for his safety shall, on conviction, pay a fine of not more than three dollars for each offence.

Sec. 2: That no person shall shoot off any gun, pistol, squib or cracker within the town . . . unless upon emergency. Fine $1.00 and costs of prosecution.

Sec.3: That all persons residing in the town of Dublin, Indiana, shall, every Thursday evening at 7 p.m., get butt-naked and fuck like bunnies.

(OK, OK, I made the last one up.) There are ordinances covering the buying of the first graveyard and the building of the Market House. The name of every merchant in the town between 1850 and 1877 is recorded, but not one of them is Irish. Every graduate of the local high school from 1875 to 1917 is recorded too, and once again, no Irish names amongst them. This was a picture that was becoming familiar. If there ever was an Irish population in this area, it had silently assimilated itself over the decades.

Back outside in the main street again, Randy and I were beginning to feel thirsty. We decided to get a beer before going on to Cambridge City to visit the library there. We walked up and down the only street in the town in search of a bar, but we couldn't find one anywhere. Was this possible? Could there be a town called Dublin anywhere in the world that didn't have even one pub inside its limits? We stopped the local postman and told him about our plight. He shook his head and grinned. 'Ain't much drinkin done around here,' he said. 'This is Bible country.'

Randy and I decided to drive on to Cambridge City, which wasn't exactly Vegas, but we did manage to procure a few beers and a pizza. After lunch Randy said he wanted to come with me to the library. So off we went together – he introducing me once more as 'a real famous writer from Ireland' – and together we looked up all the old books about Dublin the librarian could lay her hands on. Here it became clear that the town's opposition to alcohol actually had a strong historical basis. Quite early in its existence, Dublin, Indiana had been colonized by whole busloads of fundamentalist Protestants who regarded consumers of alcohol as being somewhat akin to Satan worshippers. Unfortunately, however, like most fundamentalist Protestants both then and now, they also regarded fundamentalist Protestants of slightly different persuasions as being somewhat akin to Satan worshippers too. The early records of the town are full of accounts of the most vicious internecine rows: 'The old battle was again begun. Many of the church members were indifferent; some entirely backslidden, others did not believe in revivals, others thought there was too much singing, some said without singing no good could be accomplished.'

In time, however, the full force of puritanism took hold on the town, and fun of all kinds was made illegal. An early catalogue for a Dublin school records that 'Dublin is a pleasant and retired village, noted for its temperance and morality, where the student is under the best social and moral influences, and free from the temptations and vices of larger towns. It is a fact worthy of remark that there has not been any intoxicating liquors sold publicly in Dublin for the past thirty years.' (Love that 'publicly'.)

An obituary for one of the town's early head honchos, the Reverend Caleb Witt, recalls how he helped set up Dublin's two schools: 'These schools along with the town's determined opposition to the sale of intoxicating liquors gave Dublin its enviable distinction as a place where intelligence and sobriety could be depended on.'

But even though the uptight Wasps ran Dublin, Indiana as though it was their own personal fiefdom, the arguments between them never stopped. A letter dated 17 May 1871, from one John Huddleston, who had been publicly condemned by Preacher Witt for ripping off money collected to buy an organ for the church, lets the old phoney have it between the eyes:

Bro. Caleb, you must be verry mutch mistaken or I must be guilty of a verry great crime. You have seen and known of stealing, lieing, swairing, drunkenness, sabbathbreaking, hoardom, quariling among proffessed christians, good church members drove out of church by unfair treatment, sinners drove to purdition that might have been saved had the church have been as pure as it ought to have been; you have seen all this, and more too, you say that you have been so powerfully hurt and grieved over an opposing spirit and ugly faces made at you so that you could not preach. You have entered heavy complaints against a brother while he was in good standing in the church. You have seen and done all the above and then say there has nothing so grieved you here in Dublin as to see me do what I have done ... You have acted so verry partially and unfairly in the organ case ... together with other weaknesses that I have lost confidence in believing that you are as perfect a christian as you would often have the people believe ... Now I propose to beg, coaks, pray, plead, urge, insist, and, if need be, be willing to sacrifice my all, that you may, for the good of the church, for the salvation of sinners, and for your own soul's sake, and for your usefullness in church, that you get immediately about setting your rongs right ...

Yet, to be fair, the Christian influence on the town wasn't all bad. A touching story included in a number of local histories records how, in early 1832, a party of Delaware Indians were moving through Indiana having been chucked out of their home in Ohio. They were on their way to Kansas, and as they reached Dublin – then only two years old, and a solidly white settlement – they stopped on the south side of the nearby river to nurse a sick child. The child died and was buried on the banks of the creek. The grieving Indians implored the local Christian settlers to keep the site sacred, which, astonishingly enough, they did. What is now Dublin, Indiana's South Lawn Cemetery grew up around the body of that unnamed Indian child.

The librarian in Cambridge City was a really lovely woman. She told me that her own favourite character from local history was one Charles S. McNichols, editor back in the nineteenth century of the short-lived but glorious *Dublin Times*. Mr McNichols, a Boston Irishman, was basically a complete crook who came to the town to make himself as rich as possible by ripping off the gullible locals. Having drunk and gambled away almost all of the cash collected by the Dubliners to invest in their newspaper, the going began to get tough, and in time-honoured tradition, Mr McNichols got going. The librarian fished around for an account of my countryman's colourful days in Dublin and when she found it, it actually made me laugh out loud. Written by Mr McNichols's former assistant, as an exercise in treading the line between diplomacy and outrageous libel, and as a glorious symphony to the ancient journalistic art of buck-passing, this is pretty hard to beat:

As a beginning it is necessary to state that Mr McNichols was formerly proprietor of the Enterprise, published at Mooresville, Indiana. This paper, from lack of support or brain power eventually collapsed, and the people of Morgan County added another chapter to the Book of Experience. Hastily gathering together a few fragments of his establishment, he made his exit, in company with H.E. Statzel, a young man from Monrovia, and started on a tramp ... Dublin was selected as the objective point. They were possessed of such a scarcity of funds that it became necessary to pawn certain articles in order to secure their passage to this place. They arrived here in the latter part of March, rented rooms, deposited their mixed type, purchased a dry goods box as an imposing stone and began preparations for the publication of a newspaper, the first number of which was soon after printed.

The people of this place responded to their calls for aid, and a liberal subscription was raised. But the confidence of the people was, in a manner, betrayed. The almost entire absence of any business tact soon became visible to those noted for observation, and the lack of energy manifested caused the most sanguine to waver in their hopes of the paper's ultimate success. Mr Statzel perceived the drift of popular opinion and returned to his home.

Mr McNichols soon saw the decrease of support and sympathy, and instead of making strenuous efforts to regain the good will of the masses, rather became more indolent, careless and unmindfull of his own interests. Although making no endeavors to merit public approval, yet he still seemed to anticipate renewed patronage. On last Thursday I handed in my resignation (for no partnership existed between us) and subsequently his eyes were opened to a contemplation of his future prospects. These were found to be sufficiently gloomy, and repeated overtures were made to induce me to purchase his office. This I positively declined to do, and he revived his drooping spirits and appeared determined to reform and try and retrieve his precarious fortunes.

On last Saturday morning he went down the street and was observed to enter his hotel. Sometime afterward he was observed traversing the railroad in the neighborhood of Straughn's station, and his destination was doubtless Mooresville, the scene of his former journalistic exploits. According to a card found in his room he had two cents in his pocket. His indebtedness here will exceed one hundred dollars, exclusive of his numerous subscribers whom he has basely and faithlessly deserted.

We hope our readers will consider Mr McNichols' youth, his inexperience, and his peculiar traits of character, and kindly throw the mantel of Charity over the scenes of the past in which he was manager and chief actor.

Wonderful wonderful stuff. Good old Mr McNichols. Now there was one early Irish immigrant who really believed in that old biblical adage: the Lord helps those who help themselves.

Some of the other news pieces from the early Dublin newspapers were just fabulous. Randy Newman, the librarian and I sat in the library falling about laughing as we read. All the following are from the final issue of the *Wayne County Register*, 4 June 1909:

Miss Edna Shepperd is in New Paris, Ohio, nursing a case of paralysis.

Mrs Mattie Owen has given her house a new coat of paint, also her lawn fence.

Gabe Griffin (coloured) of Indianapolis was here this week greeting his many friends. He was a former resident here, but for many years has been head janitor at the store of L.S. Ayers, and has been a very faithful servant.

Howard Champe went to Indianapolis Monday morning and expects to get employment in one of the business firms in that city. Loren Champe has gone to Indianapolis to attend business college.

I mean, they're *news* stories, for God's sake. Here's my absolute favourite: 'Mr Edmund Morgan is in a critical condition, and no hopes are entertained of his recovery. Old age with a broken down constitution resulting from hard toil all his life leaves nothing to build on.' Edmund Morgan, you poor old bastard. I mean, imagine waking up and feeling poorly and reading that about yourself in your morning newspaper. You'd just say your prayers, keel over and kiss your ass goodbye.

Randy and I stayed a few hours in Cambridge City, and early that afternoon we hit the road again for Columbus, Ohio, the last stop on the first stage of my trip. We drove through a heavy shower of sleet, through East Germantown, Pennville, Centerville, Spring Grove, and crossed the Indiana–Ohio border at Richmond.

We were still on old Interstate 40, which was beginning to play merry havoc with Randy's suspension. The sleet stopped falling and the sun began to crawl out from behind the grey-blue clouds. We sped on through New Westville, Gettysburg (not that one), Bachman, Dodson, Arlington, Englewood and the beautifully named town of Vandalia. All around the tiny airport at Phonetown little planes were buzzing in the sky.

At the small town of Brandt, Ohio, Randy decided his springs had taken enough punishment, and we turned south on to Interstate

70, through Sulphur Grove, Medway and Beatty. At Limecrest, we met up with Interstate 40 again, and continued through Harmony, South Vienna, Brighton, Summerford, Lafayette, West Jefferson, New Rome, Lincoln Village. At about four o'clock in the afternoon we turned on to Columbus, Ohio peripheral highway 270 and drove around clockwise to Dublin, a large affluent suburb north-west of the city.

The houses in Dublin, Ohio were very different to those in Dublin, Indiana. Randy and I toured around for a while just looking at them. They were huge great stone and glass monstrosities on stilts, with swimming pools and tennis courts in their gardens, and several cars parked in their garages. Despite the fact that it had been raining all day, sprinklers were playing on a good number of the lawns. Many of the houses had fabulous gardens, full of tall evergreen trees and thick shrubs. In one garden I saw three middle-aged black men, down on their knees with trowels and turning over the soil in a flower bed. One or two of the houses had prominent notices outside announcing that armed guards were patrolling the grounds and that intruders would be shot on sight.

Randy and I were tired now and we fancied a cup of coffee. We drove around Dublin for a while but the place really didn't seem to have a centre. Eventually we pulled up in the car park of an enormous upmarket shopping centre called the Dublin Plaza, which, I couldn't help noticing, had been built right next to a graveyard. We went into the graveyard for a quick look around. I took some photographs of graves with Irish names on their headstones, but I was a little sick of hanging around in graveyards by now, and Randy said it was getting late and he wanted to get back to his wife in Indianapolis. 'I had the best day I've had in years, Joe,' he said, 'and I feel real bad for taking your money.' I insisted that he was to take it, and he gave me a big hug and a slap on the back which almost shattered my spine, and then he jumped back into his taxi and sped away down the road.

Alone in the vast central hall of the shopping centre, I watched a clown with a mop of pink hair and large yellow lips emptying buckets of water over a miserable little sidekick in a top hat and striped suit. All the kids roared 'Yeah, yeah, yeah,' whenever the tall guy asked, 'Should I do it?' After the fourth or fifth soaking the little guy jumped up and ran to the table, grabbed a bucket and emptied it with a howl of joy down the back of the big guy's trousers. Then he grabbed another bucket and took a run at the crowd of kids, blowing his whistle and yelling 'OH YES OH YES OH YES,' as they scattered out of his way. He cornered a hapless looking kid with pudgy legs and dumped the bucket over his pleading face. It turned out to be full of confetti.

Apart from the clowns, the mall itself was kind of unpleasant. There were pizza parlours and burger bars and little circular public toilets that looked like pods from which an alien might emerge in a horror movie.

I went into a coffee shop and looked over the notes I had made in New York about the Irish in Ohio. There wasn't much, and what little there was told the same old story of assimilation. One Irishman, J. Fitzgerald, had written in August 1860 from the city in which I now found myself:

All things nearly are done in this country in a different way from Ireland ... America is a land of opportunity with no aristocracy or rank but what money establish, [however] every man must depend upon his own individual efforts. He must be active, up with the Times and away ahead of them for progress, cents and dollars are the order of the day. If an Irishman abroad be quick, active, enterprising, disposed to labor hard, get rid as soon as possible of National peculiarities and set himself down to adopt the ways and customs of the people he is certain to succeed ... But if he cannot divest himself of his old way of doing things, if he cannot flow into the great current of American life he will never succeed.

Mr Fitzgerald knew what he was talking about. The Irish who would come here in such large numbers in the middle of the nineteenth century would slowly disappear over the decades. Gradually, even the influence of the Catholic Church was to decline in this area, as in many others. Indeed, one Ohio Irish Catholic priest had written dolefully as far back as the 1870s, 'Scarcely one out of ten of our Irish on the railroad goes to his [religious] duty . . . one half are grown up to 20–25 years & never made their first communion [and] know nothing of their catechism.'

I finished my coffee and went off through the mall in search of a bookshop. After a while I found one which had a large and promising section of songbooks full of songs about Ohio. I must have spent an hour looking through them all from cover to cover. Out of two hundred folksongs about Ohio, one was Irish.

> An exile, I fly to the land of Ohio
> Where gloomy dark deserts bewilder my way
> Where fell snakes are hissing and dire monsters screaming
> Where death pregnant lightnings are dreadfully gleaming
> And direful contagion destruction proclaiming
> Infest every vale and embitter each day . . .
>
> Oh, man! thou art fretful, contentless and wavering;
> Thy blessings are countless, but thou mean and vile;
> The hand of Jehovah extended and favouring
> Peculiarly visits the Emerald Isle
> Yet outcast of Nature, how blind to true pleasure
> Thou bart'rest of enjoyment for base sordid treasure
> And home thou forsakest, though dear beyond measure
> Where friendship and freedom in harmony smile.

I guess, for the Irish, Ohio just wasn't that much fun.

It perhaps says a lot about Columbus, Ohio that it has no connection whatsoever with Christopher Columbus. It is called Columbus just because the city fathers decided long ago that Columbus would be a nice name for an American city. You might detect a slight lack of self-confidence in such a cop-out and you might very well be correct.

Like the yuppie suburb of Dublin, the downtown area turned out to be one large shopping mall. All the stores had façades of precast concrete, lurid plastic tiling, fake wooden planks, imitation white or dark green marble, painted aluminium, distressed stucco. Behind these, you could still see the remnants of the older buildings, beautiful brick houses and stone office buildings with carved roof panels and large windows. All forced into retreat, for the sake of the supermarket.

I remember reading somewhere that when Nikita Khrushchev first entered an American supermarket he had tears in his eyes as he peered along the endless aisles, each one devoted to a single type of food. The shopping mall, he told an aide, was the reason why Communism would ultimately fail.

Susan Marling's book *American Affair* points out that the origins of the shopping mall are actually European. The mall has its roots in the early nineteenth-century arcades which were built to house luxury shops for the Florentine middle class. But it took American engineering to bring the mall to its glorious conclusion. The development of cast-iron allowed the galleries to be lofty; glass roofs let in the daylight and kept the rain off the shoppers. The mall became a place where you didn't just shop. It became a place in which to spend that most American of currencies, leisure time.

The American version of the mall came into being only in the fifties. The war was over, building land was relatively inexpensive, car ownership was soaring, in most American states there was almost full employment and money to spend. Victor Gruen, the architect widely credited as the inventor of the mall, poignantly hoped that the shopping centres he imagined would eventually become integral social centres in the rapidly growing suburbs – a string of pleasant oases in the unending deserts of prefabricated housing and spaghetti-junction motorways. The dream did not come true. The malls remained unashamedly commercial, and like all such buildings, irredeemably ugly. But by the time Allen Ginsberg got around to serenading the greatest poet of democratic America, where did he envision him? Not in a street, or a park, or a church, or a bookshop, but in what, by the sixties, was the most American of locations, a supermarket:

What peaches and what penumbras! Whole families
shopping at night! Aisles full of husbands! Wives in the
Avocados, babies in the tomatoes! – and you, Garcia Lorca,
what were you doing down by the watermelons?
I saw you, Walt Whitman, childless, lonely old grubber,
poking among the meats in the refrigerator and eying the
grocery boys.

'We are the prisoners of infinite choice,' wrote the Irish poet Derek Mahon, and he might well have been thinking about the shopping malls when he did so. In the shopping mall everything is available to the consumer. These are places removed from history, geography, context. Perhaps, I thought, as I strolled through Columbus that day, perhaps in the end, the malls were the ultimate symbol of America's immigrant past. In the mall, there is nothing bizarre about wandering into a restaurant done out as a Mexican cantina, emerging to find a gang of Greeks in traditional costume doing gymnastics in the mock-Georgian lobby, dropping into an Irish pub for a pint of green Guinness and then browsing around a jeans shop decorated like an Eskimo's igloo. The unending clash of visions makes you dizzy with exuberance. It tells you that you are everywhere, and nowhere. It tells you that you can create yourself.

The real problem is that whole generations of American youth have become more accustomed to growing up in the shopping mall than in the real world. Some American sociologists actually contend that teenagers now come of age in the mall. The mall experience has become one of the restless rites of teenage evolution. It is where the young first go to meet each other, to get away from their parents and teachers, where they learn how to drive, where they first spend their own money, and all too often, as any urban American police officer will confirm, where they go to buy drugs. According to a large number of surveys, as well as any number of anecdotal narratives, the car park of the local mall is where most young Americans first have sex. You see funeral parlours and wedding chapels in American malls now. You could practically get born, get married, have children and die without ever having to leave the building. The mall has replaced the school, the church and the dancehall in the new architecture of social cohesiveness.

Cities like Boston and New York have strong enough personalities to resist the seductive lure of the mall. But what does that lure mean for an otherwise soulless city like Columbus, Ohio? Marling's *American Affair* quotes one contemporary architectural critic:

> Shopping malls ... are ... examples of the new stage of hyper-reality – the falseness that is better than reality. Reality always has its detrimental aspects, like crime, homeless people, dirt. In a situation of hyper-reality like a shopping mall, everything is reduced to a set of agreed-upon themes, so people feel more comfortable here than in a real situation. The accurate urban reality is replaced by the falsehood of the shopping mall.

A whole country full of people in love with a dream, rather than a reality. But an American dream, I suppose. An American dream, after all.

Next morning I slept late and when I woke from a deep and dreamy sleep I really wasn't sure whether I was in Columbus or Indianapolis or somewhere else. I got up and took a shower and sprayed the last of my Irish Spring anti-perspirant under my weary armpits, and stepped out into the day.

The morning was fresh and breezy and I decided to go for a walk. There was nothing of much interest in the downtown area so I thought I would wander back up towards Dublin and have another look around the shopping mall and maybe pick up a few souvenirs. I was going home to Ireland tomorrow. I was looking forward to going home.

But I never made it back to the Dublin Plaza, because I got lost. I turned down a few of the beautiful suburban avenues, their houses all decked out with decorations for Thanksgiving. In one driveway, an anxious looking father was helping his two young daughters wash his car with a wildly undulating hose. I turned another corner. I walked on. I turned again. And there tucked into a few little side streets just down the road from the mall were the remnants of Old Dublin. It was like walking on to a film set. The lawns were neat, the little picket fences were gleaming with fresh white paint, the street lights were of the old-fashioned gas-lamp variety, the golden leaves lying in neat piles by the sidewalks looked like they'd been laundered and pressed. There was a Shamrock Barber Shop and a County Kerry Tea Rooms. Most of the other shops on the street displayed harps or round towers, Irish tricolours or posters of the Irish soccer team on their walls, laughing leprechauns or lamenting colleens in their windows. And then, just as I thought I had died and gone to some sort of terrible Hibernian Hell, a police car turned the corner and swept down the street. The police car had the words 'Dublin Police' painted on the side, beside an enormous emerald green shamrock. I had seen everything now.

I wandered into a gift shop which specialized in Irish and Scottish products, Aran sweaters and tartan kilts and tapes of Irish musicians singing the kind of rebel songs which people back in Ireland would find faintly embarrassing. The man in the shop was kindly and soft-spoken. He told me I was very welcome to Ohio. He had been to Dublin, Ireland many times, he said. It was an extraordinary place, it was one of the world's great cities. We chatted about Ireland for a while, and then I bought a T-shirt from him which featured a Stars and Stripes flag, done out in a green, white and orange design. It was the most tasteless thing I had ever seen in my life.

'You like our street?' he asked me.

'It's certainly unusual,' I said.

'We like to think it's a little piece of the real Ireland,' he smiled. 'We like to think it's authentic.'

'This isn't the real Ireland,' I told him. 'Leprechauns and fairies and inflatable shamrocks.'

He peered into my eyes and laughed softly. 'I go to Ireland twice a year,' he said. 'I've been doing that for twenty years. Twice a year, regular. The wife and me, we have to go, for the business, you know. We go on buying trips. And you go to any city in Ireland now, it's got places like this and stores like mine all over. I mean all over. I never saw the phoney Irish thing anywhere in the world till I went to Galway last summer. Jesus, even the nuns were wearing Aran.'

Outside on the street, the shamrock-painted police car swept past once again. 'This is the real Ireland all right,' he grinned. 'Maybe you just don't like what you see.'

'Maybe,' I smiled, and I said goodbye to him and got the bus back into downtown Columbus.

PART 2

THE COAST OF GOLD

For love and whiskey make a young man older,
And love and porter make him old and grey.
What can't be cured, love, must be endured, love,
And so now I'm bound for Amerikay.
For the sweetest apple is the soonest rotten
And the hottest love grows the sooner cold.
What can't be cured, love, must be endured, love
And so now I'm bound for the coast of gold.

From 'Love Is Teasing',
traditional Irish song, nineteenth century

2 a.m. Wakened by a boy with message from bartender to bail him out of jail. 3 a.m. Back to bed. 6 a.m. Fire engines, up and off to the scene to see my election district captains tending the burnt-out tenants. Got names for new homes. 8.30 to police courts. Six drunken constituents on hand. Got four released by a timely word to the judge. Paid the others' fines. Nine o'clock to municipal court. Told an election district captain to act as lawyer for widow threatened with dispossession. 11 to 3 p.m. Found jobs for four constituents. 3 p.m. An Italian funeral, sat conspiciously up front. 4 p.m. A Jewish funeral – up front again, in the synagogue. 7 p.m. Meeting of district captains and reviewed the list of all voters, who's for us, who's agin. 8 p.m. Church fair. Bought ice cream for the girls; took fathers for a little something around the corner. 9 p.m. Back in club-house. Heard complaints of a dozen push cart pedlars. 10.30 p.m. A Jewish wedding. Had sent handsome present to the bride. Midnight – to bed.

From the diary of George Washington Plunkett,
New York Irish politician, late nineteenth century

Now the Kellys run the statehouse and the Kellys run the banks
The police and fire departments sure the Kellys fill the ranks
Dan Kelly runs the railroads, John Kelly runs the seas,
Kate Kelly runs the suffragettes and looks right good to me.
Well I went and asked directions from a naturalized Chinee
And he said, but please excuse me, for me name it is Kell Lee.
And there's Kelly from Dublin, Kelly from Sligo,
Little Mickey Kelly who came from County Clare.
Sure Kelly built the pyramids with good old Galway granite,
And when Kelly discovered the North Pole
Didn't he find Pat Kelly there.

Irish-American vaudeville song, 1920s

CHAPTER 11

Venezuela My Ass

I could not obteyne any [Irish servants] for the thing at present seems
new and forraigne to them, & ... they have been so terrified with the
ill practise of them to the Carribda Ileands, where they were sould as
slaves, that as yet they will hardly give credence to any other usage.

Letter from Robert Southwell, agent, explaining his inability
to entice Irish servants to Virginia and Carolina, 1669

America would be a grand land if only every Irishman would kill a
negro and be hanged for it. I find this sentiment generally approved –
sometimes with the qualification that they want Irish and negroes for
servants, not being able to get any other.

Edward Augustus Freeman,
English historian, 1881

The woman behind the Visitors Information counter in the arrival
terminal at Atlanta airport had a face like a well-spanked arse. She
was reading a copy of the *National Enquirer* and talking to somebody
on the telephone. She frowned at me as I stood there. Finally she
put the telephone down and glared. Crabby is not quite the correct
word for her expression. The bitch practically had pincers.

'I need some information about getting a hotel room in Atlanta,'
I explained, smiling with the sweet sense of unreality induced by
spending ten sleepless hours on an airplane next to a person with a
bad cough.

'No hotel rooms available at this time,' she said.

'Sorry?' I said.

'No hotel rooms,' she repeated, turning a page of her magazine.
'WOLF BOY SPOTTED IN FLORIDA' was the headline, I noticed.

'So what do you think I should do?' I asked.

'You could call 'em up yourself,' she said, 'but I don't think you'll find a hotel room at this time.'

I felt hot, tired, tense and jetlagged. 'Could I have some change for the phone please?' I enquired.

'No,' she said. 'I can't do that. You'll have to try the booth next door.'

'The booth next door is closed,' I pointed out.

She shrugged again. Boy, could this dame shrug. She could shrug in seventeen different languages. Thus it was that, fresh off the plane from Ireland, and en route to Dublin, Georgia, I had to wander up and down the arrivals terminal of Atlanta airport accosting total strangers and pleading with them to change a dollar. One man I stopped turned out to be a photographer for the local newspaper. He was panting, out of breath, red in the face. He gave me a quarter and asked me if I had seen Claudia Schiffer. Not recently, I told him. He laughed. No, he had been told Claudia Schiffer was arriving at Atlanta airport around now. He was desperate to get the first photograph of her. I had no idea how much money he could get for a photograph like that. His eldest son was graduating from college this afternoon, but he had decided to skip the ceremony on the off chance that he would get a really good picture of Claudia Schiffer. It was great to be back in America.

The day I arrived in Atlanta the weather was pretty bad for April. Rain was pouring, thunder was booming, lightning was doing what lightning does. The city was in the grip of a full-scale tornado warning. One important thing to know about Americans is that they are exceedingly good at coming up with gradations of weather, and a full-scale tornado warning, as gradations go, is pretty darn serious. It is the level immediately below 'OHJESUSCHRISTALMIGHTYRUNITSA FUCKINGTORNADOMOTHER!'

The taxi driver was in laconic humour as he explained all of this to me. We eased through the rain and the rush-hour traffic, the voice of the radio announcer becoming more tense all the time. I was very excited about the prospect of the tornado. I had never seen a tornado myself, except very briefly in the opening scenes of *The Wizard of Oz*, and I thought it might be a fine thing to observe, experience and then write about in a travel book. Great, I thought. Only in the country an hour and already a bit of local colour.

The taxi driver was called Sergei and he was Russian, from St Petersburg, or Leningrad as he still called it. I asked him if he ever missed home and he shook his head and said Atlanta was his home now. 'There are more dumb fucken assholes in Leningrad than any place else in the whole world,' he said, 'except maybe Los Angeles.'

'Spasiba,' I said, as he dropped me off at my hotel.

'Pazhalsta,' he replied, and he smiled at me.

Those are the only two words of Russian I know. The first means thank you and the second means please. (As in, oh, please don't feel you have to thank me, that's quite all right.)

Just to get the trip off to a great start, the hotel had never heard of me or the reservation I had made from the airport. The desk clerk simpered and rattled the keys on his computer terminal, but there was really nothing he could do. There was a convention in town this weekend, he said. This was Atlanta, American capital of the weekend convention. There was always a convention in town.

Standing on the side of a motorway soaked to your underwear and trying to hail a taxi is a miserable enough experience, let me tell you. When I finally managed to stop one and get in, we drove up to Buckhead through the gathering storm. The wind screamed under the bridges and the rain was coming down horizontally now. I felt sure I was getting pneumonia.

All the hotels along the route seemed to be full. Finally the taxi driver suggested the Embassy Suites, slap in the middle of Buckhead. It was a little expensive, he said, but he felt pretty sure they would have a room.

The nice man behind the counter said no, there were no rooms available, but there were suites for $139 plus tax and deposit. It was a hell of a lot more than I had budgeted for, but by this stage I didn't care. Blubbering with gratitude I flung a bundle of banknotes across the counter and went out to collect my suitcase from the back of the cab.

The room was very nice. I mean, to be absolutely honest, for $139 plus tax and deposit I felt it should have contained a jeroboam of champagne, a side of smoked salmon, a large pack of ribbed condoms and an attractive nymphomaniac recently released from a year in solitary confinement. But still. What it did have was two televisions. One for me, and one for Claudia Schiffer, I thought, just on the off chance that she might show up after all.

I lay on the bed and turned on Claudia's television. I watched the local station reporting the latest news on the tornado, which was creeping along the northern edge of the city like a burglar intent on mischief. It became clear pretty quickly from the pictures that tornadoes are not that much fun after all. Buildings on the outskirts of town had already been demolished, and several people had been seriously injured out in the countryside.

'Wayne,' the newsreader said to the weatherman, 'what exactly is a full-scale tornado warning?'

'Well, Bob,' Wayne chirped, 'it's a warning that a tornado is going to happen soon.'

'And what should the viewers do, Wayne, if the tornado comes their way?'

'If the tornado comes their way, Bob, they should not go outside.'

That seemed like pretty good advice, I reflected, as the wind made the windowpane shudder and rattle in its frame. 'Go down to the basement of your house,' Wayne said, 'and stay there.'

'And if you're outside already, Wayne?' asked Bob.

'Bob, if you are outside already, you should hide in a ditch immediately.'

I had a sudden and terrible vision of wide-eyed farmers cantering up and down their fields frantically searching for ditches. To help me get over this, I went downstairs to the bar and joined the queue for cocktails. There was a pleasant atmosphere in the lobby. People seemed to be very happy. What was causing this, I wondered. Then, with a quite indescribable surge of joy I realized. The drink was free. You could go up to the bar and just have whatever you liked. The drink was absolutely free! This was staggering, I thought, and I gleefully anticipated doing a bit of staggering myself later.

I remember having four tequila sunrises. I remember talking to a couple called Kim and Kerry. Then I remember nothing much, except the sound of the wind, howling outside my window, and the sound of myself, howling in the bathroom.

Quite early the next morning I got up and went into town. It was a Saturday, and so I reckoned that town would be pretty lively. It was lively all right. Teams of firemen and city workers were wandering through the streets sawing up fallen trees and clearing collapsed masonry. Poor old Atlanta looked like it had gone ten rounds with Mike Tyson.

I say poor old Atlanta, although, in truth, Atlanta is quite a young city. Founded in 1847, it was frankly a pretty unimportant little railroad town until the Civil War, when its location made it the ideal place for the Confederates to set up enormous munitions factories. The Atlanta Underground was built around that time. A complex maze of subterranean streets in the centre of the city, it was relatively safe from bombardment. It was a very important place during the American Revolution, and so now, obviously, it has been rebuilt as a enormous shopping centre.

There weren't too many shoppers around that Saturday morning, however. I wandered about for a while, trying to find something worth buying, but after half an hour I gave up. I think the problem is that I've never liked being under the ground. It makes me feel like some sort of burrowing mammal. However, as soon as I emerged into the daylight, the morning began to look up. There, across the street from the main entrance to the Atlanta Underground, was the world Coca-Cola headquarters and museum. This, it seemed to me, was a must.

The Coca-Cola museum is a truly extraordinary place. As soon as you enter you encounter something called 'The Bottling Fantasy', an enormous kinetic sculpture which, according to the brochure, 'blends reality and illusion to illustrate the bottling process and create the fanciful sights and sounds of an imaginary bottling plant'. In other words, it bears no relation whatsoever to a real bottling plant, it just clanks and rattles and looks good and, if you go to see it early on a Saturday morning with an appalling tequila hangover, it makes you feel vaguely queasy.

The exhibition itself begins in 1886 with Dr John Smyth Pemberton, the chemist who developed the still secret formula for Coca-Cola. Dr John was a bit of a genius but also, it seems, a complete nerd, in that he invented Coca-Cola but was absolutely positive that nobody would ever buy it in bottles. Thus, he sold the right to bottle the stuff to a far-seeing Atlanta wideboy, Asa Griggs Candler, for one dollar. One dollar. How come stuff like that never happens to me?

The centrepiece of the Coca-Cola museum is an 'authentic 1950s Soda Stand' which has been lovingly recreated in the middle of the building. The sign outside says: 'You'll feel just like folks did back when they met in soda shops like this to greet and chat with friends.' I rushed in, looking forward to greeting and chatting with a few friends, but there was nobody there except a good-looking man behind the counter who was pretending to be a 1950s teenager with a part-time job in a soda fountain. His performance was astounding. I mean, there were only the two of us in the room, like I say, and I was really interested in who he was in real life. But he wouldn't tell me. He absolutely refused to acknowledge the fact that this was 1993 and he was an actor and we were in a skyscraper in downtown Atlanta. It was all Chevvies and Elvis and whitewall tyres and hep cats. He just wouldn't let up, not even for a second. And he kept using the phrase 'soda jerk' to describe himself. This was fine at first. It was when he began to abbreviate it that I started to get a bit giggly. 'Being a jerk is a good job, you know, a lot of people would like to be jerks, but being a jerk takes training, you know?'

The final room in the exhibition is full of bizarre facts about

Coke – 'If all the Coca-Cola ever produced was placed in average size bottles, laid end-to-end they would stretch to the moon and back 1,045 times' – and more interestingly, it has dozens of taps dispensing free cola from lots of different countries. You could thus rot your teeth in all sorts of international ways. My own favourite flavour of gum decay was Chinese blueberry.

It says a lot about how Atlanta is run these days that every single tourist map of the city features the Coca-Cola museum, while hardly any of them even mention the fact that Martin Luther King was born in the city and preached there. To find the location of the King museum involved a good deal of wandering up to strangers and asking for directions in a furtive manner, as though I was looking to buy half a ton of heroin. Eventually, somebody told me how to get there. I would have to walk, she said. There was no bus. Can you believe that? There is no bus from downtown Atlanta, where all the tourist hotels are, to Martin Luther King's birthplace. Phew, how the South is changing these days.

Having hiked the necessary several miles over rough country, vacant lots and attractive building sites, I have to admit I was a little disappointed to see that Dr King's final resting place was not particularly attractive. The mortal remains of the great man are interred in a white marble vault on a little stone island in the middle of a memorial pond which has a sky-blue tiled floor. The overall effect is reminiscent of nothing so much as a giant swimming pool. I wasn't sure whether to pay my respects silently or plunge in and try to break the hundred-yard butterfly record.

Nevertheless, the exhibition in the adjoining building of King's life is very moving. There are papers and books and film extracts of his speeches, and I have to confess, there were tears in my eyes watching some of them. What a guy. The kind of guy, you might think, that you would want all your tourists to come and find out about. But never mind. Who needs civil rights when you can have blueberry-flavoured Coca-Cola?

Perhaps the most telling exhibit in the entire museum was donated by Senator Ted Kennedy to Dr King's widow, Coretta Scott King.

It is simply a piece of official US Senate headed paper which records how each of the senators voted on the question of whether or not there should be a national day of celebration in memory of Martin Luther King. It was a salutary experience to look down the list of names and realize that I was standing in a country where democratically elected representatives could still actually vote against something like that.

The King family house, just down the street, is open to the public and is one of the poshest in the area. I was surprised to discover that Dr King's family was actually pretty well off. His father was minister in the local Ebenezer Baptist Church, and young Martin came from a long line of smart, tough and educated people. The house is nicely done up, although, as with the Coca-Cola museum soda fountain, some considerable effort has been put into making it all 'exactly just the way it was forty years ago'. Looking at it, I really hoped I would never become famous myself. If I were to die suddenly tomorrow, and if the authorities were to preserve my flat in Dublin exactly the way it is now, I think I would die all over again with the embarrassment. Can I just say now, in case it ever happens, please, please let my relations in first, to remove my dirty socks from the sink and to burn the Bay City Rollers albums I keep hidden at the back of the fridge.

When the tour of the house was over I went back out into Auburn Avenue and just stood there for a while, smoking a cigarette and vaguely wishing I was black. After a few moments, my fantasy of being either Muhammad Ali or the lead guitarist in James Brown's backing band was rudely interrupted when an enormous red limousine pulled up outside the King house. This was a limousine of the type you only see in America, a good ten foot longer than your average Mercedes, with tinted windows and a forest of aerials bristling from the roof. A tall black chauffeur in a uniform and a peaked cap stepped out gracefully and opened the back door. A young and quite gorgeous-looking white woman got out and handed the driver a camera. She then went and stood in front of the house, where she put her hands on her hips and pouted in a Jaggeresque fashion while her chauffeur took her photograph. Then, when he had finished, she jumped back into the limo, and thirty seconds after it had pulled up, the car revved up and slid away down Auburn Avenue. I really thought that meant something, but I wasn't quite sure what.

I strolled across Auburn and went into the National Parks Department office, where they were showing a slideshow all about the history of the area. The show was interesting and clearly organized, developing into a brief history of the civil rights movement in America. There was a particularly memorable section about the elderly Alabama seamstress Rosa Parks who refused to obey that state's racist law which made blacks and whites travel on separate buses. When the show was over I went back outside and got talking to the friendly young woman from the Parks Department who sold tickets and ran the office. She asked where I was from, and I told her Ireland.

She said she had been to Ireland once, but she could not remember where exactly. I asked whether she had been to the north or the south, but she could not even remember that. I found this amazing. I wondered whether she was lying to me, but she seemed so nice that I couldn't imagine her telling bare-faced lies to strangers for absolutely no reason whatsoever.

'Are you sure you can't remember?' I asked.

She stared at the ceiling and shook her head. Then she smiled. 'But I liked that movie, *The Commitments*,' she said.

'Yeah,' I said, 'me too.'

Now, I should explain that most Irish novelists are haunted by Roddy Doyle in a way that is almost impossible to describe. I mean, how do you deal with this guy? Here is a guy who sells hundreds and hundreds of thousands of copies in hardback. Here is a guy whose first novel was filmed by Alan Parker, nominated for Oscars, hugely successful all over the world. And he's nice! That's the awful thing. He's apparently very nice. I mean, if all the money had gone to his head, if he had booted the wife and kids out of the house and installed a harem of buxom teenage floozies, or if he had moved to

LA and turned to the drink or the cocaine, that would have been great for the rest of us. But no. Roddy Doyle is nice and no matter where in the world you take yourself now, people want to talk to you about him. It is truly awful.

'That was one swell movie,' she said.

'Sure was,' I said. 'So anyway, this museum is beautifully organized.'

'"Mustang Sally",' she crooned, '"I guess you better slow-ho, that mustang down. Oh Mustang Sally now baby, I guess ya better . . ."'

'Ha, ha, ha,' I tittered. 'So, anyway, that was a very moving slideshow.'

'Oh yeah, thanks. Listen, you remember that bit in the movie where the kid wants to put the horse in the elevator?'

'Yeah, yeah,' I said. 'Hilarious. Anyway, did Dr King ever—?'

'What was that guy's name?' she said. 'The guy that wrote that book?'

I swallowed hard. 'Roddy Doyle,' I said.

'Roddy?' she said.

'Doyle,' I said.

'And he's Irish, right?'

'He certainly is.'

'And he's doing real good?'

'I believe he's certainly surviving,' I said.

'I sure hope he is. I hope he's makin piles of money. You know him?'

'No,' I said.

'Aw,' she said. 'Shame.'

'Well,' I blurted out, 'I met him once.' (Oh sweet Christ, I thought, what a sad bastard you are. Step forward please, The Man Who Met Roddy Doyle Once.)

I told her that I had met Roddy Doyle on the night he had won the Booker Prize. She didn't know what the Booker Prize was, so I said it was like the Pulitzer. 'That's big, right?' she said, and I confirmed that yes, the dimensions of the Booker were indeed not inconsiderable. I told her that Roddy Doyle had thrown a big party in London that night and I had ended up going to it.

'You see,' I pointed out, 'I write novels myself actually. So anyway, tell me, did Dr King really—?'

'You ever won it?' she said.

'What?'

'That thing. The Booker? You ever won that?'

'Well, not exactly,' I said.

'Aw, shame. Guess you ain't as funny as him, huh?'

'Well, I—'

'Guess nobody's as funny as him though. Gee, he's really funny. Guess I wouldn't even *try* to be as funny as him.'

'Actually, I—'

'Yeah, yeah,' she said, 'well, that was one swell movie. You see him again, you tell him I said that, OK? Man, did I laugh or what? That really was one hell of a funny movie. I think it's the best movie I ever saw in my whole life. Period. *You tell him I said he deserved all the success in the world now, OK?*'

'Yes,' I said. 'Goodbye now.'

On Saturday night in Atlanta I went out to a club called Blind Willie's Blues Bar. (It is not, incidentally, named after President Clinton, but after the ophthalmologically challenged popular chanteur, the late Mr Blind Willie McTell.)

Blind Willie's was a nice little place in a trendy part of town. I sat down near the back, and the waitress came over and told me her name was Sandra. 'Sandra,' I said, 'what a lovely name.' I was in a good mood, you see. 'Where you from, sugar?' she asked. 'Venezuela,' I told her, because I was afraid if I said Ireland she would turn out to be a big Roddy Doyle fan. 'You talk real nice,' she said. 'So do you, Sandra,' I said. Things were looking up.

By about ten o'clock the place was pretty full. A couple of white kids appeared on the stage with guitars and began singing about being poor and ornery and how they wuz gonna jump in that ole ribba and drown theyselves cuz they dun had doze blues so bad. To judge by their appearances, I felt their only real experience of the blues was probably not having received enough orthodontic treatment as teenagers. Shortly after this, Magic Slim's band came on minus their leader and began to romp efficiently through a selection of Chicago blues standards. It was nothing hectic, but it was pleasant to hear it all the same. Sandra passed by and winked at me.

'Que pasa?' she said.

'Nothing much,' I said.

'I thought you were from Venezuela,' she said. 'Don't they speak Spanish in Venezuela?'

'Ha ha ha, Sandra,' I said. 'Portuguese actually.'

'Really?'

'Yeah, the part I'm from, we all speak Portuguese.'

'I never heard that,' she sighed. 'You see, I majored in Spanish in high school. I just love guys who speak Spanish, you know?'

'Oh,' I said. 'Really? Well, you know, I do speak—'

'Portuguese,' she interrupted. 'Oh well. Vaya con Dios.'

She turned and disappeared into the crowd, and if I had known that I would not see her again for the rest of the night I would have had the presence of mind at least to order up half a dozen cervesas before she left, por favor. Hindsight is a great thing. Anyway, just as she left me for ever, Magic Slim sloped up on to the stage and plugged in his guitar and the audience began to get excited.

You can always tell when Americans are getting excited. It's the small things really. The way they get up on their seats and start swinging out of the lampshades and hollering and screeching and kicking their legs in the air. Magic Slim remained fairly calm in the face of such a spontaneous display of affection. He lashed into his first number, which would have gone a whole hell of a lot better if his amplifier had been working. He stopped and tried to start again. His amplifier began to make a loud farting sound. The audience continued to scream and howl, but nothing Magic could do would make his amplifier work. It was when he took off his hat that I really sensed all was not well.

The show was temporarily halted while Magic's roadies came on to the stage and started displaying their considerable technical expertise. This involved a good deal of getting out screwdrivers and hammers and spanners and then proceeding to batter the shit out of the amp with them.

Mission accomplished, Magic came back on and started up again, and this time, as Confucius once said, he was cooking with fucking gas. I was just beginning to enjoy myself when two very large people came and stood right in front of me. The man was short and stocky and he was wearing a tartan shirt. The woman was spectacularly tall and had on a stripey frock. They were trying to talk to each other, so it was obviously a first date situation. The woman was holding the man's hand very tightly and swinging it in time to the music, and to judge by the way he was tenderly sticking his enormous tongue in her ear and wiggling it about, he too had been deeply pricked by Cupid's famous dart.

Now, I am not one to get in the way of true love, but I really did feel that I had not forked out ten bucks to stare close-up at two arses. I mean, all alone, in a distant city, short of entertainment and company, I could imagine that one night I might conceivably do this. But this was not the night, and these, most certainly, were not the arses. These particular arses were so rotund that you could have played handball against them and parked your bicycle afterwards between their cheeks.

As Magic Slim paused for a between-song breather, I reached out and lightly touched the man on the back. He turned around and stared at me. 'You gotta problem, bub?' he said.

'No,' I said. 'I just wondered if you could move over a little.'

'Oh, you did, huh?'

'Yes, I did. Please.'

He sniffed. He took a swig from his bottle. 'Fuck you,' he said, and he resumed his oral exploration of his beloved's auditory channel.

'Fuck you too, you redneck, shit-kicking moron,' I said. To myself. Really quietly.

Up on the stage, Magic Slim was getting going again, but the evening had been spoilt for me. I debated getting up and giving the tartan-wearing tosspot the hiding of his life, but then, luckily for him, I remembered that I don't really believe in physical violence. It would be better, I felt, to make a quiet and dignified exit and thereby allow the pair of obese sheepfuckers to steal my seat so that at least one out of their four buttocks could be comfortable.

I stood up and said, 'Excuse me, please' in a very threatening manner and pushed my way forward through the bopping crowd and towards the door of the bar. The last thing I saw was Sandra the waitress, propped up against one of the speakers, with her arm around a hairy tattooed guy in a leather jacket.

'Venezuela my ass,' she said, as I disappeared into the night.

The Limerick Junction Irish bar was just down the street and I wandered in for what I hoped would be a few quiet drinks. It was very crowded. There was a signpost on the wall which said 'Limerick 6000 miles'. There were framed posters of 'Irish' sayings. 'May you be in heaven half an hour before the divil knows you're dead.' That kind of thing. I mean, I am Irish myself, and I have never once heard anybody say that.

On a small stage down at the back, a young pimply man in an Aran sweater was strumming an acoustic guitar and singing an Irish song called 'Whiskey in the Jar':

As I was going over
The Cork and Kerry mountains
I met with Captain Farrell
And his money he was countin'
I first produced my pistol
And I then produced my rapier
Saying, stand and deliver
Or the devil he may take you
With your ring-dumma-do dumma-da
Wak-fol-the-daddy-oh, wak-fol-the-daddy-oh
There's whiskey in the jar.

This is a song you hear a lot at really sad weddings in the parts of rural Ireland where people marry their first cousins. It was about as authentically involving as a detailed speech by Henry Kissinger on the finer points of the South Moluccan economy. And it was about as depressing as shit.

The next morning was a Sunday and so I rose early and went back to Auburn Avenue, to the Ebenezer Baptist Church, for the ten forty-five service. I am not a religious person, as you will know by now, but still, I wanted to see what a genuine southern Baptist service would be like, in case one of my grandchildren would ever ask me such a thing.

I had thought that the congregation would be full of visiting liberal whiteys like myself, but Ebenezer is very much a functioning local church and almost all those present were black. Most of them were middle-aged or elderly, but a good number were my own age. The men were all dressed in smart suits and ties, the women in soberly coloured dresses and wide-brimmed black hats. As the church gradually filled up, people in the congregation sat in the pews and chatted to each other. It was nice. Before a mass in Ireland, nobody would dream of chatting inside a church. Chatting inside a church in Ireland is a criminal offence.

At ten forty-five on the dot, five women came up to the front of the church and began to sing a cappella gospel songs. Now, sinful hedonistic pagan as I am, there are few noises in the world as likely to stir the emotions as a cappella gospel singing, I find. The women sang a song called 'Count Your Blessings', and they swayed from side to side as they sang in beautiful harmony, clicking their fingers or clapping. When they had finished there was a rousing round of applause from the congregation. That's another thing that would never happen in an Irish church. Applause in an Irish church is actually punishable by death. I thought they were bloody marvellous, I must say. I certainly thought they could have blown Magic Slim off the stage any day of the week.

The J.R. Roberts Memorial Male Voice Choir came in next and they sat in the benches at the back. These guys were dressed in sober suits and dark ties and long black robes and they looked a lot more self-important than the women. Just as they started to sing their beautiful solemn hymn, the pastor swept into the church and went up to join them. Pastor Roberts – he turned out to be the son of the J.R. Roberts after whom the choir was named – was a tall, full-figured and handsome man, with a beautiful warm bass voice. They all sang together, leading the congregation, and the volume of the singing threatened to lift the rafters off the building:

Look ye saints, the sight is glorious
See the man of sorrows now:
From the fight returned victorious
Every knee to him shall bow.
Crown the saviour, angels crown him:
Rich the trophies Jesus brings
In the seat of power enthrone him
While the vault of heaven rings.

Sinners in derision crowned him
Mocking thus the savior's claim;
Saints and angels crowd around him
Own his title, praise his name.
Hark! The bursts of acclamation.
Hark, these loud triumphant chords.
Jesus takes the highest station,
Oh, what joy the sight affords.

After the hymn, Pastor Roberts told the congregation to sit down and relax. His assistant, Brother Ken, read out a few announcements, and then a piece from the book of Romans. When the reading was done, the choir stood up and sang another song, with a mournfully beautiful air:

Spirit of the living God
Fall afresh on me
Spirit of the living God
Fall afresh on me
Melt me, mould me, hold me, fill me
Spirit of the living God
Fall afresh on me.

When they had finished singing, everybody clapped and cheered and yelled 'Amen' or 'Praise the Lord'.

The organization of the service itself was interesting. It began with a section where people prayed specifically for loved ones who were ill. 'Oh Lord,' said the Pastor, 'some here, Lord, have received bad news from the doctor this week, but you said by your stripes are we healed.'

'Yes Jesus,' came the cries from the congregation. 'Amen, amen, amen.'

Next there was a portion of the service called 'The Welcoming of the Visitors'. All of us who were visitors to the church had to stand up and identify ourselves. The choir sang an upbeat song while the congregation surrounded us and shook our hands and hugged us and made us all feel welcome. Pastor Roberts came down and asked me where I was from. When I told him, he threw his arms around me and exclaimed, 'Praise the Lord'. (I think I said 'Praise the Lord' too, because Pastor Roberts didn't even mention Roddy Doyle.)

All this had been great fun and very moving. But the really good stuff was to come. Pastor Roberts's sermon turned out to be the utter business. He began gently, carefully explaining the intricacies of his chosen biblical text. God had paid the price of our justification, he told us. We were saved. All we had to do was trust God. Even if we had sinned, all we had to do was repent and trust God's mercy. His voice was calm and measured. There was nothing at all about hell or damnation. He stressed the compassion of God again and again, the beautiful mercy of God. There was no sin that could not be forgiven. He cracked a few jokes here. Even adultery could be forgiven. 'Some of you out there been nibblin the green grass in someone else's yard,' he said. 'Don't think I don't know that, and yet God has paid the cost of your justification!' Slowly, gradually, his voice began to rise and quiver with passion. Black people had always been made to feel inferior, he said. All through the centuries they had been made to feel bad. It was still going on now. That was why there was so much war in the African countries, so much crime in the inner cities of America. Because black people had been taught to hate themselves. And this was wrong. This was not what God wanted. Only God could give people back a sense of what they were really worth.

'Because when they cut us, and when they made us feel we were debased, and when they told us we were worthless, some poor black slave standing in the field got up one day, and he just cried out, "Over my head I feel music in the air, there must be a God somewhere." Yes he did. He said, "You will not enslave me, nor will you define the conditions of my servitude!" Yes. Praise Jesus. He cried out, "Before I'll be a slave, I'll be dead in my grave, and go home to my Lord and be free."'

There was loud and long applause at this point, and cries of 'Yes Lord' and 'Amen' and 'Say it, Preacher'. Pastor Roberts took a deep breath and started to give it the full welly.

'And that's the reason our people were able to make it through the dark time. That's the reason Sojourner Truth could make it. That's the reason Martin could make it. The reason Rosa Parks could make it. That frail little seamstress. That old lady. They told her not to sit on that bus. She said no. Amen! She just said no. And you couldn't see him, but I believe the Lord sent down an angel and said, "Rosa, just sit there!" Amen! "Just keep on sittin there, girl, and you will lead your people to freedom." Do you believe in angels, people? Read your Bible! Read it! Every new morning, new mercies I see there . . . Our brother Martin, Dr King, he could have preached at Riverside Church. Any fancy church in town. He could have taught at Harvard University. Anywhere. But he heard the cries of his people for freedom. And God worked through him. Can I get a witness here? Oh Lord, I wish I had a witness!! Is there anyone out there feels the spirit working today? Amen, Jesus. Are you full of the spirit this morning?'

Three full hours after the service began I walked out into Auburn Avenue. And I don't know whether I was full of the spirit or not. But I don't mind telling you, I felt better than I had for months.

That Sunday afternoon after lunch I spent a happy few hours driving round and round Atlanta's peripheral highway and repeatedly missing the turn for the southern highway that would eventually take me to Dublin, Georgia. Whatever the events of the morning, the spirit was certainly not leading me now. When I did finally manage to leave Atlanta on Interstate 75 South, I stayed on the motorway for a whole ten miles, before accidentally turning off again on to Highway 23, which is kind of parallel, except that it runs in the opposite direction.

People will tell you that driving in America is easy, but this is an outrageous and terrible lie. America must be the most mapped country in the world, and the maps make it look like the very picture of simplicity. Yet the full-scale reality is a hell of a lot more complex. America is the world capital of the hidden turn-off, the unmarked sliproad, the incredibly important signpost which you see only as you are speeding past it at seventy miles per hour.

When I finally got back on to the correct road, I felt about ten years older than I had when I'd left Atlanta two hours earlier. I drove through the Panola Mountain Conservation Park without stopping, then through Stockbridge, Flippen, McDonough, Blacksville, Locust Grove, Jackson, Flovilla, Indian Spurs, Juliet, Jarrel Plantation, Popes Ferry and Payne, before stopping for a break in Macon.

Macon was a lovely little town, full of small hot squares and clean streets. I had a bowl of guacamole and a cold beer in a pavement café and then I went for a walk. The walk was only slightly spoilt by all the posters announcing that Magic Slim was playing in Macon that night. Bad enough Roddy Doyle following you around. Now it was Magic bloody Slim.

I managed to get out of Macon with surprising ease, turning on to Interstate 16 East for Savannah. After a few miles of straight road I felt so confident that I turned off the main road and on to the old Highway 80 West which was a lot more scenic. I drove through Dry Branch, Fitzpatrick, Jeffersonville, Danville, Allentown, Montrose, Dudley and eventually came to Dublin, Georgia.

By the time I got to Dublin dusk was falling. The first sight of the town was pretty disappointing, I have to say. I wasn't expecting fireworks or a marching band or anything, but Dublin, Georgia seemed just like a lot of the small Georgia towns through which I had passed in my attempt to get there. It had one long main street and a load of agricultural supply stores and a couple of gas stations and that was about it. I drove down the one long main street and discovered that it led to a separate town called East Dublin, which was, in all respects that I could see, a carbon copy of Dublin proper.

I found a motel and checked in. I was really very tired now, and I asked whether there was a bar. The woman behind the desk said there was indeed a bar, and a very fine bar at that, but this being Sunday, it was closed. It was the county law, she explained. No alcohol could be sold in Laurens County Georgia on a Sunday. The spirit was really moving within me now. I would have sold my pet puppy to Satan for the suck of a bottle of Bud.

I went out and had dinner in a restaurant just down the road. I had better not name the restaurant because it was so utterly vile that their lawyers would definitely try to sue. Suffice it to say that the steak was swimming in a pool of greasy blood, and the air conditioner was turned up so high that even before the blood had congealed on my cutlery my teeth were already chattering. Worse than this, the fucking table was slanted. When you're tired and hungry and cold and pining for alcohol, a slanted fucking table is pretty much the worst thing you can imagine.

The waitress was a very nice Austrian woman who was married to a local man. She said she really loved living in Dublin. I asked her what a person could do for a good time around here.

'A good time,' she said. She repeated the phrase, as though she had never heard it before.

'You know,' I said, 'bars for instance.'

'We got the bar here,' she said, 'and the bar at the Holiday Inn. But they're both closed, of course. It's Sunday, you see.'

'That's it?' I said.

'Well yes,' she said, 'but who has to drink to have a good time after all?'

'Well,' I said, 'I know one or two people like that.'

'Not me,' she laughed.

Back outside the restaurant everything was closed and the streets were deserted. I tramped down the Interstate for a while, cursing and blaspheming and hoping to find an open gas station with a convenience store. After a few miles of brisk walking, I succeeded. I went in and filled a basket with all kinds of junk. Biscuits, peanuts, two packets of dental floss. At the last minute, just as I was about to approach the cash register, I slipped a couple of six-packs of Rolling Rock into my basket with a contrived air of innocence so total that it would have made one of the Waltons seem seedy.

The man said he couldn't sell me a six-pack until a minute past midnight. Oh no, really? I looked at my watch. It was now ten to midnight, I pointed out, and I wouldn't tell anyone if he didn't. He shook his head and said he couldn't do it. I was a tourist, I said, I didn't know the rules. That, he said, was as may be. He couldn't do it and that was that. I laughed lightly and began to explain some of the more basic concepts of existentialism, for instance, the funda-mentally Sartrean notion that as mature human beings we can, and indeed must, make our own moral choices and construct our own ethical identities if we wish to be, in any meaningful sense, human. 'Yeah,' he sniffed. 'Well, I said I can't do it, and I guess that means I can't do it.'

I went back to the motel room, where I cried myself to sleep with the air conditioner on, and woke up with a terrible headache two hours later. Out in the motel car park, a gang of truck drivers seemed to be having a party. For one awful moment I was going to get dressed and go out and ask if they would sell me some beer, but I thought they might bludgeon me to death just for sport, so in the end I decided against it.

Next morning after breakfast, I went on my usual trek down to the town library to try and find some information about the God-forsaken lousy joyless dump, I mean, sorry, the town.

The librarian was very helpful. She explained that following the Revolutionary War, Georgia had been divided into eight large counties. A movement soon began to create new and smaller counties, in order to centralize the local economies. In the area around what is now Dublin the subdivision movement was particularly strong. Most of the local farmers were owners of vast estates which could easily be broken up and sold to the poor gullible half-wit immigrants who were eagerly looking for arable land close to waterways.

The town was thus incorporated on 9 December 1812, the smallest town ever created by the Georgia legislature. 'The incorporation,' reads the original deed, 'shall extend to and include all the inhabitants living within 250 yards of Broad Street and within 400 yards of the courthouse.'

There are two theories about how the town got its name, and praise the Lord, neither of them have to do with inns or horses. Theory number one is that Dublin's founder, one Jonathan Sawyer, hailed from Dublin, Ireland. (There is no doubt that he was Irish, but nobody has ever been able to establish for sure which town he was from.) The second explanation is that Sawyer married the eldest daughter of a family who came from Dublin, Ireland, and named the place thus in order to impress the babe. I decided that I would plump for theory number two, on the basis that it was more sweet and romantic. Dublin, Georgia had been named as a token of love. Pass the sickbag, Alice.

After its foundation, the history of Dublin pretty much mirrors that of the whole South. The town and county became very prosperous, which prosperity may in some small way have been related to the fact that most of the people doing the work were not actually being paid, whereas most of the people who weren't doing the work were drinking a hell of a lot of mint juleps. In 1845 there were 3,258 whites and 2,760 slaves in Laurens County, a ratio which would put even antebellum Alabama to shame.

By the turn of the century the town was booming. The railroad was extended to Dublin from Macon in 1891. Tourism became big business. There was a big theatre at the corner of Madison and Monroe Streets. By 1912, there were twenty-two passenger trains daily into Dublin. This is the kind of thing small town librarians in America are really good at. Ask them where the really hot local bars are and they look vague. Ask them about trains and they can quote you bloody timetables from 1912.

When the librarian had gone back to her office, I pottered around the shelves for a while and found a book of statistics about the town. Even though the figures had been compiled within the last twenty years, they still revealed a pretty shocking picture of racial segregation. In one part of town there were almost a thousand white people and only five blacks. The compiler had noted, with gruesome unselfconsciousness, 'there are relatively few blighting influences in this study area'. (Yes, you fascist prick, I thought, what you really mean is that there are only five of them.)

It was a lovely spring day, but I have to admit I was getting an unpleasant feeling about Dublin, Georgia. So far I knew only two things about it. One, getting a drink was difficult; two, black people were clearly regarded as being one short step up from alcoholics. I noticed that the car was running very low on gas, so I drove up and down the main street looking for a gas station. I couldn't find one that was open, so I decided to turn down a side street.

The scene that greeted me would have made the poorer streets around Auburn Avenue seem like Beverly Hills. The houses were small and in terrible condition. A lot of them had been repaired with enormous sheets of corrugated iron. This was only April, but the afternoon heat was already close to unbearable. I tried to imagine what the houses would be like in the middle of August. All the people on the street were black. All of them. Without exception. I pulled into a gas station, got out and filled up the car. When I went into the station to pay, I noticed a hurriedly scrawled notice on the wall which announced: 'We take welfare cheques and food stamps'. It was the first time in many trips to America that I had ever seen such a sign.

I drove back up on to the main street of Dublin, Georgia and I went into a Dairy Queen where I ordered a sandwich and a cup of coffee. A young black man in a uniform was mopping the floor. He caught my eye and gave me a friendly smile.

'You from outta town?' he said.

I told him I was from Dublin, Ireland.

'No kiddin. You guys have green beer over there, right?'

'No,' I said, 'I've never had green beer in Ireland.'

'I thought you guys had that green beer in Ireland, no?'

'We don't usually,' I laughed, 'but I'll tell you the truth, I wouldn't mind any colour beer right now. Do you have bars here in Dublin or what?'

'Not too many,' he grinned. 'You tried Shoney's or the Holiday Inn?'

I said I'd tried both and I didn't much like the look of them. But I thought I had seen a couple of bars in the side streets last night, on my way into the town. It was dark but I was sure I'd seen some bars. Down in the side streets? He shook his head.

'You don't wanna go over there,' he said.

I asked why not and he shrugged.

'We got our own places back there,' he said, 'you know what I'm sayin?' He glanced at me for a second and then he tried to smile again and he looked away. And I did know what he was saying. In Dublin, Georgia, he was saying, black people had their own bars, and white people had theirs.

Just then an elderly white policeman came into the restaurant. He said hello to the young black man and sat down at a table by himself.

He was a tall white-haired man who looked like he might have once been handsome. When he noticed that I was alone he nodded across at me and said hello.

'He's from Dublin, Ireland,' the young black man said.

'Well you're mighty welcome,' the policeman said, and he came over to my table and held out his hand.

'You bin to Georgia b'fore?' he said, and I told him no.

'Most beautiful state in the whole union,' he said. 'You can go anywheres you please, but if you're lookin for pretty as a picture scenery, well Georgia's th'only place.'

I asked him what it was like being a policeman in Dublin, Georgia and he told me there were times when it wasn't that great. There was a severe drug problem in the town, and the police hadn't got the resources to fight it. I said I couldn't believe this, that a town this size would have a drug problem, but the policeman explained that Dublin is right on the main highway from Florida, the state through which most illegal drugs come into the US.

The policeman looked over his shoulder to make sure that the young black man with the mop wasn't listening. Most of the drug addicts in the town were, you know, coloured. He didn't mean to be prejudiced or anything, but that's just the way things were. 'I mean, don't get me wrong,' he said. 'Your heart'd go out to 'em. I mean, I don't get it m'self now, the drug thing. How you take one of them syringes and load the sucker up and then squirt that mother in your arm, man, I don't get that for one short minute. But I guess I'm a little too old to be a swinger, you know?'

I said I knew what he meant. Then I looked at my watch and said I really had to go.

'Yeah,' he said. 'Well, you be real sure'n come back agin to Georgia now, y'hear?'

I told him I would, but from the look in his eyes I think he knew I was lying.

CHAPTER 12

The Devil in Disguise

He [Elvis] was ahead of his time because he had such deep feelings, because he was so deeply loved by his mother, Gladys. He was able to appreciate profound beauty in sounds. He started a musical revolution.

They say all revolutions start from love.

Imelda Marcos

Rock 'n' roll is part of a pest to undermine the morals of the youth of our nation. It is sexualistic, unmoralistic and . . . brings people of both races together.

The North Alabama White Citizens'
Council, 1955

The flight to Nashville was short and enjoyable. From the plane I could see the Mississippi River winding through the countryside, breaking into lakes and enormous tributaries and then flowing back into one vast watery highway again. All the fields far below me were large and ruthlessly square, and the white roads ran in straight lines as far as the eye could see. Only the river broke the unremitting geometry of the scene as it curled and snaked and wound through the grid of the landscape like a great big living reminder that human beings may do their best to impose something like order on the elements, but Mother Nature is a feisty old dame who does more or less what she damn well feels like.

There wasn't a town called Dublin in Tennessee, but I still felt I had to visit the place. Someone had once told me that Elvis Presley had Irish blood, and I wanted to find out if this was true. Also, I simply wanted to hear some wonderful music and, if that's what you want, Tennessee is really a must.

The taxi driver told me I was welcome and asked me where I was from. When I said Ireland, he reached over and shook my hand and said, 'In that case, friend, you're double welcome.'

He loved Ireland, he told me, and he had been there several times. He had no Irish blood himself, but his wife's people were 'Scotch-Irish' (this was the description the Ulster presbyterian immigrants gave themselves in order to disguise their ethnic origins). But even though he wasn't Irish, he was a big fan of Irish music. The Irish traditional music group the Chieftains were among his absolute favourites. He told me proudly that the Chieftains had recorded an album in Nashville the previous year, with Emmylou Harris, Chet Atkins, Ricky Scaggs, Willie Nelson, Don Williams and a whole pantheon of other country music superstars. I told him it sounded pretty interesting but I hadn't heard it. He pulled a tape of the album out of his glovebox and pushed it into his cassette deck.

A series of truly amazing sounds came bursting from his speakers. The American country standard 'The Wabash Cannonball' segued seemlessly into a traditional Irish reel called 'Father Kelly's'. The Elvis classic 'Heartbreak Hotel' was punctuated with a long and wild blast of 'The Cliffs of Moher Jig'. The last track on the album went on for about fifteen minutes, a joyous incorporation of Irish dance music with bluegrass, jazz, blues, boogie-woogie piano playing and classical motifs. It was like listening to all the clamouring voices of immigrant America condensed into one huge and glorious chunk. When we got to my hotel the taxi driver and I just sat in the car park for half an hour playing bits of the tape all over again. I had never heard anything quite like it in my life. I was dazzled by it. When I went to get out of the car, the driver insisted on giving the tape to me. I went rooting through my rucksack for a tape of the Irish singer Christy Moore singing the astoundingly lovely New Orleans song, 'The Lakes of Ponchartrain'. The song tells the story of an Irish soldier in the Yankee army at the time of the Civil War who gets lost behind enemy lines and falls in love with a black woman who rescues him. When I found the tape, I insisted that he take it as fair exchange. He shoved the cassette into his deck and we both sat there entranced in the car park, smoking cigarettes, as the mellow voice of Christy Moore filled the car:

I said my lovely Creole girl
My money is no good
And if weren't for the alligators
I'd sleep out here in the wood.
You're welcome here kind stranger
Our house it is very plain.
But we'd never turn a stranger out
On the shores of Ponchartrain.

She took me home to her mammy's house
And treated me right well.
The hair across her shoulders
In jet-black ringlets fell.
To try and paint her beauty
Would only be in vain;
As handsome was that Creole girl
By the shores of Ponchartrain.

That night I went out to eat at the Stockyard Bullpen Steakhouse in downtown Nashville, a restaurant which had been warmly recommended to me by the taxi driver. 'They give you a steak there you'll never forget in your damn life,' he had said, and as it turned out, he wasn't joking. The steak, when it came, was the size and thickness of a your average Bible, and I'm talking the King James version. It took a good half an hour to eat, and by the time I finished it I really felt that I was going to explode.

When the meal was over I waddled out into the street and found a club where a country band was playing. I sat at the bar and listened for a while, drinking double Jack Daniel's and trying to make myself feel thin. The music was interesting. There were no songs about horses or trains or lonesome trails or failed crops. This was the modern hybrid music known as New Country. The band played an eclectic mix of cover versions, from Glenn Miller's 'In the Mood' to Burt Bacharach and Hal David's 'I Just Don't Know What to Do with Myself'. There was a brass section and a synthesizer. Nobody was wearing a Stetson. The musicians could play more than three chords. I remember thinking that if the ghost of Hank Williams were suddenly to materialize through the floorboards, he would have found it all very strange indeed.

Which was odd. Because just as I was thinking this, someone in the audience called out for a Hank Williams song. 'Oh yeah, Hank,' drawled the singer, 'which Hank number you wanna hear?' The call came back for the tender spiritual, 'Just a Closer Walk with Thee'. The band began to titter like naughty schoolboys. 'OK,' said the singer. 'You got it, sister.'

The band struck up the introduction and the singer clutched his hand to his breast in an attitude of respectful reverence as he closed his eyes and began to whine:

Just a plate of butter peas,
A toasted sandwich with Swiss cheese,
Just a nice big steak, oh please,
Gimme just a plate of butter peas.

This, for a traditional country music buff, would be every bit as blasphemous as Sid Vicious singing 'My Way' was to Frank Sinatra fans. But here in the Stockyard Bullpen bar, everyone laughed loud and cheered as poor old Hank's most heartfelt number was briskly stripped down, tied up and beaten to within an inch of its life.

As the song finished in a wail of feedback and thundering drums, the man beside me at the bar was cackling so loud I feared he might rupture himself. I ordered a beer. My neighbour nodded at me and then he nodded across the bar in the direction of the barlady, an attractive blonde woman in her early thirties.

'She's cute,' he said. 'Ain't she?'

I confirmed that yes, she was certainly of pleasing aspect.

'Yew like her?' he said.

'She seems like a very nice person,' I said.

'Oh she ain't that,' he tittered, 'she ain't naahce at all, friend. She's damn naisty in fact, I can tell yew that much, hoo hoo hoo. She's th'original good time's bin had by all.'

I tried to concentrate on my drink. He nudged me.

'She'd give you a keeyuss if you tawked like me,' he said. 'She don't like furrners, see. She jest loves that Suthen axaint. You jes try it now when she gaits back here witcher beeyah. You jes say, thankee kindly, honey, like me, and she'll give ye a big keeyus.'

I told him I didn't actually want a kiss.

'Jest try it for fun,' he cackled, 'you jest say, howdee sweetie pie, and she'll gait that ole look in her eye and next thing yew know you mo be out back and stokin.'

'Stokin?' I said.

He put his hands on his hips and began to thrust his pelvis back and forth.

'Stokin,' he replied. 'Doin' the wild thang.'

'Oh right,' I said, 'Listen, I'm just here for the music actually.'

He threw back his head, opened his mouth and gave a wolf-like howl. 'Oh main,' he said, 'if it's music yew want, she's the one. Yew be stokin her, I'll tell yew, it's music yew gonna hear. She's like a ole steam train goin throo a tunnel man, yes siree.'

The barlady came back with my drink. Her very physical proximity seemed to reduce my new friend to a quite terrifying paroxysm of mirth. 'Look at the hooters on that,' he sighed, as she took my money and went off to the till. 'She ain't never gonna fall flat on her face, is she, friend?' At this point I was going to give my enthusiastic companion a brief summation of the main ideological tenets of contemporary feminism, but then I just looked into my beer and I thought, oh, fuck it, and after a while he stood up and went away.

The imminent arrival of a singer called Flaco Jones was announced from the stage, to a great roar of approval from the audience. Flaco is the Spanish word for skinny, but to judge from Flaco's appearance he had clearly been named ironically. The man was the size of a basket balloon. He waddled up to the stage with his guitar under his arm, panting and huffing and dripping with sweat. His neck was the most disgusting thing I had ever seen in my life. It looked like a packet of frankfurters. Flaco's flowery shirt looked like it had been hired out for the night from Rent-A-Tent, and his trousers could have comfortably accommodated a whole family of gypsies. Everything about him was big. His hands were the size of most people's heads. His thighs were the width of Canadian redwoods. He had on a pair of cowboy boots which must have been made from a couple of Aberdeen Angus bulls. But when he started to sing, Flaco had the gravelly dark-brown voice of an angel after a day trip to Purgatory:

You'll get tired when I want to go out dancin'
You'll get tired when I say we'll go to bed.
You'll get tired when I want to be romancin'
And you'll say you gotta bad pain in your head.
We once had a sweet and true love but we lost it
We once had a real and special thing so rare.
But every time I turn to you now you're exhausted
So next time you turn to me, I won't be there.

The barlady came over to me and pointed at my glass. She raised her eyebrows in a silent question. I put my hand over my glass to indicate that I was fine. She turned and looked up at the stage. Flaco's voice was quivering with feeling.

Cos now I'm tired of all your cheatin' and your foolin'.
And I'm tired of all the lies and mizzer-ee.
You must get tired of all those guys,
And all those phoney alibis.
But won't you ever just get tired of hurtin' me?

Flaco finished his song to a surge of applause so heartfelt it was reminiscent of a jumbo jet taking off in a toilet. He unplugged his guitar and wobbled from the stage, almost tripping up on his boots. The barlady turned to look at me.

'Now ain't he got a purty way with words, sugar?' she said.

I lit a cigarette and took a deep breath. 'He surez hail duz, darlin,' I replied.

One of the most . . . er . . . interesting things about Nashville is that it contains the world's only full size and exact replica of the Parthenon in Athens. Now, you might think that this begs at least one obvious question, namely, why? But actually, the Nashville Parthenon is quite sweet. Only in America, I thought, would people go to so much trouble and expense and effort to build an exact copy of something that is falling to bits in Greece. Perhaps, I mused, the Greeks could learn something from this? Perhaps present-day Athens should put up a model of the Empire State Building, complete with its own Cretan King Kong?

When I had finished admiring the Parthenon, I went for a walk downtown. I found a little gospel record store near the centre, and I went in and wandered around the racks for a while, just listening to the music which was blasting out over the speakers. An acappella group sang a song called 'I'm So Glad He Lifted Me', and I was so touched by it that I decided there was really nothing for it except to whip out my wallet and spend some money immediately. (Most of the Christian Churches, now that I think of it, have always understood the close relationship between piety and money.)

I picked up CDs by the Soul Stirrers, the Reverend Alex Bradford and His Congregation, The Five Original Blind Boys of Mississippi, James Cleveland and the Meditation Singers, Johnnie Taylor, Dorothy Love Coates and the Original Gospel Harmonettes, Bessie Griffin and the Consolators, the Chosen Gospel Singers. I went up to the counter with an armful of CDs.

'Shoot,' said the assistant. 'I guess you're fixin to spend some today, huh?' He looked through my CDs, adding up the prices.

'Well, you got good taste,' he said. 'They're mighty fine artistes, all of 'em.'

We did the usual thing then, where are you from, Ireland, oh really, et cetera et cetera. Bert asked me where I had been so far on my trip and where I was going to go. I told him that I was looking forward to going to Graceland and he nodded and said that Graceland was 'real special'. He said he had always considered Elvis a truly great gospel singer. I was surprised at this, but he told me that before his rock and roll career took off Elvis had auditioned for a popular Tennessee gospel outfit called the Blackwood Boys, who were looking for a bass singer. The king's voice wasn't deep enough to sing bass, but next to blues, southern quartet gospel singing had always been his biggest influence. Indeed, Bert told me, Presley's long-time backing band the Jordanaires had actually been a regular gospel band before they joined up with the king.

I said I had often heard that Elvis had Irish blood in his veins, and I was interested in finding out whether or not this was true. Bert laughed and said he had heard this himself, most often from Irish visitors to Nashville, but he didn't really think there was anything to it. 'But I guess maybe he had a Irish attitude,' he said, 'I guess he was an old hell-raisin rebel, huh? The way you guys are in Ireland?'

He added up my bill and insisted on giving me a 10 per cent discount, on account of my Irishness. He waved off my protestations and continued to speak.

'The thing about Elvis,' Bert said, 'we get 'em all here in Tennessee, from all over the world. Man, we get Chinese fellers and Russians and all. We get Orstralians and Jews and Hindu folks and you name it. And they all love Elvis. Don't matter where they're from. So I guess the king belongs to everybody, huh? So you can say Elvis was Irish if you want to.'

Bert laughed and put my CDs into a bag. And then he said something really interesting. The thing was, Elvis probably did have some Irish influences, whether he knew it or not. There was country and Tennessee hillbilly music, of course, which had a big Irish traditional strain in it. But even the kind of gospel Elvis liked had a bit of an Irish history to it. I asked Bert what he meant. He went off into a back room and rummaged around and came back with a cassette tape which he put into a machine on the counter. This was a tape of a man called Robert Ackers, whose family, Bert thought, had been of Irish descent. The tape was of such poor quality that you could barely make it out, but Bert explained that Ackers's performances had been truly extraordinary. Not for him the polite harmonies of typical southern gospel. Ackers had gone in for hysterical tears and frantic screaming and wild flights into speaking in tongues. It wasn't really gospel singing, in any normal sense, and whether this was prompted by Bert or not I can't honestly say, but the little of Ackers's vocal pyrotechnics I could make out on the tape reminded me a lot of the traditional 'keening' or mourning singing which used to go on at funerals in rural Ireland. Bert told me that Ackers was one of the first white gospel singers in the whole South to work with a band which featured electric guitars, drums and piano. His performances had apparently been truly legendary, but sadly, he had never made a record.

But it was thought by some that Ackers had been a big influence on both Elvis and Jerry Lee Lewis, Bert said. Certainly, a lot of early rhythm and blues was basically gospel with the words changed. He went off into his back room again and returned with a cassette of a television programme which he played for me. There was an amazing sequence of Jerry Lee Lewis performing a gospel number called 'God's Not Dead, He Is Alive', which borrowed the exact chord sequences from Ray Charles's classic R and B number, 'What I'd Say'.

'Gospel and rock and roll,' Bert said. 'See, it's like the same thing. I mean, if Jerry Lee was up there singin I love ya honey, stead of I love ya Jesus, you wouldn't get too much of a difference, would you?'

Bert fast-forwarded through the tape to a scene of a performer called Mickey Gilley, who, he thought, was also part Irish. Like Robert Ackers, Gilley went in for 'the shoutin typa gospel', Bert said. 'He liked to stir em up a little.' Gilley was a cousin of both

Jerry Lee Lewis and the fundamentalist preacher Jimmy Lee Swaggart, whose own highly accomplished records of gospel singing and piano playing, Bert told me, had sold more than even Hank Williams.

'You gotta see this part,' Bert said, and he fast-forwarded again, giggling as he did so. He stopped at a sequence where the clean-cut fifties pop singer Pat Boone was talking about gospel in general and Jimmy Lee Swaggart in particular, making the point that Jimmy Lee could have been a highly successful wild-man rock and roller like his first cousin Jerry if he had really wanted to be.

'Cos the thing is,' Boone said, 'Jimmy can duplicate most of what Jerry does.' He paused and looked into the camera for a moment. 'Except, I don't think he plays the piano with his ass, of course.'

Bert was really getting going now, on the subject of gospel and rock and Irish music, weaving together the threads. Most forms of American music had at least a little bit of Irish in them, he said. Even some of the blues had what he called 'an Irish heart'. He went yet again into his store room and this time he came back with an extraordinary book called *I Say Me for a Parable*, the dictated autobiography of the little-known Texas bluesman, Mance Lipscombe. He pointed out an intriguing section where Mance was talking about the influence on the blues of what he called 'seance', or supernatural ability, and how it was possessed in America by the Indians and the Irish as well as the blacks.

> Mama was a Indian woman. About half or little bettern half. She didn know nothin about the way a life a colored people. What we called ourselves, my daddy called hisself African. They do thangs a whole lot funny than other nations a people. Irishman do thangs whole lot funny than other nation. Everbody nated to his nation. His instain, thats seance too, see. Got it inside.

I left Bert alone in his record store, happily humming along to 'Jesus Is a Rock in a Mighty Weary Land' by The Five Original Blind Boys of Mississippi. I was glad that I had met him. He was living proof that, contrary to popular opinion, the devil doesn't really have all the best tunes.

The driver on the Homes-of-the-Nashville-Country-Stars Bus Tour was a talkative little redneck called Hiram. ('Just call me Hiram and fire'em,' he chuckled.) At first I quite liked him. He was all goshdarns and y'alls and spitting out the window. It was like he'd been sent along to drive the bus by Central Casting. But after a while, I noticed that he kept addressing the women passengers as girls. 'Now, girls, ya'll mo be real interested in this.' That kind of thing. I mean, I don't usually get uptight about stuff like that, but I have to admit that the fifteenth time he said, 'Now, girls, if you look to the right there, ya'll gonna see another shopping mall, yes sir, and we all know how you girls like to shop till you drop, yes indeed, girls,' I did begin to wish that one of the girls on the bus was Andrea Dworkin.

The tour was a bit of a disappointment, I must say. Nashville millionaires' houses are pretty much all the same as each other and once you've seen one you've seen y'all. I had hoped to be invited in to tea by Tammy Wynette, but no such luck. She wasn't even in the garden hanging out the washing. And the thing is, most really big country stars don't live in Nashville any more. They've all moved away to California where the real centre of country music recording is now located. Still, we saw Dolly Parton's front wall and Hank Williams's former back fence and we passed the school where Pat Boone graduated and the house where he was brought up. Hiram assured us that Mr and Mrs Boone still lived in this house and that they were wonderful people who 'truly loved the Lord'. That was a relief, I can tell you.

After a while, Hiram's commentary became pretty toe-curling, to say the least. He told us a long and lurid story about how some country singer who had been killed in a plane crash — I know that doesn't really narrow it down much — had been found with 'three of his fingers missin and th'other two clutchin onto a five dollar bill'.

And then, as we passed the home of some Memphis merchant banker or another he said, 'Well now girls, been serious here for a moment, that feller's wife lost her breast there last Christmastime I guess it woulda bin, and heck, that's no picnic for any girl, Lord knows.'

From time to time on the tour we were also treated to brief sidelong glimpses into Hiram's views on the racial question, which views had, shall we say, a distinctly southern character. 'See that house there, laydies and gennelmen, that's a three-million-dollar home right there, yes it is. And I'll tell you whut. It's owned by a black feller, yes sir. Imagine that now. Whut'll they want next, huh?'

After about an hour of offending just about everybody, Hiram pulled up the bus near Music Row and we were invited to go and spend some money in the local stores, all of which seemed to be owned by country singers. Sorry, I thought, as I gazed on the scene, but I am not spending my hard-earned greenbacks buying inflatable Stetsons from Randy fucking Travis. For those who did not want to do this, Hiram informed us that there was a church nearby which contained a larger-than-life-size woodcarving of Leonardo da Vinci's famous painting of 'The Last Supper'. Leonardo da Vinci was, he clarified, 'an Eye-talian feller, lived mebbe three hundred years ago over there I guess'. Hiram really did want us all to go and see this aesthetic marvel. 'Because if you love the Lord, and I know you do, why, y'all gonna sit there with the tears just streamin down your face.' I decided to give it a miss and go for a walk instead.

Off I set, in no particular direction. At the end of Music Row I found myself strolling past a large and loudly decorated striptease nightclub. There was a huge flashing neon sign up on the wall. 'Fifty Beautiful Girls and Three Ugly Ones'.

That had to be worth a visit, I felt. But sadly, it was only three o'clock in the afternoon, so they were closed.

★

The Country Music Hall of Fame turned out to be a pleasant surprise. It has all the naffness you would expect – Elvis's 24-carat-gold grand piano, for instance, and one of his many Cadillacs, complete with television set in the back - but the museum also records in scrupulous and fascinating detail the musical contribution of the Irish and Scottish immigrants to the popular culture of America. In addition, it has the original stage of the Grand Old Opry on which you can stand and walk around and utter a silent 'yeehaw, pardners' to yourself. It is my kind of museum, basically.

After you've finished in the Hall of Fame, your ticket allows you free entry to RCA studio B, which is just a few hundred yards down the street. This is a tiny and cramped and, frankly, rather ugly little three-room one-storey building which would doubtless have been knocked down many years ago and turned into a themed shopping mall were it not for one thing: Elvis Presley recorded there.

You can walk in and wander around and look at Elvis's guitar and stand in the little booth in which he stood while doing his vocal tracks. Elvis used to record very late at night, sometimes at three or four in the morning. When you visit the studio they play you tapes of him rehearsing and messing around with the band in the middle of the night. It is an eerie feeling to stroll around the tiny room and listen to his ghostly voice on the studio out-take tape, laughing and cracking dumb jokes and crooning through brief snatches of gospel and country tunes and generally gearing himself up. It's strange, because the songs he sang, you've heard them so often that sometimes you forget that a real human being actually walked into a room one day a long time ago and sang them into a tape recorder. It's like they were always there. It's like they just evolved, like mountains, or the Mississippi River. But here you are now, in the room where those songs were made. And you're all by yourself. And then the guitars begin softly strumming and the harmonies kick in and the voice starts up in earnest, and it cuts straight into your heart, even though you've heard it a million times before.

I'll tell you honestly, there are very few times in my life when the hair on the back of my neck has actually stood up, the way it always does in books. But that afternoon, listening to Elvis in the tiny dark room from where he changed the world, it wasn't just standing. It was practically going for a walk round the block.

In the bar down the street from my hotel in Nashville there was a dance on that night. The band was pumping out zydeco tunes – 'Johnny peu'pas danse', 'Les Flames D'Enfer', 'L'Anee Tu Partit', 'Je suis com sa' – their lyrics and titles all in the strange dialect of French so guttural and harsh and grammatically incorrect that it is spoken by only two racial groups in the whole world, the Louisiana Cajuns on the one hand, and English presenters of the Eurovision Song Contest on the other.

I sat at the bar knocking back tequila slammers with a couple of English guys I'd met on the Homes-of-the-Stars Tour that afternoon and we just watched the people dancing to this astounding music. The men and women held onto each other tightly as they shimmied across the floor and kicked and swivelled and shook their torsos and thrust their thighs together. Whatever the hell was going on out there, it had very little to do with dancing.

Cajun music was born on the banks on the Atchafalaya River, just outside Baton Rouge, Louisiana, but it has spread from there all over the American South. This is old time party music, and it sounds like nothing else in the world. It is hard-driving, incessant, based on pumping rhythms, scatological lyrics and blistering accordion solos, full of joyful two-steps, frantic polkas and tongue-in-cheek melancholy waltzes with self-mockingly sentimental lyrics. Many surviving early Cajun songs are lewd versions of ancient European ballads, full of earthy sexual puns and fabulous imagery. Characters from Chaucer, Shakespeare and Greek mythology all appear in the original Cajun music, but in the nineteenth century, as the Irish migrants who flooded into New Orleans and the southern states popularized the use of the violin and accordion in the folk repertoire, Cajun became predominantly a dance music, performed at 'fais-dodos' –

Cajun house parties – or country picnics. Even the very names of the great Cajun performers – Boozoo Chavis, Aldus Roger, Don Montoucet, Denise Lasalle, the Lafayette Playboys, Sheryl Cormier, Blackie Forestier, the Cajun Aces, Camey Doucet, Beausoleil, Good Rockin Dopsie and the Cajun Twisters – sound like brash and raucous dance music.

Outside of the American South, the only place in the world where Cajun has anything like a mass audience is Ireland. Dublin bands like the Cajun Kings and the Fleadh Cowboys regularly command vast audiences in urban nightclubs and rural Irish country dances. Perhaps something of the anarchism of the ceilidh days is evoked in the spirit of the new Cajun sound. Perhaps it is that in the sheer foreignness of that sound the Irish recognize something oddly familiar. I don't really know. But when the Cajun Kings are playing their glorious cross-cultural hybrid music in a bar on the banks of the Liffey, if you closed your eyes for a second you would swear Louisiana was just outside the door.

Certainly, Cajun is an interesting example of the way in which differences between racially and ethnically based American folk musics have always been blurred. Southern dancehalls became integrated a long time before restaurants and schools ever did. Thus, in the early years of this century Cajun began very quickly to absorb influences from other American folk traditions, particularly Irish, country and western, boogie woogie, western swing and Dixieland jazz. A sub-music, zydeco, the predominantly black form of Cajun, borrowed heavily from the tradition of the delta and Chicago blues, with artists like Clifton Chenier taking the music in new directions. And in the fifties a Cajun-tinged form of pop sometimes called swamp rock experienced an upsurge in popularity, before almost disappearing again in the sixties.

But modern Cajun is back again now, bristling with multifarious influences, yet still abounding with the rollicking riotous spirit that makes it unique. Recordings by early purist Cajun artists like Nathaan Abshire, Harry Choates and Leo Soleil, as well as more experimental bands like the rockabilly-influenced Wayne Toups and the Crowley Aces, sell in very healthy numbers all over America. The great Cajun band Good Rockin Dopsie and the Cajun Twisters appeared on Paul Simon's platinum-selling album, *Graceland*. More recently the Grammy-award-winning top ten American hit for Mary Chapin Carpenter, 'Down at the Twist and Shout', brought Cajun to a massive and nationwide young audience. Back home in Ireland, you had to turn off the radio every fifteen minutes if you wanted to avoid hearing it.

Perhaps another reason for this music's popularity in Ireland is that its fuck-it-all-let's-party spirit has been shaped by the unspeakable harshness of Cajun history, a history so full of exile, struggle and oppression that it can't help but recall our own. The Cajuns were poor farmers who hightailed out of France in the seventeenth century to settle in the Canadian provinces now known as Nova Scotia and New Brunswick. Their colony was originally called 'Acadie', after Arcadia, the idyllic Ancient Greece. ('Cajun' is a corruption of 'Acadian'.) The poor old Acadians had a tough time when they were caught up in the war between the British and the French, and when they refused to swear allegiance to the perfidious Limey crown they were kicked out of their homeland. They drifted south, most of them finally settling in tiny farming, fishing and trapping communities in southern Louisiana. For almost two centuries they were the only immigrant American community not to assimilate at all. They lived in desperate poverty and isolation, eking out a precarious living in the swamps and bayous. Cajun cooking is now very popular all over America. It's all stews and broils, ragouts and spicy casseroles. But the cuisine, like the music, was born out of poverty and necessity. 'A Cajun will eat anything' is an old Louisiana proverb, and if you think about that for a minute or two, it tells you quite a lot.

But history seemed very far away that night, as I sat in a bar in downtown Nashville listening to that thundering apocalyptic sound come roaring down from the stage. The place was packed to the rafters. The floorboards were quaking. The bass throbbed through the walls. The accordion player squinted and gritted his teeth as his fingers raced up and down his keyboard. The singer howled into the microphone: 'Laissez Les Bon Temps Roulez!' OK, so it wasn't grammatically correct, but who really needs grammar, after all? This was a music that had looked death in the face and laughed. The people roared and bawled and boogied around the floor until the sweat had reduced their clothes to wet rags. After about an hour, even the English guys were politely tapping their feet. I smiled and ordered another round of tequila slammers, as one of them got up, took off his jacket and began to dance.

He was born in a shack. He was the King of America. He was the most popular star ever in the history of pop music. He never learned to play the guitar. On stage he moved like no white performer ever had before. He clutched at his groin, caressed his face, swivelled his hips, swung his ass, thrust his pelvis, clawed blindly at the air around him. Offstage he was so shy that he could hardly speak without stammering. He was pilloried and condemned and widely banned for wanting to destroy American youth. He was a regular church-attender. People said he was anti-authoritarian. He spent four years in the US Army. People said he was a dangerous anarchist. He voted Republican. He took drugs and seduced underage girls. He couldn't go to sleep at night unless he had spoken to his mother. He sold more records than anyone, ever. If you laid the records he sold in a continuous line on the ground – I don't really know why you'd want to do that, but this is the way Americans tend to put things – they would stretch around the equator two and a half times. He was a poor white nobody from a shitty little town nobody ever heard of, Tupelo, Mississippi. He was, and still is, and always will be the definitive voice of the twentieth century.

Eighteen years after his death, his record and video sales are still enormous. His last album, a collection of mediocre and trashy love songs all of which had been previously released, sold half a million copies in Britain alone. One of his fans once wrote him a letter saying, 'There is nothing that anyone could ever say about you which could possibly discredit you in our eyes.' Nothing. Elvis Presley attracted the kind of adulation usually reserved for gods and dictators. The fact that he was a little bit of both shouldn't really surprise anybody.

It is perhaps a little cynical to say that death has been a good career move for Elvis Presley, but people do say that, and in a way it is true. In 1979, the annual income of his estate was about $1 million. Financially, things had not been terrific for the King for some years. All his early records were – and are still – owned by RCA, having been sold to them early on for a relatively small amount by the king's mercurial and Svengali-like manager 'Colonel' Tom Parker, a man who entered showbusiness as the proprietor of a fairground dancing chicken act. (The Colonel used to make the chickens dance by heating up a metal plate and placing them on top of it, and from there his business ethics went down.) In the early 1980s, Presley's executors spent half a million dollars on his former home, Graceland, before throwing its doors open to a salacious public. It is said that they got their money back in thirty-eight days. These days, Graceland alone brings in $15 million a year. It is by far the biggest tourist attraction in the American South.

And yet there is nothing morbid about any of this. The city of Memphis is extremely proud of its most famous son, and what is now known as the Graceland Visitors' Centre is surprisingly tasteful. OK, so it's not exactly the Sistine Chapel. But for the home of a pop star it's not as vulgar as you might think.

The house itself is surprisingly small. When you arrive you are told that on no account are you allowed to go upstairs. 'This,' the tour guides tell you, 'is in respect to the privacy of the late Elvis Presley.' You are shown his living room and his dining room. There are stained glass images of peacocks in a panel on the wall. Peacocks, you are told, are a symbol of immortality, and Elvis 'really believed in immortality'. You are allowed to take photographs as long as you do not use a flash. 'Please don't lean on the bar,' the guide says.

From there you are brought downstairs to the pool room. Then there is the television room. There must be twelve or fifteen television sets all lined up on shelves on the wall. He believed in immortality and he watched a lot of TV. You are then brought back upstairs and into the jungle room. A miniature waterfall trickles down a brick wall. Fake animal skins hang from the ceilings. 'Elvis used to play his hi-fi in this room,' the tour guide says, 'so he had it sound-proofed out of consideration for the family.' It occurs to you that there might have been other less wholesome reasons for the sound-proofing of the king's private room, but you don't say that. You are vaguely ashamed of yourself for even thinking it.

His father Vernon was his press officer. He helped run his son's career from a shed in the back garden. You can see the shed now. There are filing cabinets and notebooks and a typewriter and a telephone. It is all just the way it used to be. You half expect Vernon to wander back in any minute and tell everybody to get the hell out, because he's busy. There is a video screen on the wall. Visitors are shown a short clip of a press conference which Elvis gave in that very same room thirty years ago, just after he returned from Germany, from his stint in the army.

What strikes you most about the young Presley is his famous shyness. 'It simply isn't easy to get more than a few clichéd comments out of the man,' the president of the English Elvis Fan Club said once. 'Conversing with the King is not unlike talking to a pleasant but not very articulate farm labourer.' There he is on the screen, at twenty-three, already the most famous man in the world, stuttering, blushing, repeatedly turning his impossibly handsome face away from the camera, giggling suddenly at nothing obvious, addressing the journalists as 'sir'. 'The way I move on stage, sir, it's just natural to me. Well, I dunno know what it is exactly, but when I'm singing my music, why, I guess it just feels right.'

I guess it just felt right to everyone else too. I stood looking at his image as it flickered on the screen, and I remembered my mother telling me that when she was a teenage girl in the working-class suburbs of Dublin all the young women who lived on her street would actually get dressed up to go to the cinema and scream at the Elvis films. I had seen a few of them myself, and I could certainly see why a person would want to scream at them. But 'it was like he was there himself', I remembered my mother telling me. If he had ever truly turned up in Dublin, God only knows what would have happened. There would have been riots in the streets. It would have been the 1916 uprising all over again.

He built a special room in Graceland in which to put all his trophies. There are thousands of gold discs and silver discs, platinum discs, awards from all over the world. There are certificates and adoring fan letters and photographs of Elvis with world leaders. There are posters and costumes from all those execrable movies he was forced to be in by the leeches and vampires and glorified pimps who surrounded him. His glittering spangled stage suits are all here too, eerily hung on headless tailor's dummies which stand in bullet-proof glass cases.

In the middle of all this paraphernalia of superstardom, you could almost miss the framed letters from the Memphis City Council recording the millions and millions of dollars he gave to the poor and the underprivileged of his adopted city. He gave to orphanages, hospitals, schools, homes for battered women and schemes to help young offenders. He seems to have simply given to anyone who asked. (One yellowed letter of acknowledgment from the Memphis City Council notes, 'We understand and appreciate that, as usual, you do not wish to have this gift recorded as a tax-deductible expenditure.')

And then there are the exhibits which point to the darker side of the King's mangled personality. As he grew older, like many rich middle-aged men from the American South, he became paranoically obsessed with guns. His rifles and pistols have been lovingly polished and placed in glass cases for his fans to admire. He learnt karate, so that he could kill with his bare hands if he had to. He adored police and military uniforms, and he became an honorary member of police forces all over the United States. There are membership cards of all these police forces with his name on them. There is a truly poignant photograph of the fallen king of white-trash rock and roll, near the end of his days now, chubby, bleary-eyed, and clearly drugged out of his mind, shaking hands with a pompous little police chief who is presenting him with a medal. There is a photograph of him shaking hands with a leering and jowly Richard Nixon – the best and the worst of twentieth-century America in one single image.

On 16 August 1977 it is said that he was alone in the house, that he sat down at the grand piano in his den, tape-recorded himself singing an old song, 'One Night With You', went upstairs and visited his bathroom. Who knows what thoughts flitted through the King's mind as he perched regally on the can for that last time. Perhaps he thought about all his wonderful fans. Perhaps he thought about his fantastic music. Perhaps – who can tell? – he began to countenance the possibility that his beloved only daughter might one day grow up to marry a man whose best friend was a chimpanzee called Bubbles. Sadly, we shall never know. For not long after the royal drawers had been dropped that evening, their owner suffered a massive heart attack, keeled over and cashed in his chips.

He is buried in a small circular grove by a pool about a hundred yards from the house. His father is buried on one side, his mother on the other. His twin brother, who died shortly after birth, is buried there too. There is a mock-classical white marble statue of two kneeling angels, and a statue of Christ triumphant with his hands outstretched in a gesture of love. There are dozens and dozens of bunches of flowers on the graves. The labels attached to the flowers bear messages from his fans. 'Thank you Elvis for so much joy'. 'Elvis, you will always live in my heart'. 'King Elvis, always yours'. 'God bless you Elvis. May You Rest in Peace'. 'Elvis, wherever you are now, may you find the peace you never could find in this world'. 'We love you Elvis. Always'.

As I stood by his grave, the woman beside me hung her head, put her hand to her eyes, and started to sob. The man who was with her put his arm around her shoulders. She clasped his hand tightly and shook her head, and her tears spilled on to the ground. 'I know,' the man said, just that. 'I know,' and then he took off his sunglasses and put his wrist to his eyes and started to cry bitterly himself.

★

From Graceland, I took a cab into downtown Memphis, booked into a motel, dropped off my stuff and wandered down to the world-famous Beale Street. Beale began as one of Memphis's poshest streets before yellow fever wiped out most of the inhabitants. The nobs were quickly replaced by hordes of poor immigrants – Greeks, European Jews, Chinese, Italians, Germans, Irish. But it was Beale Street's black culture which was to give the place its greatest fame. Slap in the middle of the south-east corner of America, black migrants from all over the country passed through it in search of work. From the Mississippi Delta and the Chicago ghetto, from the Texas prairies and the slave fields of Alabama, they brought their music with them. If the blues was conceived in a thousand places across the wide continent, it was on Beale Street that it was finally born.

And it was still very much alive, I could see, as I arrived on the corner of Beale that hot day, to find a three-piece busking blues band setting up in the shade of an enormous plane tree. Workmen were cutting the grass nearby, and the foddery smell of freshly cut vegetation filled the air. A huge crowd of black schoolkids sat on the steps eating a picnic with their teachers and waiting for the band to get going.

Time passed and the morning got even hotter. The white stone slabs on the floor of the nearby square seemed to suck the heat into themselves. As soon as the band struck up, the kids threw down their sandwiches and started to dance. The music was authentic Mississippi Delta blues, raw, powerful, built on a chugging bass rhythm and a lazily insistent drumbeat. The words were spectacularly politically incorrect.

Sugar Baby, Sugar, what's the matter with you?
Sugar Baby, honey, you don't treat me like you used to do.
Sugar Babe, oh Sugar Babe, it's all over now.

All I want my baby to do
Make three dollars and give me two.
Sugar Babe, oh Sugar Babe, it's all over now.

Goin to town, gonna get me a line.
Whip my gal till she change her mind.
Sugar Babe, oh Sugar Babe, it's all over now.
Sugar Babe, Sugar Babe, I'm so tired of you.
Sugar Baby, darling, ain't your honey but the way you do,
Sugar Babe, oh Sugar Babe, it's all over now.

I watched enthralled for a while, until the heat got too much and the pounding beat began to give me a headache, and then I set off to amble down Beale and have a look in the store windows. I went into Schwabs Dry Goods Store, number 163. This was a big dark cool shop which smelt of spices and peppermint and mothballs. There were racks and racks of cheap clothes. There were huge stacks of hats, boxes of shoes. At the front of the shop to the side was a whole section specializing in voodoo products. There were Ward-Off-Evil soaps, there were love potions of various kinds. There was a 'Money-in-three-days air-freshener' and a 'Come Back Husband Shampoo'. There were skull-shaped candles and mojo hands, good luck tokens similar to rabbit's feet, the mystical origins of which lie in West African religion. There were statues and pictures of John the Conqueror (or John the Conqueroo), a mysterious but reputedly very powerful sprite in the voodoo culture. (Blues fans will recall that Muddy Waters sings, in 'Mannish Boy', about 'little Johnny Conqueroo'.)

Back out in the street an enormous black man who was completely bald and wearing black leather from head to toe seemed to be waiting for me. He grinned and nodded and walked up quickly when I came out of the store and into the sun. 'How's it going?' I said.

'Straight on, brother,' he said. 'You Irish?'

I said yes, I was Irish.

'Me too,' he said. He put his hand in his pocket and handed me my passport.

'You left it down there,' he said, nodding towards the tree where the band was still playing.

I was speechless. 'Thanks,' I said.

He shrugged. 'Straight on,' he said, and walked away.

I took a few aspirins and went into a bar and ordered a beer and a large plate of jambalaya. It was cool in the bar and the place was almost empty. A tattered Stars and Stripes hung from the high wooden ceiling. Through the open windows the blues music was still pounding in from the hot street outside. I listened to the words and they made me smile now. I could not believe the size of the plate of food when it arrived. The oysters had the dimensions of golf balls, the prawns were fresh and spicy, the yellow rice was moist and fluffy. I took a spoonful and my tongue felt like it was going to explode with delight. The music was hot. The beer was cold. I took another big mouthful of food. This was the real America, I thought, as the music and the applause drifted in from the street. This was living.

Oh ashes to ashes and dust to dust
Lord, the whiskey don't get you then the women must.
Oh tell me how long, how long must I wait?
You're playin' in my orchard, now don't you see
If you don't like my peaches stop shakin' my tree.
Oh tell me honey, how long, how long must I wait . . .

★ ★

There was a bit of a buzz in B.B. King's Blues Club on Beale Street that night, because B.B. himself had turned up to play on the previous two evenings, and the talk in all the bars was that he might show up again tonight. I arrived early and got a good seat. After a while a man who did admittedly look a little like B.B. – except that he was perhaps five stone lighter – ambled up on to the stage wearing a purple sequinned jacket and carrying a guitar under his arm. The audience shouted up to ask him was B.B. coming and he just smiled and said he didn't know, but he was going to play a few tunes anyway. He played unaccompanied, with a delicate touch on his guitar and a lot of care and consideration for the music. He would step up close to the microphone and lightly croon a phrase and then step back and punctuate the singing with a short clear guitar burst of startling clarity. But he played with humour too, cleverly drawing out the wit and pathos of the lyrics:

Bought you a brand new Ford.
You said, baby, how 'bout a Cadillac?
Bought you a ten dollar dinner.
You said honey, why thanks for the snack.
Gave you a penthouse apartment.
You said darlin, gee thanks for the shack.
And I gave you seven children.
And now you want to give 'em back!!

After the guy had finished his set, B.B.'s house band came on and began hammering into Chicago blues tunes with efficiency and verve, but the audience had started to finish up their drinks now and drift out into the night. It was clear that the big man was not coming after all. I threw back my beer and headed off too. I had enjoyed what I'd heard but I wanted to hear something different now. Memphis, after all, was not just the adopted home town of Elvis, and the stomping ground of W.C. Handy, the first man ever to record the blues. It was also the home of Stax Records, the greatest soul record label of all time, and I was in the mood to hear some soul.

I walked up and down Beale Street for a while, looking for some soul music, but at first it was a depressing experience. In one of the tourist bars, a tall thin white guy in a ludicrous purple suit was singing a blues song, and there was just something wrong with it. I mean, he could sing, and he could play the guitar a bit, but he looked and sounded like somebody doing an impression of something he just didn't fundamentally get. There was a tall thin woman behind him, playing an electric keyboard with a built-in drum machine and grinning maniacally. She looked like something out of the *Muppet Show* house band. I guess that didn't help.

Out into the street I went again. Across the way in another luridly painted bar done up like a Hawaiian native village, a young guy who looked like a car salesman was singing Elvis tunes into a booming mike. I stayed for a while and listened to him murder 'Hound Dog', 'All Shook Up' and 'King Creole'. He wouldn't have been too bad, but for the fact that he kept going 'uh-huh-huh' in between the lines and, I mean, nobody but nobody can go 'uh-huh-huh' the way the king did.

I walked right down to the south end of Beale and found nowhere that interested me much. I turned around and crossed the street and went back the way I had come, all the way up to the quieter north end. A party of sailors in white uniforms came singing around the corner. I looked through the windows of an enormous pool hall where young black guys in denim jackets were swigging beers and laughing and shooting racks under the fluorescent blaze of the table lights. There was only one bar down here, a small place where the entire front was open on to the street. But it seemed to be closing early. The chairs were stacked up in the far corners, the window shutters in the gable wall were half closed. A hip-looking black guy in 501s and a red T-shirt was standing behind the counter adding up the till receipts. Every once in a while he would close his eyes and bend his head low and mumble something to himself. There was one of those blue electric fly-lamps on the wall behind him, and every few seconds it sparked and spat as it claimed another kill. A beautiful distracted-looking waitress with red lips and long red hair tied in a bun wandered from table to table, collecting glasses into a huge tower. A neon sign on the back wall flashed out the message ROCK AND ROLL, I GAVE YOU ALL THE BEST YEARS OF MY LIFE. And the jukebox was playing Elvis, the beautiful mellow voice echoing and distorting in the empty little bar.

You look like an angel,
You talk like an angel,
You walk like an angel,
But I got wise.

Cos you're the devil in disguise,
Oh yes you are,
The devil in disguise.

★   ★

Down the other end of the street in the Rum Boogie Café, I finally
got lucky. At last! Here was a place where the house band was
playing soul tunes. There was a three-piece brass section, a fellow
playing a wailing Hammond organ, two guitarists, a drummer and
two singers, a black man in a beret and black leathers, and a young
white woman in a purple swirly skirt and cowboy shirt. The trumpet
player was a tall handsome black man who was dressed so sharply
that I was afraid he might cut himself. He played his trumpet with
one hand, the other thrust into the pocket of his suit. As I walked in
and sat down, the band were doing a Sam and Dave song, and the
audience were already on their feet and yelling along with the
chorus, 'Hold on, I'm coming, Hold on, I'm coming'. This, I
thought, was going to be my kind of place.

As soon as they had finished this number, the guitar player, a
lanky white chap with long blond hair and glasses, ripped into a
scorching version of Stevie Ray Vaughan's 'Pride and Joy'.

Two corpulent assholes from Missouri were sitting at the next
table, whooping and screeching like deranged monkeys. I mean, I
am all for people enjoying themselves, particularly if they are
unfortunate enough to be from an infamous shithole like Missouri,
but these specimens would have made Beavis and Butthead seem
like Wildean sophisticates. After a while they really started to get on
my nerves.

While the band were taking a breather I noticed a busker who I
had seen earlier on the street come into the Rum Boogie Café and
stroll up to the stage. He was an elderly black man in a bowler hat
and a shabby evening suit with an overbloomed scarlet rose in the
lapel. His name, the guitarist announced, was Ruby Williams, 'one
of the real Beale Street bluesmen', and Ruby wanted to sing. The
band members came back up on stage and struck up a slow New

Orleans-style funereal blues, all heavy mournful brass and heavy bass drum and wailing clarinet. The joyful party-time words which Ruby sang made a brilliant counterpoint with the dirge-like music.

> Don't stand there gawpin'
> Talkin' your trash
> You wanna have some fun,
> Gonna have to spend some cash.
> So let the good times roll.
> Let the good times roll.
> Make no difference you're young or old
> Get together and let the good times roll . . .

When Ruby finished his song, the place went wild, and the band opened their final set of the evening the way dynamite opens a safe. They did 'Try a Little Tenderness' and 'Sittin' on the Dock of the Bay' by Otis Redding, 'Midnight Hour' by Wilson Pickett, 'Soul Man' and 'I Thank You' by Sam and Dave, 'I Feel Good' and 'This Is a Man's Man's Man's World' and 'I Feel Like a Sex Machine' and 'Living in America' by James Brown. And then, just as I was about to expire with happiness, something unforgettable happened. The young woman singer stepped up to the microphone and started very gently to sing an Aretha Franklin song. I mean, it was nothing more than that. But she clutched the microphone stand and closed her eyes, and she swayed from side to side as she softly sang the tender words, as though she was the first person in the world who had ever done so. I think it was Bob Dylan who first said that black soul music was the only real poetry of modern America, and listening to this young woman, I could really see what he meant.

Sometimes, just sometimes, when great or even good singers sing soul music, an odd thing happens. The thing the guy in the record store in Nashville had talked about. The feeling goes beyond passion, beyond excitement. Mystery takes over. You are reminded that this music was born out of gospel, that before soul ever took on its great themes of money and success and black freedom and political struggle and sexual love, it was concerned with the search for the divine. That's what happened, watching this woman sing. A condition of mystery approaching the condition of prayer. It must have been the five hundredth time she had sung the song, but she sang it like the first time. Her whole body was trembling with emotion. The veins in her neck were throbbing. Her hands clutched at the air as she hit the highest notes and she shook her head and beamed with pure helpless joy as she seemed to wrench the words out of herself, 'You make me feel like a natural woman' and one of her hands clenched into a fist as though she was trying to squeeze juice from the air. The band swelled and soared behind her. The brass harmony kicked in. The Hammond organ wailed. Her dark eyes were wet, I noticed, and she rubbed them with her fingers, and pushed her hair away from her face and sang again. And by the time the last verse came around even the two obese assholes from Missouri were standing up beside me and singing too, in earnest falsetto, 'You make me feel, you make me feel, you make me feel like a natural woman,' with the tears flowing uncontrollably down their pink and chubby faces.

When she finished a roar of applause filled the Rum Boogie Café. People stood up and yelled for more. The brass players put down their instruments and clapped. The guitar player put his hands to his face and shook his head. The drummer put his fingers in his mouth and whistled. The saxophone player came over and took the woman by the hand and kissed it several times and stepped up to the microphone.

'The healin music,' he cried, 'soul power, the healin music,' and he threw his arms around her and hugged her tightly, burying his face in her hair.

CHAPTER 13

Honky Tonk Angels

Dear Brother Michael, I was very glad to hear that you and all the family in Cratloe were well. Michael, I am in first rate health. I was never better in my life. This Rocky Mountain air agrees with me first rate. I have everything that would tend to make life comfortable. But still at night when I lay in bed, my mind wanders off across the continent and over the Atlantic to the hills of Cratloe. In spite of all I can never forget home, as every Irishman in a foreign land can never forget the land he was raised in. But alas! I am far away from them old haunts.

Letter from Maurice H. Woulfe,
Irish immigrant, 1870

The city of Dallas was being battered by freak spring rains as I drove into it for the first time, en route down to Dublin, Texas, and followed the signs around to Dealey Plaza and Elm Street. Shoppers and workers ran through the streets, a moving forest of umbrellas. The gutters overflowed at the sides of the roads. Rain beat on the roof of the car like applause and when I finally got to Dealey and pulled over and parked, there was hardly anyone around. This was odd. The scene is so familiar, the very streetscape is so deeply etched into your consciousness, that seeing it now without blurred speeding limousines and running Secret Service men and terrified members of the public shaking with tears on the grassy knoll, was eerily anti-climactic.

What I had always wanted to know about the JFK assassination was this: did anyone ever ask Lee Harvey Oswald if he remembered where *he* was the day Kennedy was shot? But this was not the time for levity. Here I was in the holiest place in Irish America, the urban Golgotha where the great saviour was cut down. Like all such holy places in the United States, a small admission price is all you need to tread in the steps of history and experience it all again. As with the soda-fountain in the Atlanta Coca-Cola museum, the room in the famous book depository from where at least some of the shots were fired has been preserved for posterity, exactly the way it was, and I have to tell you frankly that I didn't like the idea of standing in the window of that room and looking down on that rainy street and imagining the terror and chaos it must have seen on that inglorious day in 1963. I didn't like the look on the faces of the people who were coming out of the building having done it either. I am not a big fan of John F. Kennedy, but really, to encourage the public to see the scene of his death through the eyes of his killer is a little less compassionate than anyone deserves.

If death was good for Elvis Presley, it turned John Kennedy into a saint. Every last detail of his funeral was planned with a careful eye on history. Jackie said she wanted the body laid out and buried exactly as Abraham Lincoln's had been. Teams of researchers were dispatched to the Library of Congress to pore through books about Lincoln's funeral. The White House was draped with black crêpe. A replica of Lincoln's catafalque was found. The muffled drumbeat, the gun-carriage bearing the coffin, the riderless horse of the lost leader, all the images which entered the culture as signifiers of the shattering of a generation's hopes were copied from Lincoln's funeral. The only modern touch was the flypast by fifty F-105 jet fighters, an oddly appropriate tribute to a self-proclaimed peace-maker who had always been fascinated by the machinery of war. The pageant went off without a hitch. The astute first lady, unable to control her husband's dishonesty and philandering during his life, set out boldly to shape his image in death. John Kennedy's funeral was a spectacle of national theatre. It was the last great Irish-American day out.

In the months and years after Oswald or the Mafia or the Cubans or the CIA immortalized the Kennedy name by blasting it into the history books, everyone talked about the sense of loss, and how they would always recall where they had been when the news had come.

The hacks and mythmakers went to work. In increasingly absurd prose, John Kennedy began to be imagined as a slain and innocent hero. He was 'a child of [King] Arthur', simpered the journalist William Manchester, and Jackie was a princess 'born of elves in a fairy glade ... dressed in magic cloth of gold'. JFK became the cultural figurehead of a new society which had never existed anywhere outside the leader pages of the liberal newspapers. Bright, young, dynamic, attractive, he and his glamorous wife and their allegedly happy family came retrospectively to epitomize the fantasy of itself which America constructed in the sixties. In life, Kennedy had never been as popular as he was in death. His presidential victory had actually been the narrowest for eighty-seven years, a fact which always injured his great vanity. But in death, Kennedy became the most popular president ever. A third of Americans still wish he was president now.

Bill Clinton understood this desire well, and largely based his own 1992 presidential campaign on an attempt to tap into the still powerful reverberations of the JFK myth. Indeed, he set out deliberately to become the inheritor of the Kennedy reformist mantle. A short clip of a home movie showing a youthful Clinton shaking hands with JFK was included in his campaign television advertisements. The message was clear. Clinton too was youngish and white and Democrat and good-looking. Oddly enough, he was especially good-looking when you put him on a stage beside George Bush and Ross 'I'm All Ears' Perot. He employed a good line in vapid Kennedy-style rhetoric which came over well in soundbites but was substantively meaningless. Hell, Bill Clinton even had Irish blood – or 'Scotch-Irish' anyway – though the campaign genealogists had to look very hard to find it.

As the campaign went on, and it became clear that the main thing 'WJC' – as his press officers dubbed him – had to offer America was his irritating 'aw shucks, me?' grin, the television advertisements got progressively shorter. They concentrated more on those flickering images of JFK pressing the Clinton flesh. That handshake became the central image of the Democrat campaign, until the rest of

Clinton's then lithe teenage body almost disappeared from the ads. WJC merged into JFK. The American public was being offered the ghost of John Kennedy as its new president, a spiritual handshake with its own imagined history.

This history has been extremely kind to John Kennedy. He has a reputation as a great humanitarian, a defender of the poor, a crusader for civil rights and world peace, a cultured patron of the arts. But the JFK myth, like most myths about modern American political power, is an utter fiction. It is an assiduously crafted historical construct, rigorously controlled by the Kennedy family and their supporters. Respected journalists like Benjamin Bradlee of the *Washington Post* have revealed that while Kennedy was alive, he threatened and manipulated the press with remorseless vigour. Since his death, the family has savaged critics, tried to censor unflattering books, refused to meet dissenting interviewers and kept many of his most important papers secret. (The furtiveness with which the Kennedy Library is run has been described as 'a scandal' by the historian Stephen Ambrose.) But from behind the smokescreen of distortions, the truth is emerging now. And the truth is that John Kennedy, in addition to being a spectacular disaster as a human being, was a second-rate president of only average abilities at best.

Such sad details of his childhood which are available make his subsequent bizarre personal life seem tragically predictable. The Kennedy family would have made the Borgias look like something out of a soap powder commercial. Both JFK's parents were clearly in serious need of psychiatric help. His father was a power-crazed thug who lied and cheated his way to wealth, and attempted to seduce his daughter's friends, while all the time continuing publicly to practise his peculiarly ultramontane form of Irish Catholicism. According to the recent biography *JFK: Reckless Youth* by Nigel Hamilton, Kennedy's mother was a religious fanatic who could not bear to embrace her children. Perhaps the frequent vicious beatings she administered were her own sadly warped way of expressing love. In private the family was staggeringly dysfunctional. But in public, the Kennedys passed themselves off as the personified culmination of the immigrant-American dream.

Joe Senior had always been determined that one of his sons would one day be president. When the favoured candidate Joe Junior died, the patriarch simply bought the hypochondriacal, penny-pinching and less talented Jack into the White House. He later admitted that, given the amount of money he'd spent on the campaign, he could have got his milkman elected. Joe's milkman might well have done a better job. There were some important successes, admittedly. Economic growth averaged 5.6 per cent annually in the JFK years, and unemployment dropped to 5 per cent. But many of the policies and actions of Kennedy's government were shocking disasters. The Bay of Pigs episode, the planned invasion of Cuba, was a bloody fiasco. The Cuban missile crisis brought the world to the brink of nuclear annihilation. There was also the small matter of Kennedy's frequent and apparently serious consideration of launching a nuclear first strike on East Berlin. Behind the dashing smile and the rhetoric of peace, Kennedy was, as the historian Richard Walton has observed, 'the most dangerous cold warrior that we have had since the end of World War II'.

But despite these truths, the icon of Kennedy is still largely in place. From the pages of style magazines and the covers of tabloids alike, the self-created gentleman prince of reforming America beams out at a world weary of political compromise and sham. Again and again, he has been fawningly compared to some sort of winsome King Arthur in a mohair suit. The Kennedy clan became almost the new holy family, with the White House their heavenly home. But despite the public performance of marital perfection, all was not quite what it seemed in Camelot.

'I'm not through with a girl till I've had her three ways,' JFK confided, according to one of his lovers, White House employee Traphes Bryant. The language of many of his other observations about women is similarly enlightened. '[I] expect to cut one out of the herd and brand her shortly,' he wrote of women students at his university. It has been suggested that his famous libidinous insatiability was the result of his appalling relationship with his mother, and perhaps this is true. In any case, Kennedy relentlessly used his family and marriage to promote his political ambitions while secretly treating his wife and his other women like a lower form of life. Many of his published letters reveal that he simply had no conception whatsoever of women as human beings. His administration certainly did nothing to advance the position of women in society, and most of the women he employed when president were his mistresses.

But like most male sexual compulsives with an Irish Catholic background, Kennedy didn't actually like women very much. He saw women as his father had seen them, as collectable trinkets. Nor, apparently, did he even particularly enjoy sex. 'I like the chase,' he once said, before adding in revealing language, 'not the kill.' Marilyn Monroe confided to a journalist that Kennedy didn't bother with foreplay because he was usually too busy. His lover Traphes Bryant recalled that JFK was the only man she'd ever met who could make love with one eye on his watch. His friend Congressman George Smathers once recalled Kennedy disappearing from a party for ten minutes of sex. 'It was like a rooster getting on top of a chicken real fast,' Smathers recalled, 'and then the poor little hen ruffles her feathers and wonders what the hell happened to her.' But when the secret parties were over, and the feathers had settled, the widely distributed propaganda photos just kept rolling out of the White House. There they were, King Jack and Queen Jackie, and their happy children playing tag in the oval office.

In foreign policy terms, Kennedy was similarly hypocritical. While he posed as a peacemaker, he plotted war. The book *A Question of Character* by Thomas C. Reeves has put forward convincing evidence that he was involved in plans to assassinate Fidel Castro. In 1975 the Senate Committee to Study Intelligence Activities revealed his illegal use of the CIA to attempt to overthrow governments and conduct covert operations in Cuba and South-east Asia. Much has been written about Kennedy's supposed opposition to American involvement in Vietnam, but there is little real evidence to support this. He was, in fact, a virulent anti-Communist who infamously refused to vote to censure the witch-hunting fascist Senator Joe McCarthy. He was also a fanatical supporter of the so-called 'domino' theory, used to justify the American imperial adventure in Asia and the resulting loss of hundreds of thousands of lives.

Kennedy's so-called progressive attitude to civil rights was equally typical of his political slipperiness. During his presidential campaign he promised to end racial discrimination immediately 'in every field of Federal activity'. Once elected, however, he retreated into a sly and amoral pragmatism. Terrified of alienating racist southern Democrats, he left civil rights issues to his brother, and simply put votes ahead of principles. He refused to keep his promise to end discrimination in public housing because it would have been politically dangerous to do so. He quarrelled with his own Committee on Equal Employment because they insisted on publishing damaging statistics on racism. 'Political expediency was a very strong force in Kennedy's administration,' a founder member of the Civil Rights Commission, Father Theodore Hesburgh, has noted. 'He did what was the politically expedient thing to do.' Kennedy quarrelled often with Martin Luther King, who later described the Kennedy brothers as 'tokenists'. 'They don't understand the social revolution going on in the world,' King said, 'and therefore they don't understand what we're doing.' On another occasion, King described the JFK government as 'the nation's highest investor in segregation'. Throughout all the thousand days of his presidency, Kennedy appointed precisely one black person to his massive staff, as a junior press secretary.

Behind the constructed myth of John Kennedy lies a mass of political contradictions, unfulfilled objectives and broken promises. It is perhaps poignant that his final resting place is not the cemetery at Arlington, but the pages of a hundred airport paperbacks each one of which has come up with a more absurd identity for the killer than the last. The trainspotters of history have adopted JFK's ghost, and perhaps it should be left to them. It is an even sadder reality that the supposedly last great hope of liberal Irish America turned out to be a gifted but damaged and ultimately dangerous man who evidently countenanced political assassinations and the brutal murder of millions with nuclear weapons. 'You're no Jack Kennedy,' Democrat Senator Lloyd Bentsen once jibed famously at Dan Quayle. But the tragic truth is, Jack Kennedy was no Jack Kennedy either. The sooner Irish America comes to terms with that, the sooner it will come to terms with itself.

Lost now in downtown Dallas, I decided to follow the signs back out to the airport on Texas Highway 97 and try to get my bearings for the Dublin road from there. It took me oooh, only an hour and a half to drive the seventeen miles as the crow flies back to the airport, which I considered was pretty good really. Now for the tricky bit, I thought.

I set off full of hope and courage and spent a further hour just trying to get on to the interstate. I drove round and round like a bastard and finally, by sheer luck, I found myself careering along merrily through Euless and then Arlington, past the Six Flags over Texas Amusement Park, then the enormous Forum 303 Shopping Mall. There it was in front of me – the Red Bird Mall, the turn off for the road to Dublin, Texas!

Practically weeping with gratitude, I swerved out on to Route 67 West, which is known, revoltingly enough, as 'The Love Highway', and at last the sequence of little towns through which I was passing began to coincide with the sequence I had written down the night before, after hours of map-studying, in my notebook. I ticked them off as they sped past my window. Cedar Hill, Midlothian, Venus (Jesus, imagine living in Venus, Texas), then Alvarado, Keene, Cleburne, Bono (yes, there is a town in Texas named after the lead singer of U2!), Nemo, Rainbow, Glen Rose and Chalk Mountain, where I saw a large sign painted on a wall: THE SOUTH WILL RISE AGAIN.

The first thing that strikes you about Texas is that it is big. I know everybody tells you that, but it really really is. It's massive. It's enormous. It's as big as something really incredibly big and then some. You drive for hours and hours and don't feel like you're getting anywhere. You could drive for an entire day in Texas and when you checked your mileage that night it would actually be less than it was when you started. That's how big Texas is. Look, it's so big, OK, that . . . Oh never mind. I think you get the message. It's big, all right?

The other odd thing about being in rural Texas for the first time is that the landscape is so familiar to you. The desert sweeps away from the road in enormous undulating waves of tan-coloured sand and ridges of outcropping black rock. Cacti and tumbleweed speckle the earth. Then suddenly the land is flat again, except for the towering crags which shimmer in the distance like ruined cathedrals or beached ships from some childhood dream. This is not just the backdrop of the cowboy movie, it's the landscape of the imagination. The reason you think you've been here before is that you have.

Tired and bored by the straightness of the road, somewhere along the way I passed an abandoned drive-in movie theatre, its tattered grey screen still standing, its car parking spaces still clearly visible, each with its own waist-high speaker on a pole. The huge hoardings along the edge of the interstate announced JESUS IS COMING or THE WAGES OF SIN IS DEATH or REPENT FOR YOU KNOW NOT THE HOUR WHEN HE COMES. There was country music on the radio now. It didn't matter which channel you tried to tune in to, it was all country.

After three long hours on the lonely road with my underwear cutting a far deeper groove between my buttocks than the one the good Lord intended, I finally passed through Stephenville and turned on to Route 377 South to Dublin.

In 1854 a group of thirteen poor farmers from Tennessee and Arkansas settled along Resley's Creek. Their campsite became the site of modern day Dublin. You will be astounded to hear that nobody in the entire state of Texas knows for sure how the town received its name. You will also be astounded to hear that at this stage I didn't really give a flying fart. I was tired of arriving in towns called Dublin and looking for spurious Irish-American connections, so I decided to abandon this approach and just start enjoying myself. Unfortunately, enjoying oneself is not a big activity in Dublin, Texas.

I checked into a nice little motel and decided to go for a bit of a stroll. I had half-planned to have a beer somewhere, but Dublin, Texas, as I was completely overjoyed to discover, is actually a dry town. Christ almighty, it was bad enough in Georgia where you couldn't get a drink on a Sunday. Here in Texas you couldn't get a drink full stop, unless you were a member of a private club. Dejected and despondent, I wandered into a diner where I ordered a coffee and a sherry trifle, on the basis that I intended drinking the coffee and then chucking away the cream and the sponge-cake in the trifle and just sucking the fuck out of the bowl. But then something happened which cheered me up a lot.

As I sat at the table and waited for my refreshments, I noticed in the local paper that Johnny Bush and his Bandolero Band were playing the City Limits Bar, just outside Dublin, that very night. This was wonderful news. Back in Nashville, Bert the gospel music store man had told me that Johnny Bush was his favourite country singer in the whole world, and that if I ever had the chance to see him play live I should crawl across broken glass to do so.

The waitress came back and told me the sherry trifle was off. I sighed deeply. But I didn't care, I told her. I was going to see Johnny Bush tonight.

By nine thirty that night the crowd outside the City Limits Bar was getting a little restless. I waited very patiently in line, but I have to say that not everybody was as philosophical as I. The man in front of me really did need to take up transcendental meditation. He kept going deep red and hammering on the door with his gigantic fists and roaring that if they didn't open it soon he'd 'kick the mother-fuckin thing in' and then 'break some sumbitch's neck'.

During one of his rest periods from assaulting the door, he turned
to me and scowled. 'Those damn sumbitches in there,' he said.
'They got no motherfuckin idear how to treat the public.' I agreed
that a course in customer relations would certainly be desirable, yes.
Thankfully, just then the doors opened and the crowd surged
forward waving their money in the air. I waited politely in line, as
being trampled to death by stressed Texans was not my idea of how
I wanted to depart the corporeal realm. Finally I reached the ticket
counter.

'It's seven dollars to come in see the show,' the bearded cowboy
behind the desk announced, 'but if you wanna buy alcohol ya gotta
be a member.'

'How much is that?' I enquired.

It turned out that it was a mere ten dollars to sign up and purchase
membership of this fine establishment. I was overjoyed. But then,
to my horror I discovered that I had come out without my wallet.
It was ten miles back to my motel, and the show was about to start
in half an hour! What could I do? I did have the seven bucks
required to get in and, stuffed in my pocket, one more crumpled
dollar bill. But that was it. I was going to have to endure the
screaming nightmare of spending the rest of the evening sober in a
place containing enough alcohol to sink a battleship. I really hoped
that Johnny Bush would be worth it.

The City Limits Bar turned out to be a vast barn of a place, with
numerous bars, a big stage and a long thin L-shaped dance floor with
seats all around the edge. I noticed immediately that I was literally
the only man in the hall not wearing bluejeans, a belt with an
enormous buckle, and a Stetson hat. I sat at the edge of the dance
floor and sipped demurely at my Coca-Cola, feeling pretty embarrassed. You do not see too many male adults drinking refreshing soft
drinks after dark in Texas, I can tell you. But still, I was looking
forward to the show.

I should explain that Johnny Bush and his Bandolero Band play
Texas country music, a variety all of its own. The instrumentation is
different to Nashville country; the bands are big. There are usually

three fiddles, a steel guitar, drums, piano, bass and lead guitar. The Bandoleros also have a four-man brass section, two trumpets, a saxophone and trombone. The singing is melodic and, unlike Nashville country, is almost all in harmony. More than strictly musicological differences, however, Texas country also has a different attitude. Not for the Texans the trendiness of the new country sound, or the relative sophistication of glitzy Nashville. This is country dance music at its most visceral.

Just after ten o'clock Johnny Bush strolled on to applause that really was thunderous, and the punters swarmed on to the dance floor.

The dancing in the Dublin, Texas dance hall was very intricate, like a cross between formation ballroom dancing and Irish jigs and reels. The men led, whirling the women around, pulling them in close, pushing them away and then clasping them tightly. They don't go in for much line dancing in this part of the world, I am happy to relate. The dancing is physical, sexual, all about touching and holding your partner. The songs are earthy too. When Johnny Bush sings 'No Wonder I'll Go to a Stranger Before I'll Go to You' you know he ain't exactly talking about popping across the road to a Tupperware party.

People in the crowd seemed to know all the words, and they sang along with Johnny and the band as he proclaimed: 'The only true friends the lonesome man knows/Are Jim Beam, Jack Daniels and Sweet Gypsy Rose.' Indeed, most of Johnny Bush's songs dealt with either adultery or drunkenness, which was odd, I thought, because the City Limits Bar seemed to be both the most sober and the most monogamous place I had ever been in my life. There was drink all right, but I didn't see even one drunk in the course of a very long and late night. There were lots of couples, all dancing together for the entire evening. You couldn't help feeling that a tap on the shoulder and a polite excuse me please would have been met with a swift upper cut to the temple followed by a brisk horse-whipping in the car park. These people really didn't look like they had any intention whatsoever of cheating on each other, but still, the cheating songs came thick and fast.

It was wonderful wild stuff, real Texas country music at its very best. When Johnny Bush finished his first set some of the men actually did cry out 'yeee-haw' and throw their Stetsons in the air. And if I'd had a Stetson myself, I believe I would have done the very same thing.

Next morning in the Dublin, Texas Post Office I saw something posted on the wall which I simply could not believe. It was a circular letter from the Texas Rural Letter Carriers' Association, giving an outline of what Texas postmen were to do in the event of an armed robbery. Here it is in full:

Q: **Suppose he (the robber) is using a gun or making threats with a gun in trying to escape.**

A: Shoot him.

Q: **Suppose the thief was apparently unharmed but was running away?**

A: Call halt twice at the top of your voice, and if he does not halt, fire one warning shot; and if he does not obey this, shoot to hit him.

Q: **Is it permissible to take off my pistol while on duty: for instance, when in a mail car riding between stations?**

A: Never take off your pistol while on duty. Keep it loaded, locked and cocked while on duty.

Q: **Is there a general plan for meeting a robbery?**

A: Yes. Start shooting and meet developments as they arise thereafter.

Q: **If I hear the command 'Hands up!', am I justified in obeying this order?**

A: No: fall to the ground and start shooting.

What a fine state Texas is! I noticed, incidentally, at the bottom of the page that the motto of the Texas Rural Letter Carriers' Association is 'Service with a Smile'.

Dublin, Texas is a quiet sort of town. You can tell this from the front page of the local newspaper. The first morning I was there it led with the startling headlines 'TICKETS STILL AVAILABLE FOR TONIGHT'S CHAMBER OF COMMERCE BANQUET' and 'TWO DUBLINITES NAMED TO GORMAN BANK BOARD'.

The main story on page two began with the stimulating line 'Fourth graders in Dublin are studying grandmothers, and what better way to study them than to sit with them, watch them and listen to them.' From this exciting beginning, the piece continued: 'We tried to think of a subject the children would be familiar with,' says Judy Gromatzky, Tarleton student teacher. 'We just finished reading a story about grandmothers so Ms Delaveaux and I decided to go with the theme of the grandmother.' I am not making this up now. Seriously, that was the lead page two story of the *Dublin Citizen* that morning.

The *Dublin Citizen* is nothing if not informative, and in the great investigative spirit of Woodward and Bernstein, I noticed that on page three of that issue the local school's lunch menus for the forthcoming week had been published in full. (Monday 25 April: French fries, tartare sauce, coleslaw, carrot sticks, milk with a side order of corn dogs. Tuesday 26 April: Steak fingers and gravy, cream potatoes, English peas, jello, hot rolls, milk, crispitos. I won't go on because your mouth would water all over the page.) I was glad to have all this information, although I did note with some concern that the article listing the school menus had been sponsored by 'Harrell Funeral Home, 112 N. Camden Street, 445–3311.' Gosh, this really was a terrific paper. Page six offered a thought-provoking and probably undeniable quote from the American Lung Association. 'When you can't breathe, nothing else matters.'

I picked up another local paper which had a much more promising front page headline: 'GUN TERROR STALKS THE STREETS OF DUBLIN'. As sometimes happens in the world of the media, however, the anticipation was a little greater than the event. The gist of the story was that some old farmer had driven into town in his clapped out truck on the previous Saturday night, following which he had somehow managed to get drunk and have an argument with a waitress. He had then got himself thrown out of whatever speakeasy he had been in. To express his unhappiness he had loosed off a few blasts of his shotgun in the town car park and then driven home in a huff. Hardly GUN TERROR, really.

It was probably the best night of his whole bloody life.

The next day was almost all spent in the car. From Dublin, Texas, I headed north on the Farm Road to Bunyan and then Lingleville. From there I went west to Desdimona, then on to Texas Route 2224 (perhaps only in Texas do road numbers get into four figures) which led to Interstate 20. Rain started to fall. A few miles down 2224 I found the town of Eastland where I turned on to the interstate. Cisco, Scranton, Putnam, Baird, Clyde, Tye, Abilene, the towns all went past in a rainy blur.

Merkel, Trent, Sweetwater. At Roscoe I turned off 20 West and on to Interstate 84 North. Thunder boomed in a dirty sky. I passed through Wastella, Inadale, Hermleigh, Snyder, Dermott, Justiceburg. After that, there was an enormous gap before Post, Close City, Pleasant Valley, Southland, Slaton Rock. I drove on through Posey, and stopped for the night, exhausted, in Lubbock, the home town of Buddy Holly, but unable to sleep because of the lightning storms which continued to rage almost until dawn.

I went to a bar and got talking to a guy who told me all about Buddy Holly, who, you will know, died in a plane crash. What you may not know is how this happened. Apparently, the great bespectacled one swapped his seat on his band's tourbus for a place on the ill-fated downwardly mobile airplane so that he could arrive at his hotel early enough to get his laundry done for the next day. The man who wrote 'Peggy Sue' died for clean underwear. There is, quite simply, no God.

Next morning I left Lubbock on Interstate 84 North. Almost immediately, the landscape started to change. The vast well-tended green fields of rural Texas disappeared. The earth seemed rockier and desolate, soon there was hardly any vegetation. Shallowater, Anton, Bainer, Littlefield, Amphers. At Sudan, Texas there was a sign saying the nearest store was thirty-one miles down the road. I drove on anyway and stopped for coffee in the ugly little town of Muleshoe.

I drove on then, through Progress and Lariat and crossed into New Mexico at the little town of Farwell. I went deeper into New Mexico on Highway 68 West. Through Clovis, Grier, St Vrain, Melrose and Taiban. And then, on the outskirts of Fort Sumner, New Mexico I noticed a large signpost saying 'THIS WAY TO THE ONE TRUE AND ONLY GRAVE OF BILLY THE KID, THE BOY BANDIT KING'. Now this I had to see.

In his brilliant essay 'The Disinterested Killer, Bill Harrigan', the Argentinian writer Jorge Luis Borges plays mischievous havoc with the legend of Billy the Kid, spinning out fables and folktales which are all the more intriguing for being at least partially invented. This was probably a fair enough thing to do to the Kid, because the most interesting thing among many about him is the extent to which he invented and manipulated his own infamous mythology. The documentary facts of his life remain as obscure today as they ever were.

Borges contends that the Kid was born thousands of miles away from the West, in New York, to poor Irish parents, and grew up there, getting involved quite early with the traditional New York activities of nastiness, burglary and doing grievous bodily harm to out-of-town visitors. He also tells us that young Billy Harrigan was a member of a streetgang called the Swamp Angels who hung out on the docks and robbed drunken sailors, and that when he wasn't doing this, he often went to the theatre. He loved the vaudeville melodramas of cowboy life, Borges says, and they were to have a profound effect on him, for he ran off to the West while still a teenager and began his career as an infamous desperado.

The only existing photograph of the Kid shows a squat and stocky fellow with a face so stupid that only a mother would have truly loved it. He had a small head, straight lips, big ears, a chubby belly and long gangly arms. He was, as one biographer tactfully notes, 'not a very attractive person'.

Opinion is still divided about whether the Kid was a Robin Hood-style folk hero who practised an early form of wealth redistribution, or rather, in point of fact, a breathtakingly psycho-pathic bastard whose hamper was several sandwiches short of the full picnic. I myself reluctantly incline towards the latter view. Borges tells us that Billy gunned down twenty-one men in his short life, 'not including Mexicans'. The twenty-one men detail is true, but not the Mexican stuff, which is Borges' idea of a good joke. The Kid actually got on pretty well with Mexicans, and is not thought to have killed any, which is always a good way of telling. But he certainly killed twenty-one Caucasian cowpunchers. Indeed, his one-time friend Pat Garrett, who finally ended their tempestuous relationship by blowing a large hole in the Kid's stomach – you'd think a diplomatically-worded telephone call would have done the trick just as well – tells us in his memoirs that Billy used to laugh hysterically as he watched his victims die in the dust.

Still, despite his bloodthirstiness, or perhaps because of it, the legend of Billy the Kid has proved to be an enduring one. The little museum beside his grave details the extraordinary number of copy-cat killers who all claimed to be the one true Billy the Kid. As late as the 1960s, one elderly man actually went to court in Texas to insist that he was the only genuine Billy and to claim the pardon to which he felt he was entitled.

The Kid's tombstone has been stolen from its location at Fort Sumner several times, but it has always been recovered in the end. A thick band of cast iron now clamps it to the ground and a metal cage encloses the entire grave. The headstone is plastered with dried dust and prairie weed. But if you get down on your knees and look closely you can still just about make out the faded inscription, which, to judge from its heroic tone, he might well have written himself. 'Billy the Kid. The Boy Bandit King. He Died As He Had Lived'.

What a guy! Good old William Harrigan, an early Irish American who really did make his mark.

After paying my respects to Billy the Kid, I sped out of Fort Sumner and on to Santa Rosa where I turned on to Interstate 40 West. It was a sixty-mile drive to Clines Corners, where I would meet the turn north for Santa Fe, New Mexico, the next stop in my journey. Clines Corners came and went, and I drove on then through White Lakes, Gonzalez Ranch, Galisteo, Lamy, on through the Santo Domingo Indian Reservation, and up into the mountains on the road towards the north.

It was late afternoon now. A heavy snow had started to fall. The road steepened as I climbed into the mountains and then abruptly levelled out so that the car started to feel a little lighter. Thunder exploded again and forked lightning seemed to rip the whole sky in half. And then, very suddenly, the snow stopped and the thunder died away. I stopped the car and got out. I was on a quiet country road. The silence was so amazing it felt as though the snow and the thunder had been stopped by some violent act. The black clouds parted and the sun began to go down. I walked down the road and sat on a rock, just watching. Pink light spread across the sky like watercolour paint spilled over a canvas. The sky turned yellow and green, then it took on a mysterious bronze light. A long arch of peach-coloured cloud hung over the mountains for a while, sur-rounded by a soft swath of light pinks and variegated reds. And then the mountains grew blacker. The last of the light faded away and suddenly the night was here.

It was very cold now. I walked back down the road to the car, got in and turned on the radio. Frank Sinatra was singing a Cole Porter song. The playfulness of the words made me smile. I switched on my full headlights, lit up a cigarette and drove on through the snow-covered hills towards Santa Fe.

CHAPTER 14

Love Hurts

It's goodbye Mick and goodbye Pat and goodbye Kate and Mary
The anchor's weighed, the gangway's up, I'm leavin' Tipperary!
There's the steamer blazin' up,
So I shall no longer stay.
And I'm off to New York City boys,
Three thousand miles away, HA HA HA!!

From 'Leavin' Tipperary', traditional Irish song, nineteenth century,
recorded by Dan Sullivan's Shamrock Band, Boston, 1926

I could then go to a fair, or a wake, or a dance . . . I could spend the
winter's nights in a neighbour's house cracking jokes by the turf fire . . .
I could have a neighbour within every hundred yards of me that would
run to see me. But here everyone can get so much land . . . that they
calls them neighbours that live two or three miles off.

Letter from Irish immigrant,
name unknown, late nineteenth century

Imagine this. Everyone in the world has a friend like this. This
person is not a hippie exactly, although he or she will probably wear
a lot of cheesecloth and know all the words of Don McLean's
'American Pie'. He or she loves you dearly. He or she is a deeply
caring person, a loyal supporter, a true friend with a heart the size of
a juggernaut. You don't deserve this person. You are grateful to
God almighty and his holy mother that they put this person in your
life, but sometimes, you must confess, this person makes you want
to run screeching into your bathroom, lift the lid on your toilet,
kneel down on the floor, breathe in deeply, open your mouth, stick
your fingers down your throat and vomit like a souped-up fruit
machine.

This person is just too nice. This person is kind to animals and good to the environment. This person has spent the equivalent of the national debt of a Central American republic on psychotherapy. He or she draws little smiley faces inside the dot over the letter 'i'.

Sometimes you meet this person for coffee. You are in a good mood. You feel wonderful. You indulge in a bit of chit-chat. Then, at some early point in the conversation, this person's eyes will suddenly become misty with concern. (Oh, fuck all the 'this person' stuff, let's just call her 'she' and be done with it, all right?)

'Are you OK?' she will say, and you will answer yes, you are. 'Are you sure?' she will ask.

'I'm fine,' you will reply.

'But I can sense that you're in pain.'

'I'm not.'

'You're in denial.'

'No, I'm not!'

'See what I mean?'

She will reach out and clutch your wrist so hard that you will wince. 'Mr Denial is in town again, huh? Well, you just need to give yourself a big hug, Mr Sad Sack. You need to give your inner child a big huggy-wuggy-smuggly-buggly treat. You need to start giving yourself permission to just tell yourself you're OK.'

'I know I'm OK.'

'Have you read that book, *I'm OK, You're OK*?'

'No, I haven't, but I've read *I'm OK, You're a Screaming Pain in the Hole*.'

'Ha ha ha. Covering up your pain with puerile humour. I used to do that too, instead of just letting myself know I was OK.'

'I know I'm OK,' you snarl. 'I fucking know that.'

'There's an airport out there called total self-acceptance,' she will say, 'and hey, listen, mister, you just get on that radio and clear yourself for immediate landing, OK?'

Well, if you could imagine a whole city planned and built and populated by people like that, what you would be imagining would be more than a little like modern Santa Fe.

For my first night in town I had booked into a new and very luxurious hotel which is owned and run by a local Indian tribe. 'I made a reservation,' I said to the clerk, 'in the name of O'Connor.' Immediately, I was seized by an attack of liberal whitey guilt. What a faux pas! I had used the word 'reservation' in front of a native American.

I apologized for being so rude, and explained that I had only just arrived in Santa Fe and was not used to its customs. The young man peered at me solemnly.

'How,' he said.

I held up my right hand in the traditional native American manner and returned his greeting.

'How,' I said. 'Right on, brother.'

'No,' he sighed. 'How did you arrive? How? By car? Do you need a car parking space or what?'

After I had finished apologizing again, I left my belongings upstairs in my authentically decorated native American lodging complete with minibar and trouser press and I went out into the night to find a restaurant. The joint I selected was vegetarian and fairly full, and the waitress told me that I would have to wait for a few minutes if that was OK. Of course it was OK, I said, and I asked her to direct me to the bar, or, better still, just get me a large Scotch. The waitress did a really annoying mock wince and told me the restaurant was actually 'an alcohol-free zone'. The management of the restaurant felt that alcohol was a dangerous and addictive drug, 'an unhealthy thing for us to put into our bodies'. But the naturally squeezed fruit juices were very refreshing, she confided, particularly the cranberry. Wacky, I thought, but hey, when in Rome. I said I would go ahead and make the ... er ... reservation, and that I would need a table in the smoking section, and in the meantime she could hit me with a double cranberry juice and a pack of Marlboro Lites. Well, the broad practically threw her cookies. She looked at me as though I had just suggested I perform cunnilingus on her grandmother. She informed me that the entire restaurant was 'a smoke-free zone'. I burst out laughing. This was too much. Fuck the vegetables, I thought. A restaurant where you can't drink or smoke really defeats the whole point.

I went out and began stalking the streets of Santa Fe in search of a good time, and I have to say it was hard to find because everything in the town seemed to close down by ten, except, of course, the psychotherapists' offices which are open twenty-four hours a day. Finally I found a little place down near the square which was open, which had an alcohol licence, and which sold meat. I almost threw my arms around the waiter.

'Smoking or non?' he said.

'Smoking,' I told him.

He sighed and shook his head. 'Wow,' he said, and showed me to a table. 'Good luck, and, hey, if you're a smoker, you're going to need it, buddy.'

As soon as he said this I made up my mind not to leave the scrawny little tofu-eating body-fascist a tip, so he was about to waste his time being nice to me. But nice he certainly was, as he explained the menu with the condescending patience of a medieval monk elucidating the mystery of the Blessed Trinity to a curious snot-nosed toddler. 'Here's some Texas caviar,' he said, when he had finished his explanations, placing a dish of chopped-up jalapeno peppers on the table.

'Fuck off, dickhead,' I said. In my mind.

Just across the floor from me, a young man with a nylon-string guitar was sitting on a high stool and inflicting the products of his dubious creativity on me and various other diners. This guy was pure dross. He was woeful. He was the musical equivalent of watching a slow-motion car crash.

He had an effects box on the floor in front of him. This is a device used all over the world by lousy guitarists with rich parents. It is about the size of a shoebox, and it has a series of buttons and knobs on it, which, when pressed with the feet, distort the sound of the guitar for long enough to make an audience think that the guitarist knows what he is doing. This poor sap had just bought the effects box that morning, and he confessed to us that he didn't yet know how to use it properly. He kept stopping in mid song, mercifully enough, and then going down on his hands and knees and unplugging wires which he would fiddle with, unravel and then plug back in again. I must confess that if he had plugged in the wrong wire and blown himself screaming through the rafters I would have burst into a cheery chorus of 'Oh What a Beautiful Morning'.

His name was Chuck – which was odd really, because that's what he was making me feel like doing – and after he unfortunately managed to get his sound system working properly he confided that he was 'doing mostly self-penned material tonight'. Well, you should have heard it. Every single song was slow, funereal, dirge-like. Leonard Cohen would have found this guy a major downer. There were lots of minor seventh chords from the guitar and lots of plangent 'whooo-whoos' from Chuck.

> Remember that night when I came in you first, babe
> And all the stars and planets just seemed to burst, babe
> Oh yeah, you didn't understand
> Hoo-hooo, you didn't comprehend
> That the whole of the universe was totally cursed, babe.

I'm all for that kind of thing in its place, but not when you're tucking into a big plate of refried beans.

'That's a song I wrote about the planet,' he said, 'and hey, I just think we all gotta, you know, get together and stop screwing around with nature, because if we keep doin it, man, hooo, nature's gonna screw around with us.'

There was a ripple of applause from the other diners at this point and a barely suppressed moan of agony from myself.

Shortly afterwards, as if things were not bad enough, a gang of college kids came in and sat at the table next to me. They had on expensive-looking jewellery and were all dressed in stylishly homeless-hostel-vibe clothes. As I eavesdropped on what passed for their conversation, I could not help but notice that Americans of a certain age use the word 'like' the way other people use punctuation, only more often.

'So I met her at six thurdy and I was like are we gonna go to the mall or what?'

'You were not, you were like, can we go back to the hotel now?'

'I was too, I was like toadly out of my face on tequila and she was like are you going to ackshlee go out dressed like that or what? I was like gag me with a spoon, dude.'

While I did my best to keep afloat in the syntactical swamp which was emanating from the next table, I suddenly noticed that there was a loudspeaker hidden in the trees behind me. With a terrible start, I realized that Chuck could be heard outside in the street. I felt that he had not exploited the comedic potential of this fact to the full. If it was me, I wouldn't have sung at all. I would have just waited for a tourist to come wandering past the restaurant vainly searching for a place to have some fun and then I would have said, into my microphone, 'Hey you, yeah you in the shirt, boy you're stupid-looking, yeah, *you*, butthead, like, who does your fuckin hair, man?'

But that was me. After a few weeks on the road, I was definitely beginning to get just a bit sad.

When I woke up next morning I switched on the television to watch the news. The local station was showing a commercial for colonic irrigation. This is a medical treatment involving large amounts of water being sprayed up your arse. Rich and famous people in America pay large amounts of money to have this done to them, when you would have thought with a bit of imagination and a length of good strong garden hose they could have done it to themselves just as easily. But anyway. Apparently it makes you feel great, and to judge by the list of venues offering this admirable service in the city, Santa Fe was practically the colonic irrigation capital of the world.

Breakfast turned out to be a truly Santa Fe experience. I came skipping down the stairs looking forward to a big plate of bacon, sausages, hash browns and eggs over easy. What a disappointment. Breakfast consisted of melon balls, bits of pineapple, various other fruits. The fucking buffet looked like one of Carmen Miranda's hats. There was no meat to be seen anywhere. If a mosquito or a fly had flapped into the dining room it would have sent me into a carnivorous frenzy. The most dangerous thing on the whole menu was cinnamon toast, and I felt that if you asked for an extra slice of that the chef would come out from the kitchen to give you a good hard scalping. Sorry, I mean spanking.

After I had wolfed down a lovely big slice of kiwi fruit – mmmm, hmmm – I strolled the few blocks down to the plaza and had a bit of a look around. There were lots of art galleries, I noticed. You cannot buy a pack of cigarettes anywhere inside the city limits, but if it's a Georgia O'Keefe-style painting of a big flower reminiscent of a vulva you're after, Santa Fe really is the place for you. There are also a large number of paintings of cowboys and an even larger number of paintings of native Americans.

The figures in these paintings tend to look heroic, tough, dreamy, sexually attractive, with thick necks like workers in Soviet Socialist Realist works. For some reason you never see a painting of a cowboy or a native American who is old, or sick, or ugly, or frail. Why was this, I wondered. And then it hit me. It was because – obviously – when you are out on the lonesome trail hunting buffalo or herding steers you eat a lot of kiwi fruit and you have a lot of colonic irrigation. Simple really, when you think.

Early the next morning I left Santa Fe on Interstate 20 South for Albuquerque. There was a heavy dew on the grass, but as the sun started to come up the dew melted and turned into steam, wrapping the mountains in a web of gossamer-like beauty which was almost heavenly to behold. I passed through La Cienega and the San Felipe Indian Reservation and the tiny town of Algodones. At Bernalillo, the Cibola National Forest loomed up, heavy sheets of snow on the lower branches of the trees. Then came Rio Rancho and Alemeda and Albuquerque.

Albuquerque seemed to be a dreadful place where suburbanitis has run completely riot. I sped past it and turned on to the Interstate, passing Pajarito on the left and the Canoncito Indian Reservation on the right. Then came a long hard morning's driving, through Laguna, Casa Blanca, Cubero, San Fidel, McCartys, El Malpais ('the bad country', in Spanish), San Rafael, Grants, Milan, Anaconda, Bluewater with the Lookout Mountains towering on the left, Prewitt, Thoreau, Continental Divide, McGaffney, Rehoboth.

Interstate 40, on which I was driving that day, runs parallel to the old Route 66, so justifiably famed in song and story. 'O public road,' wrote Walt Whitman once, 'you express me better than I can express myself,' and it might well have been Route 66 he was envisioning. Almost immediately after it was named in 1926, the great road found its special place in the heart of the American public. At first it is hard to understand how something like a road could have achieved such superstardom, but part of its attraction must have been its sheer length; it stretched a distance of some two thousand miles, all the way from Chicago, Illinois to Santa Monica, California, meandering on its way through Missouri, Arkansas, Oklahoma, Texas, New Mexico and Arizona, through several changing eco-sytems, climate regions and time zones. The geography through which it moved was spectacular, incorporating the extremes of both the Colorado plateau and the great plains. Indeed, at its height, you could drive most of the way across America without ever leaving Route 66, and a hell of a lot of people did.

But from the day of its birth Route 66 meant something even more than epic scale to those who had eyes to see these things. Size, in roads, is not everything. The shape of Route 66 was also the shape of American history. Its very existence told the eloquent story of a people who had always seen moving west as something worth doing. The names of the towns through which the asphalt river flowed – St Louis, Springfield, Carthage, Joplin, Tulsa, Oklahoma City, Amarillo, Vega, Tumucari – were the great geographical markers in the history of American immigrant movement towards California.

Route 66 was a hell of a road. Travelling down what is left of it today, you can almost sense the dreams and fears of the millions of poor migrants who travelled it before you. But the speed with which it acquired its mythical significance is truly extraordinary. The first full-length book about the road – Jack Rittenhouse's Route 66 guidebook – was published in 1946, a mere twenty years after it was opened. The famous song '(Get Your Kicks on) Route 66' was written the same year. How many roads ever get songs written about them? Will the M1 motorway ever have a hymn of praise written about it, never mind one as joyfully innocent, as unforgettably evocative, as 'Route 66', the pop song which made of the placenames of America as joyful a paean to human freedom as Whitman's *Leaves of Grass*?

I remember once being in a bar near the Nevsky Prospect in Leningrad. There was a pretty dreadful rock and roll band playing on a small stage. They did all the usual stuff, 'Twenty Flight Rock', 'Back in the USSR', 'Long Tall Sally', 'Jailhouse Rock'. But when they played 'Route 66' the place went wild. They played it again at the end, twice. I don't think I will ever truly forget the sight of one teenage boy from Leningrad, with the word 'AMERICA' painted in red on the back of his leather jacket, and his arms around the main amplifier, and his mouth open, screaming the words of 'Route 66'.

After the gig that night I got talking to the lead singer, a young woman from Moscow. She knew a bit about Irish rock music, she told me, she liked U2 and the Boomtown Rats and a punk band from Belfast called the Stiff Little Fingers. I asked her why her band didn't do some of these songs, why they played all these old songs. I asked her why they did 'Route 66', for instance, and why the crowd had liked it so much. She shrugged. 'The greatest thing about America,' she sighed, 'is that the people can go anywhere they want. Imagine that! A country where you can go wherever you like. And that's why we sing "Route 66". Because for us, it is a protest song.'

Route 66 was the road that would take you almost anywhere you wanted to go, the highway that ran without stopping through the American dream of itself. Steinbeck immortalized it in *The Grapes of Wrath*, renaming it the Mother Road. Jack Kerouac and Neal Cassady traipsed up and down it. Bob Dylan sang about it and Woody Guthrie wrote talking blues about it. In the 1960s Route 66 even achieved the only true fame worth achieving in America, when it got its own 200-episode-long TV show.

Having been allowed to live and celebrate the very idea of America for a mere sixty years, Route 66 officially ceased to exist on 27 June 1985, when it was 'declassified' by the incredibly imaginative and brave men and women of the National Association of Highway Authorities. As an act of aesthetic and cultural terrorism it could perhaps only be equalled by declassifying the Rocky Mountains. Route 66 was killed off by bureaucracy and, once dead, was buried beneath the wonderfully modern and undeniably efficient and spectacularly soulless surface of Interstate 40, and they didn't even leave an identifying marker for those who wanted to mourn and pay their respects. Route 66's beautiful shield-shaped yellow marking signs were removed and dumped or melted down for scrap by the authorities, or sold off as souvenirs. But it is heartening to drive into one or other of the many small towns along the site of the old route and see these little icons of American freedom, rescued from the trashcan and nailed back up to the lamp-posts, or stuck in the windows of the shops. Nobody in these towns tries to rip you off, hawking the ghost of the road for profit. There are no T shirts or baseball caps. There's nothing much for you to buy, except maybe a slim pamphlet on Route 66's short but brilliant history, which the man in the gas station at which I stopped was happy to give me for nothing.

'They cut out the heart of America when they killed Route 66,' he said, shaking his head. 'It never shoulda happened.'

I went into his gas station to use the bathroom. There, on the wall, was an old map of Route 66, printed in shades of red and yellow which must have once seemed lurid, but which were not faded and pale. There were some handwritten words on the wall underneath the map. Someone had underlined the words with a thick black marker pen. They read, 'June 27, 1985: The Day The Music Died'.

I had just crossed the border into Arizona when the road signs started to appear. Twenty foot long, ten foot tall, red and yellow billboards, screaming 'CHEAPEST CIGARETTES' in enormous lettering, or 'GAMBLING' or 'INDIAN JEWELRY' or 'TRIBAL ART', sometimes 'MOCCASINS' or 'SKINS' or 'SILVER' or 'GOLDWARE'. Almost all the signs had the words 'VERY CHEAP' in large characters. The local native Americans had erected these signs to entice visitors off the interstate and on to their reservations to buy souvenirs and ornaments. (Cigarettes are cheaper on the reservation because they are exempt from US National Tax. Likewise, gambling is legal on most reservations, even in states which have anti-gaming laws.) Sure, the Indians have to make a living like the rest of us. It's just that on some stretches of the highway, these signs appear every hundred yards or so for a distance of several miles. And then after a while they get even closer. It was absolutely ironic to drive along the highway and realize that you couldn't see the landscape properly because of these bloody signs. I could really see how the native Americans had got their famous reputation for caring for the environment.

The afternoon became an unending succession of small towns. Lupton, Houck, Sanders, Chambers, Navajo, Painted Desert, Sun Valley, Holbrook (elevation: 5,075), Joseph City, with a tiny airport just on the outskirts. I felt myself getting sleepy behind the wheel and I turned on the radio to wake myself up. The first station I could find was playing country and western. They had on a song by the Irish country star Gloria, called 'One Day at a Time'. It was funny to hear Gloria in the middle of rural Arizona, but it was kind of heartwarming too.

I drove on through Winslow, Leupp Corner, and then a long and lonely stretch passed before Winona, Arizona. The landscape was tragically beautiful to look at now, full of blasted trees and twisted shrubs and enormous gnarled chunks of brooding rock which looked like they were just waiting for the sun to go down before springing into terrible life. I got a bit weary of the country music and started flicking through the channels on the radio dial, but I couldn't find anything at first. The speakers crackled and spat. Gradually I managed to tune in to a jazz station which was playing Miles Davis's 'Sketches of Spain'. Almost immediately the music was interrupted by a woman's voice which spoke in an urgent tone. We were going over to Washington, DC for an important item of national news. There was a brief pause followed by a short piece of solemn orchestral music and then the newsreader came on and said that Richard Nixon was dead.

There followed tributes from old friends and adversaries and colleagues. President Clinton said that he had been a good man who had achieved much in the field of foreign policy and survived much that would have put a lesser politician out of business. Henry Kissinger came on and said in a trembling voice that he believed history would remember Nixon as one of the greatest American presidents ever. To me, this was astonishing.

To me, Richard Nixon had done more to destroy the idea of America than any one single individual in the twentieth century. The history of American parliamentary democracy had been the history of a wonderful and revolutionary idea. Governments were to be accountable; if the people didn't like them or agree with them, they would have the chance simply to say so in a free and fair election, and the government would stand down without further ado and be replaced. It was an idea which had spread to the furthest corners of the planet, and one which had greatly influenced the revolutionary movement which had brought a large measure of freedom to my own country. Richard Nixon had taken that noble idea and dragged it down into the muck, for no other reason than his obscene love of power. Very simply, he had cheated. He had broken the rules, and he had never even had the guts to admit plainly that he was a cheap little hood who couldn't stand to lose.

He bent the rules so hard that in the end they broke, never again to be fixed. For it became clear listening to the tearful words of ordinary Americans on the radio that afternoon that Nixon's half-assed little corruptions were regarded as relatively benign compared to the grand-scale lies of the Reagan and Bush years. He had done a terrible thing, but he had paid the highest penalty any person could pay, people felt. He had been the first citizen of the greatest country in the world and he had been forced to stand down in disgrace. America is still a deeply Protestant society, a country which believes in the possibility of redemption almost more than it believes in anything else. And maybe that's not such a bad thing. Because if even Richard Nixon could be redeemed, I thought, crossing Arizona that day, there was certainly hope for the rest of us.

Shortly after I heard the news about Nixon on the radio I found myself driving into the town of Flagstaff, Arizona. Outside the post office, I noticed that a man in a uniform was busily lowering the Stars and Stripes to half mast. He did this and then stood to attention for a moment before saluting the flag and bowing his head.

I was so tired now that I knew if I stopped I wouldn't manage to start again until morning. So I just kept going. I turned right at the edge of Flagstaff on to Highway 180 for the Grand Canyon. The route to the canyon takes you through the desolate loveliness of Riordan State Historical Park, where it is fifty-one miles from the entrance to the first junction. Ten minutes on to the road snow began to spatter on the windscreen and before long I was driving through a fully fledged blizzard.

From the edge of the park I drove the twenty-two miles more to Kaihab National Forest, then into Tuscayan, the last town before the Canyon village itself. The snow was still falling steadily and the sun was just beginning to go down as I pulled up at Mather Point viewing station and got out of the car.

I had heard an awful lot about the Grand Canyon. I had watched friends who had visited this greatest natural wonder in the world go goggle-eyed and speechless as they tried to explain its grandeur, its majesty and its sheer mind-numbing size.

But this was not a great day to see the canyon. The weather was lousy and the light was dull and you could see only about a third of it with any clarity. The sky was a dirty grey colour now and a mass of thick low cloud had sunk into the eastern section of the canyon, completely obliterating the view. Still, what I could see was breathtaking. What I could see was one of the most amazing things I had ever seen.

Trying to describe it in words is pretty close to impossible. It is a little like trying to pour a gallon of water into a half-pint glass. If you could imagine an enormous mountain turned upside down, hollowed out and driven into the earth you might be close. There are statistics of course. Americans love statistics, and they have measured and explored the canyon just about every way it is possible to measure something like that. But the statistics are so awesome that they crumble in your mind and become meaningless. The canyon is eighteen miles wide and over a mile deep. Manhattan island would fit into it comfortably and leave room for more. You could put the entire city of London into it several times over. Look, for God's sake, it's almost as big as Camille Paglia's ego, all right?

As I stood looking into it, the fog began to roll in from left to right like an enormous grey curtain and the view gradually disappeared. But to tell you the truth, I was kind of glad. There was something vaguely awful about it. It was so large and deep and silent. A picture I had once seen as a schoolchild flashed into my mind. It was a painting of one of the saints – possibly St Teresa, or St Bernadette – having a vision of Hell. That's what the canyon reminded me of. A vision of Hell, yawning, unending, profound.

I drove up to the Grand Canyon village and managed to get a

room in one of the lodges there. But I didn't sleep well. I kept waking up feeling acutely aware of the canyon's proximity. Call me old-fashioned, but I had never before spent the night a few yards away from a mile-deep hole in the fucking ground and I just didn't feel too good about it.

Next morning I went up early to have another look, but the fog was so thick that you couldn't see anything at all. I got chatting to one of the national park workers who look after the area, and it turns out that the Grand Canyon is indeed a pretty dangerous place. Falling into the bloody thing is the least of your worries, although people do, at the rate of about one per month. I wondered how this could be possible. How in the name of God would a person of even subnormal intelligence manage to plan routes, save up for a vacation, drive all the way to the Grand Canyon, take one brief look and then promptly fall over the edge of it? I asked the guard about this. 'I guess people are basically dumb,' he shrugged. 'You gotta hole in the ground, folks are gonna fall into the sucker.'

The guard gave me a copy of the safety guidelines for visitors. This was a nice gesture, but many of the guidelines were pretty damn obvious to say the least. 'Do not pitch tents or place sleeping bags in proximity to rodent faeces or burrows or near possible rodent shelters.' Oh, right then. That really wouldn't have occurred to me.

'Do not disturb dens (such as pack rat nests).' Well, that's a helpful tip. I mean you're really likely to do that, aren't you. 'Hey woah, kids, guess what, I think there's a whole nest full of pack rats over here, let's call Mom and go flush a few of those cuddly little rascals out.'

I asked the guard what it was like working at a place like this. He said it was a great privilege, but he felt that the poor old canyon was in for a tough time over the next few years. The great contradiction of the place, as he pointed out, is that what attracts people to it is its isolation and its stark beauty, but the sheer volume of tourism is now so enormous that the canyon is beginning to show the strain. Great efforts have been made to preserve it, but you just can't have three million visitors a year without it leaving some mark.

Surely, I said, the public would never let anything do serious damage to the canyon. All the authorities had to do was educate them to respect the place.

'The authorities,' he nodded and scoffed, 'oh yeah, see they want the canyon all right, but they don't care about air quality, they don't care about wilderness, they don't care about aircraft overflights, they don't care about ecosytems, they don't care about any of that stuff.'

·He laughed again, more softly now. 'I dunno what's gonna become of the poor old girl. And the way things are going in this country now, sometimes I think one day some dumb-ass politician up in Washington's gonna just suggest gettin a whole shitload of concrete and just fillin her in.'

'The Grand Canyon desert car park,' he sighed. 'S'kinda gotta Republican ring to it, don't it?'

As I left the Canyon village and headed south on Highway 180 the sky was a messy wash of dark greys, with swirling black clouds rolling in slowly from the south. At the junction with Interstate 64 I turned south for Williams. I had a long day's driving ahead of me before reaching Las Vegas, where I planned to spend the night, before flying on to San Francisco and the last Dublin, just outside Berkeley, California.

Even though the weather was awful the drive was pleasant enough. The little red steam train from Williams to the canyon chugged along parallel to the road. Huge graceful darkly coloured birds whirled around in the sky. I sped through Red Lake, stopped at Williams to buy water and cigarettes, and then turned out on to Interstate 40 West. About twenty miles down the highway the Picacho Butte Mountain loomed up in the distance, tiny skiers moving slowly over its lower slopes. At Seligman, the Juniper Mountains appeared on the southern horizon. It was a 250-mile drive to Kingman, with nothing in between except the beginnings of the Mojave Desert.

The sun began to come out and the desert took on a golden

amber glow. The yellowish sandy earth swept away from the road on both sides and into vast wave-shaped dunes. The road was so straight now that I felt like I was playing an amusement arcade driving machine rather than driving a real car. At Kingman, I turned on to 93 North for Las Vegas and drove on, passing through a tiny town called Chloride. Mount Tipton appeared on my right, 7,000 feet of menacing treacherous-looking rock. At milepost 27 on Highway 93 just a few miles south of the Hoover Dam and the Nevada border, I came to a roadside diner called the Oasis Restaurant and stopped.

The place was huge but completely empty. As I walked in and sat down a radio was playing a languid country song. After a few moments a woman in her thirties came into the restaurant and gave me a menu. She was warm and very welcoming and when I told her where I was from her eyes lit up in a lovely twinkling smile. I ordered a coffee and an omelette and I asked her what it was like living out here in the desert.

'Oh, we love our desert countryside,' she told me. 'It's not as dead as you might think. We got coyotes, roadrunners, quail, blacktail deer, bighorn sheep, burros.' (Burros, she explained, were wild donkeys.)

But what about the vast distances, I said. How could a person ever get used to those?

The woman said that if you were from a city the desert distances could admittedly seem pretty awesome. But here where she and her husband lived was within a comfortable drive of 'two of the most glamorous places in the whole United States'. They could drive to Lake Mead or Willow Beach in half an hour, and just a few minutes longer would get you to Vegas.

'All these folks who live in the fancy cities,' she laughed, 'they can't say that, can they? Can't say they're only an hour from Vegas?'

'No,' I said, 'they can't.'

True, she admitted, they couldn't exactly go dancing on a whim or send out for a pizza to be delivered. They had to do a little more planning than city folks. But it was worth the minor inconvenience to your social life to see the most beautiful sunsets and glorious sunrises anyone could want. 'Not to mention that we breathe the cleanest air in America.'

I asked if she and her husband didn't miss having neighbours.

'We have neighbours!' she laughed. 'You just don't see huge tracts of houses out here because we all cherish our solitude. But we have a social life that's great fun. And the weather out here's real nice too. Your summer high temperature's 100, 110 maybe, but with real low humidity and a nice breeze. Even in the high summertime the nights are cool, and the winter's just kinda pleasant. We don't get snow here.'

She looked at me and pretended to put on a cross face. 'So when folks say how could you live in this Godforsaken desert country we just say "God blessed it" and you would too if you have the eyes and time to see it.'

When I had finished my meal I went out and got into the car and started driving again. My back was aching and my eyes were beginning to sting. I came to the wide expanse of the Colorado River and drove across what must be the most spectacular border anywhere in the world, the Hoover Dam road. I crossed over, slowly, carefully, trying not to look down into the swirling grey water, and then I sped on again, through Henderson and on to another stretch of isolated desert highway. Las Vegas was still thirty miles away, but I could already see the glow of lights in the sky.

The MGM Grand Hotel in the middle of Las Vegas is the largest hotel in the world. It has 4,000 bedrooms. I was told this when I ambled up to the counter and innocently enquired, 'Do you have a room?' The assistant grinned at me. 'I think we can just about fit you in,' she said. In addition to 4,000 bedrooms, the MGM Grand also has eleven restaurants, four casinos, five bars, four tennis courts, a swimming pool with artificial 'real sand' beach, two full-size theatres, a 15,200-seater Grand Garden for large scale concerts and events such as boxing matches, a 30,000-square-foot amusement arcade and a seven-storey replica of 'the magical city of Oz'. Back home in Ireland, people live their whole lives in towns that don't have eleven restaurants and five bars and two theatres and an artificial 'real sand' beach. You could live in the MGM Grand Hotel for the rest of your life.

There is nowhere in the world quite like Las Vegas. The city is to bad taste what Florence is to Renaissance painting. The main boulevard has fake pyramids, an enormous glow-in-the-dark sphinx, an imitation Greek classical statue of a woman spouting water from her breasts, a gigantic 'medieval' castle so horrendously over-the-top that even mad King Ludwig of Bavaria would have found it a tad excessive.

The casinos have to be seen to be believed. In Caesar's Palace, the waitresses are dressed in togas; in Excalibur's the staff are required to address customers as 'My Lord' or 'My Lady'. There are casinos done out as tropical rainforests, Wild West towns, native American villages, pioneer settlements, but for all the staggering variation in decor, each casino is fundamentally the same as the last.

The noise is what strikes you first. The clanging, jangling, buzzing, wailing, rattling cacophony of tens of thousands of slot machines. There are plenty of ways to lose money in Las Vegas. Even the humble slot machine comes in a breathtaking range of versions. There are slot machines which take nickels and those that take special ten-dollar coins, there are multipliers, machines which accept more than one coin before playing. There are multi-liners, offering payouts on the top, middle, diagonal or bottom lines as well as the centre. There are speciality video slots on which you can play almost all of the casino table games. There are Lions Share Slots, $1 slot machines, each capable of paying out jackpots exceeding a hundred thousand dollars.

If you don't want to play the slots, that's no problem, the casinos will be happy to suggest something else. You can bet on football or basketball or baseball or ice hockey. There is horse racing, of course. The MGM casino will take any bet, of any size, on any horse race, anywhere. The Sports Book counter will take any bet on any professional or college sporting event in the continental United States. There is Big Six, a version of the fairground big wheel. There is poker played by any recognized set of rules you like. There is Pai Gow, a game played with three-dimensional cards or dominoes, and Pai Gow poker. There is Keno, a game of guessing numbers, and there is baccarat and blackjack and craps and roulette.

After the noise, what strikes you next is the sight of the gamblers. They are not the diamanté-dripping vamps and tuxedo-clad smooth-ies of Hollywood mythology. In the main they are ordinary working people, on vacation from other parts of the United States. You see plenty of middle-aged couples, plenty of people by themselves. You see a lot of people just like the woman I had met in the Oasis Café. Food is cheap in the casinos and alcohol is free to those who are gambling. There are no windows and no clocks. It is always the same time in Las Vegas. Huge blinking neon signs flash out the dubious message that it is possible to win a million dollars from a twenty-five-cent bet on a slot machine.

I watched one man of my father's age playing a machine in the row next to mine. He was dressed in slacks and a cardigan, and his wife, who stood beside him holding his hand as he fed the machine with his other hand, had on a pair of jeans and a cowboy-style frilly shirt. For a while they seemed happy. They would laugh and joke each time the machine buzzed and spat out a few coins, and sometimes she would kiss him or affectionately ruffle his hair. But then, after a short time he began to lose. I saw the woman go away and return with more free drinks and a big plastic Coca-Cola cup full of quarter coins. One by one the man pumped the coins into the machine, and he kept losing. He lost the whole cup full of coins. He started feeding dollar bills, and then five-dollar bills into the machine, and still he kept losing.

After a while his wife went away and did not return. It was only when I looked at my watch and saw it was one in the morning that I realized she must have gone to bed. But he was still there, alone, gorging the machine. He must have fed five hundred dollars into it in the space of a couple of hours.

Out on the strip the roar of noise is even louder. People rush up to you and hand you leaflets. There are flyers for casinos, for cheap hotels, for strip clubs, for restaurants, for escort agencies, for massage parlours, for wedding chapels: '*Las Vegas Weddings, $75 Chapel Fee: Includes free video tape of ceremony, free music, free Bouquet for Bride to Carry, free witness, free twelve Photos – All Different Poses, free Minister Set Up. $75. Includes all the above. Indoor Chapel or Outdoor Gazebo with Nearby Waterfall and Brook. Shalimar Wedding Chapel, Inside Shalimar Hotel, 1–800–255–9633 toll free!!*'

There are flyers and posters everywhere for lookalike performers and pop stars, fakesters who are huge stars in the ultimate city of the fake. Here in Vegas, if you've got the dough, you can see Madonna, Buddy Holly, Sammy Davis Junior, Dolly Parton, several Elvis Presleys, Roy Orbison, Liberace, Cher, Joan Rivers, the Blues Brothers and Little Richard. (To make things even more confusing, the real Little Richard is also playing Vegas at the moment, only his show, people say, is not quite as good as the impersonator's show. What?!!)

I went into a bar and had a beer. But there was no escape from the slot machines. They were lined up against the wall and set into the bar itself. There were slot machines in the men's bathroom and slot machines around the edge of the dance floor. I picked up a newspaper and began to read it, but even the newspaper horoscopes in Vegas are about gambling. I looked up my own sign, Virgo. 'Shoot craps this month. If you win one, get up and run. If you win two, you're not quite through. If you win three better stay where you be. Wear white and you will win. Play the pass line.'

Back inside the casino, enormous banks of video screens bombard you with images of the city's success stories: 'Denny Witt of Los Angeles was playing the Black Gold $5 slot machines at the Tropicana when he lined up three black gold symbols in a row. The winning result? $41,216.'

'Pamela McCrary, an education services specialist for the US Department of Defense from Florida, put six quarters in an IGT red, white and blue slot machine at the MGM Grand and drove out of the hotel in a new Chrysler Le Baron Convertible.'

By about two in the morning I had lost two hundred dollars playing blackjack. I strolled out on to the strip again to get some air. Prostitutes were strolling up and down in miniskirts and thigh-length boots and clinging shirts. Music screamed from every doorway, heavy metal and rap, disco and Dixieland jazz. The main street was so clogged with traffic that you would have thought it was rush hour and not the middle of the night. Police cars were parked in a long line down the middle of the boulevard, not moving, but with their rooflights flashing and their sirens wailing. It seemed as though the police, not being able or willing to do much else, just wanted to add to the noise and the lightshow. They stood in little groups around their cars, laughing, chatting together, smoking cigarettes.

A young man in a well-cut suit and expensive-looking shoes approached me on the corner of the strip. He asked me if I was alone and I said yes. He took a folder out of his briefcase. Inside the folder were sets of photographs of young naked women, each photograph with a letter of the alphabet next to it. Girl A was one hundred dollars an hour, he explained, Girl B was one hundred and ten, Girl C was ninety, and so on. It was like looking at a menu. If I saw nothing I liked on his list, he explained, he could arrange more or less anything else. If I wanted two or three women that would be fine. If I wanted a boy that could be arranged. If I wanted an underage girl that would be a little more difficult, but that, too, would be possible. Anything, basically, was possible.

When I went back into the casino the place was still completely full. I wandered around for a while and watched a man playing roulette. The minimum bet was ten dollars, and he kept betting on the same number – fourteen. He told me that if it came up he would win thirty-six times his ten-buck stake, three hundred and sixty dollars. He had lost one hundred and forty dollars so far, he said, but he was sure of his system. It was only a matter of time. I wasn't so sure myself. I was never much good at mathematics, but even I could tell that at ten dollars a throw he had a mere twenty-two more chances to win, and even then, he would only get his stake money back. He explained that there were thirty-six numbers, so that he had a one in thirty-six chance of winning every time he played. He had not calculated for the possibility of one number coming up twice or three times in the course of thirty-six spins, the chances of which are surely higher than every number coming up once.

'Where you from, pal?' he asked me.

'Ireland,' I said.

He laughed. 'I knew this Irish chick once. Black chick, but she had Irish blood. We had a thing for a while, you know. She had this Irish expression she used to say, what was it? Oh yeah, "How's your ass for lovebites?" She used to say that all the time. You ever hear that expression?'

I told him I'd heard something like it, yes.

'"How's your ass for fucken lovebites." That's what she used to say. She went to Ireland on a trip once, see, and I guess somebody said that to her over there. She was one wild chick.'

'Indeed,' I said.

'You know what she liked? In the sack?'

'What?'

He leaned towards me and whispered. 'She liked tyin you up and then whippin you.'

'No!'

'Seriously. She'd tie you to the fuckin bed and then beat the shit outta you with a tennis racket.'

'Well,' I chortled, uncertainly, 'they do say that love hurts.'

'Yeah, right. It fuckin does. And then she liked pissing on you. I'm not kidding. Man, she was wild.'

'Pissing on you?' I said.

'Yeah, sure. Pissing on you. And then she liked you to piss on her. And I mean, that's not always so easy, ya know what I'm sayin? Like, this one time, she wants me to piss on her and I can't, so I have to sit there drinkin big glasses of water with her screamin her tits off for a whole hour before I can do it. Big fuckin glasses of water.'

I congratulated both him and his urethra on their dedication.

'Ya like Vegas?' he asked, as he chucked in another chip.

'Well, it's certainly unique,' I said.

'Sure is,' he said, 'the most American city there is. Vegas.'

I asked him what he meant.

'You take a desert,' he said, 'nothin but the desert for two hundred miles around here, and ya build a place like this, a great big beautiful city like Vegas, outta nothin but the dirt of the desert.' He threw in another chip. 'It's the American spirit of free enterprise is what you got here. God created the world, but only an American could create Las Vegas, am I right?'

'Yeah,' I said. 'You're right.'

'Yeah,' he said. 'How's your ass for fuckin lovebites. Ain't that the wildest thing ya ever heard?'

I was tired now and I'd had enough. On my way up to bed I saw the slot-machine man again. He was playing two machines now, one with each hand. It was late and he was still losing, but he was still pumping in the coins, one after another. I don't think I will ever quite forget the look I saw on his face as I passed him by. It was a look of the most unspeakable fear.

CHAPTER 15

The Long Way Home

I dreamed I held her in my arms as in the days of yore
She said, Johnny, you're only joking like so many times before
The cock he crew in the morning, he crew both loud and shrill
And I awoke in California, many miles from Spancil Hill.

From 'Spancil Hill',
traditional Irish song, nineteenth century

Goodbye Mursheen Durkan, for I'm sick and tired of workin,
No more I'll dig the praties, and no more will I be fooled.
For as sure as my name is Kearny, I'll be off to Californee,
Where instead of diggin lumps of dirt,
I'll be diggin lumps of gold!

From 'Mursheen Durkan',
traditional Irish song, nineteenth century

I was quite keen to go to San Francisco, because it is not every city that can claim to have simultaneously invented peace and love, flower power, the Grateful Dead, a goodly smattering of Beat poets, the Manson murders and a punk rock band called the Dead Kennedys, while still somehow persuading Tony Bennett to leave his heart there.

I was also pretty interested, because the Irish had played a major part in the city's colourful history, and, indeed, there was a town called Dublin just outside San Francisco which I intended to go and visit. The Irish, in fact, were among the very first settlers in the bay area. As early as 1828, when California was still part of Mexico, a Mexican-Irish chap with the wonderful handle of Don Timoteo Murphy bought a parcel of land near San Rafael and settled down to a happy life of green Guinness and tequila sunrise.

The great California gold rush began twenty years later, and in the development of the city that grew up around the gold, the Irish were in on the ground floor. An Irishman, Peter Donahue, made a multi-million-dollar fortune out of designing, manufacturing and building San Francisco's first street-lighting system. A cousin of his, John G. Downey, who had arrived in California from County Roscommon in 1849 with only $10 in his pocket, opened the city's first pharmacy. Thirteen years later he was state governor. Such stories are typical enough. Generally the Irish achieved great economic success in the city by the bay, and they assimilated with phenomenal speed into the swirling current of San Francisco life.

I stayed in the Cartwright, a tiny hotel on the corner of Sutter and Powell. It is a very pleasant place, with yellowed old copies of the *New Yorker* in the lobby, linen pillowcases in the bedroom and a yellowed old concierge who nods amiably and beams when you come in or out, whether you want him to or not. It is small and intimate, and after the breathtaking excess of the MGM Grand in Las Vegas, the Cartwright seemed like dying and going to hotel heaven.

San Francisco is built on a big slab of land wedged in between the bay and the Pacific Ocean, with the undulating hills around Oakland and Marin providing an admirably scenic backdrop in the distance. The place started out as a port city and perhaps because of this history it has always had a reputation as a centre of bohemianism, diversity and tolerance. Modern central San Francisco is a wonderful place. The streets are organized on a grid system, so it feels a little like Manhattan with charm. For an American city, the centre is tiny, a mere seven miles long, and it thus has the ambience of a small town threatening to burst at the seams.

On my first night I strolled down to Geary Street to have something to eat. The restaurant's smoking table – yes, table, singular – was around the corner of the L-shaped dining room and boasted a really good view of the car park. There was a television playing in the corner, showing repeated images of young Middle-Eastern men being whipped, beaten and chained. For a moment or two, I had the impression that I was watching some kind of sado-masochistic pornography channel. Hey, that's just fine, I said to myself, I'm being made to feel like a leper for smoking a legal substance on which I pay tax, but I have to watch these guys getting their thrills by kicking the living shit out of each other. After a time, however, it became clear that what was actually playing was a documentary about the miraculous Shroud of Turin.

I asked the waiter if he could possibly turn the television off. He looked surprised and asked if it was bothering me. I said yes, funnily enough, I didn't actually enjoy seeing a person being flayed and nailed to a cross while I was eating spaghetti bolognaise. He got a bit sulky then.

After dinner I ambled back down Geary Street, feeling tired. I had fully intended to go back to the hotel and get a good night's kip, but I found myself stopping outside a little bar called the Blue Lamp. It looked warm and dark and pleasant and inviting. Oh, fuck it, I said to myself. Just the one.

Three weary-looking guys were up on a stage at the back playing very rude blues numbers on acoustic guitars.

I'm gonna put on brand new rubbers
Then I'm gonna poke under your hood.
Gonna put on brand new rubbers
Then I'm gonna oil you up good.
Your motor's a little rusty baby,
But I'd take you for a good long ride if I could.

Gosh, I thought, isn't that beautiful. Who would have thought that automobile maintenance could offer such promising territory to the aspiring songwriter. A very handsome middle-aged man was wandering around the bar making a horse's ass of himself with various young women. He kept staggering up to them and trying to kiss them, and despite his enviable good looks, he kept getting fobbed off. Finally he fell over in a heap and started crying about his mother. To the great gaiety of the crowd, his mother arrived to collect him about a half hour later.

The woman behind the counter was a genial person. We talked for a while about the music. There had once been a time when she liked the blues, she said, but not any more. I asked her why not. She grinned and told me to go look at a postcard which had been stuck on the wall near the door. The postcard had a cartoon which showed three frogs sitting on a stage wearing sunglasses and playing guitars. The caption read 'Woooh, my baby's left me and I done got put in jail. I got the greens so bad, oh yeah, I got the greens.'

'Since I came to work in this place,' she said, 'that's every single night of my damn life.'

San Francisco really is hilly, and so maps of the place do not help the aspiring walker much. Your destination might only be seven blocks away, but to get there on foot you will expend the effort it takes to scale one of the minor Pyrenees. Sometimes it all gets a bit much. Sometimes it makes you depressed. Sometimes you can't help feeling that if you erected a very large brick wall in downtown San Francisco and painted a yellow dotted line down the middle, people would assume it was a street and try to drive up the bloody thing.

I ambled around for the afternoon with nothing much to do. After a while I found myself in a shop which was full of hippie memorabilia. There were posters of Jimi Hendrix and Janis Joplin, tie-dyed T-shirts and dope-pipes and luminous decals with peace symbols stamped on. There was also a fifteen-foot-high figure of a beaming and rotund President Clinton with a joint in one hand and a saxophone in the other. I said to the guy behind the counter that I really liked it. 'Yeah,' he sighed, 'I'm just not sure whether that display is really working with any kind of integrity.' That's the kind of shop it was.

After this, I walked up to the world famous City Lights bookstore, where I bought a copy of Charles Bukowski's short stories, just in case I found myself having too good a time later on in the evening and I wanted suddenly to depress the shit out of myself.

I had been told by a friend that Dublin, California was 'a really famous kiss and ride town', so, as you can well imagine, I looked forward to the prospect of visiting there with the keen enthusiasm of a medieval martyr anticipating being flogged, crucified or burnt at the stake. A kiss, after all, does not come one's way just any old day of the week in the course of writing a travel book, let alone – as I feel sure Colin Thubron, Jonathan Raban or Dervla Murphy would confirm, if they are honest – a ride, except, perhaps, on a bicycle. Sadly, however, it turns out that a kiss and ride town does not mean in California what it might mean in my own dear shamrock-encrusted homeland. A kiss and ride town merely means a special kind of suburb, twenty miles, say, or thirty miles from a large city.

The derivation of the phrase is rather sweet, in a pass-the-sickbag-Mother-before-I-hurl-up-my-hashbrowns kind of way. Your partner, spouse, moll or chap kisses you goodbye in the morning just before you ride into town on the train. Thus, Dublin, California is a kiss and ride town for San Francisco. Slough, I suppose, would be a kiss and ride town for London, but I don't really think we want to get into that too much.

Anyway, Dublin, California turned out to be a pretty dreary sort of place, with the emphasis on the dreary rather than the pretty. It is a ninety-minute drive from San Francisco, and when you arrive there you cannot help wondering why you bothered. It is a vast and seemingly unending sprawl of shopping malls, discount furniture warehouses and drive-in establishments of one kind or another. There are drive-in banks, drive-in restaurants, drive-in beauty parlours. Any business into which an overfed yuppie could possibly drive they have in Dublin, California. Except garages. I don't think I saw a drive-in garage anywhere. A drive-in garage would, I imagine, be a little too common.

In 1862, three immigrant Irish farmers, Michael Murray, Jeremiah Fallon and James W. Dougherty, settled in this area, on parcels of one José Maria Amador's Rancho San Ramon. The place had no name for some years, but that didn't seem to bother anybody. Then, it is said, one day a passing traveller stopped Murray on the road and asked him what the area was called. 'For all the Paddies living there,' Murray sighed, 'you might as well call it Dublin.' The name stuck. Dublin it was.

But the place has certainly changed a good deal since then. The town is now inhabited more or less exclusively by wealthy Wasps. House prices, I noticed, are a tad on the high side. A semi-D with a couple of bedrooms in Dublin, California would easily set you back half a million smackers.

The historians tell us that Napoleon III, following his enforced exile from France, died in terrible agony in the South of England, where a lot of people, funnily enough, live in terrible agony. Well, I imagine a lot of people are living in terrible agony in Dublin, California also. The town has the brain-dead and tranquillized ambience of all West Coast American suburbia. A walk up and down the enormous motorway which passes for the main street is a salutary experience. The inhabitants of Dublin would make the Stepford Wives seem like raving individualists. There is, shall we say, a slightly glazed look in the eye, reminiscent of the finer moments of former Vice-President Quayle, or of a long weekend in a seaside town with nothing to do except watch MTV in your underpants and drink warm neat gin out of a styrofoam cup. Most of the natives of Dublin, California looked to me like the victims of advanced neurosurgery that had gone terribly wrong, as they tottered up and down the avenues of the Dublin Mall, listening to Eagles tunes on the tannoy system and, no doubt, trying to buy Prozac in low-fat strawberry flavour.

Desperate for some sort of sensory stimulation I wandered into a horrific-looking café and plonked my weary body down at a table. The service was uncommonly slow. Usually, in an American restaurant, the staff have the bread rolls out on the table and the bib tucked into your collar before you can blurt out that actually you only came in to see if you could use the bathroom. But not in Dublin, California.

The waitress, when she finally appeared, had the worst skin of anyone I have ever seen in my life. I had always thought hurling was a traditional Irish sport until I caught my first glimpse of this woman. I mean, I do not wish to be cruel here, but seriously, her face was absolutely astonishing. I will not dwell on the dermatological details now, suffice it to say that as soon as I clapped eyes on her ruined visage I decided I would be taking a raincheck on the all-you-eat-pizzarama-special after all.

American waiters and waitresses usually fawn all over you and insist you call them by their first names. But Constance – for such was the miserable creature's moniker – had the odd habit more usually possessed by European waiters and waitresses: she seemed to respond to any request I might make with either a bemused smile or a pained wince. When I asked old Pineapple Chops if I could have a teaspoon, for instance, she peered at me as though I was some kind of imbecile. And when I asked if I could possibly have a little more coffee, when she was absolutely ready, of course, she glared at me like I had just asked for a bowl of fresh flambéed snot.

After my pleasant repast, I strolled up to have a look at Dublin Prison. It was here that infamous former junk-bond bigwig Michael Milken opted to serve his two-year jail sentence. Dublin's low-security slammer is particularly popular among America's new community of gold-plated criminals. A former army barracks, it now boasts lovely lawns and flowerbeds full of big daisies and a regime which is famously severe. Prisoners are only allowed access to the brand new running track and volleyball court once a day and if they want lobster thermidor for dinner they have to order it an hour in advance.

I tried to get into the prison but my credentials weren't good enough as I wasn't wearing Giorgio Armani. So I walked around Dublin for the whole afternoon, attempting to find something interesting. There wasn't a museum. There wasn't a theatre. The one bookshop I managed to find seemed to sell only Bibles. Kiss and ride, indeed. You could kiss and ride every last person with a personality in Dublin, California and believe me, you'd still be well able to run a marathon the next day.

California, of course, does have within its proud borders one or two jails which do not appear in the Egon Ronay prison guide. The most famously grisly of them all is Alcatraz, and for no reason at all except perhaps morbid curiousity I decided that I simply had to see it.

The first thing you notice when you get to Alcatraz Island is a large hand-painted sign announcing that the place is 'Indian Land'. There had recently been a big local controversy in San Francisco about this, someone on the ferry had explained to me. It seems that the California Indians want Alcatraz Island back from the state government, presumably so they can set up a duty-free cigarette shop on it.

Alcatraz was the prison within the California prison system. You had to be a pretty serious villain to end up here, stuck on a rock in the middle of San Francisco Bay, with the wind screaming in off the ocean and no prospect of early release. The cells are absolutely tiny and are even more lacking in basic facilities than motels in rural America. The thing is, however, some of the prisoners here really were baddies. It turns out that the famously sweet birdman, Robert Stroud, for instance, was actually a ruthless killer, a complete and utter fruitcake so dangerous that he had to be locked up in solitary confinement for thirteen years. He was such a total prick that even the other prisoners hated him.

In all the years of Alcatraz's official existence, only three men ever managed to escape. It was reported in the newspapers at the time that they had successfully tunnelled their way out of the most secure prison in the entire country using teaspoons purloined from the dining room. It turns out, amazingly enough, that this was a less than truthful story which was put out by the Department of Correction. In fact, the men had bribed a number of senior prison officials to give them drills, hammers and other items of inconspicuous light-engineering equipment. As a nice touch, the fugitives also made dummies of their heads out of papier-mâché, which they placed on their pillows to fool the guards. These dummies still survive, and all I can say is that if the dummies are in any way accurate representations of the three men, I think they should have been locked up for ever purely for being so eerily ugly.

There was no evidence that the three desperadoes had survived the swim to the mainland, the tour guide said. Well, there wouldn't be, I thought. I mean, you wouldn't bust your way out, do a brisk butterfly stroke all the way over to downtown Frisco and then canter about Ghirardelli Square singing, 'Coo-ee, look at me, I'm a really dangerous sociopath who's just gotten out of Alcatraz.' Of course they had made it, I figured. I had a sudden startling image of these three retired hoods, now living quietly somewhere in American suburbia and writing their memoirs. Possibly even living in Dublin, California, in fact, where one of their daughters is working as a waitress in a café.

In the square in front of the town hall, the Cinco de Mayo festival was in full swing. This is an annual celebration of San Francisco's enormous Latin American tradition, but the endearing thing about it was that people of all races seemed to be involved. As I wandered through the square I saw stalls selling Polish hot dogs, Chinese food, take-away sushi. On a vast stage, a posse of black rappers was whipping up the young crowd. At the far end of the square, under a grove of luxuriant trees, a troop of young boys and girls wearing traditional Irish costumes danced Irish jigs and reels. They wheeled around in their emerald green skirts and their green sashes embroidered with little Celtic swirls. It was pure corn, but I have to confess that it was kind of sweet to see them. I was clearly getting homesick now. Either that, or the drugs were beginning to work.

★

On my last night in America I had planned to go and see a comedy show in a downtown San Francisco club. The first set was sold out, so I had to come back at eleven and queue up for the second show. This was fine. I had time to kill. It was just that when I turned up and got into the line for the second show, I saw all the people coming out of the first show and they looked amazingly depressed. I mean, they looked like they had just been to see *Schindler's List* and not a hilarious comedy gig. So I decided to give it a miss.

I went across the road to an Irish bar. Generally on this trip I had tried to avoid Irish bars, but I was going home tomorrow after all. What the hell, I figured, it couldn't possibly do me any harm.

The little pub was full of people. A traditional Irish music session was in progress. Little sweating plump-faced men in their shirtsleeves played fiddles and melodeons and banjos and mandolins. A tall scrawny youth in a black leather jacket pounded away at an acoustic guitar. There was a man with a bodhran and a woman with a flute. An elderly uillean piper sat on the edge of the circle, his right arm pumping the bellows of his pipes, his fingers racing over the holes in the chanter. Large whiskeys and creamy pints of Guinness were passed over the heads of the crowd to the musicians. The room filled up with the wild melodies and frantic rhythms and the sound of feet stamping out the tempo on the floor. Whenever the musicians took a quick break for a slurp of beer or a drag on a cigarette, a man in a suit would stand up and introduce the next tunes. 'Two reels now,' he would shout. '"The Bird in the Bush" and "The Galway Rambler".' Off the musicians would go once more, only to have him call out as soon as they had finished: 'We'll have a little jig next, "The Banks of Newfoundland",' or 'Now for two fine hornpipes, first "The Home Ruler" and then "Dinny Moloney's", named after Dinny Moloney from Broadford in the lovely county of Limerick!' There would be cheers and shouts of encouragement and the rollicking music would start up again.

After a while somebody called for a song. A beautiful young black woman strode up from the back of the pub and entered the circle. She would sing unaccompanied, she said. She had a California accent, but the song she sang was pure Irish, 'A Stór Mo Chroi' ('Love of My Heart', in Gaelic), a slow and desperate ballad of emigrant longing. I had heard the song many times before, but I had never heard it sung by a black woman in California. The way she sang it, and the fact of her singing it at all, brought a new level of meaning to the song which was both humbling and moving.

A stór mo chroi, when you're far away
From the home that you'll soon be leaving.
There'll be many a time by night and day
That my heart will be sorely grieving.
For the stranger's land may be bright and fair
And rich in its treasures golden.
But you'll pine, I know, for the long ago
And the love that will never grow olden.

A stór mo chroi, in the stranger's land
There is plenty of weeping and wailing.
Where bright gems adorn the great and grand
There are faces with hunger paling.
When the road is toilsome and hard to tread,
When the lights of their cities blind you,
Oh turn, a stór, unto Erin's green shore
And the love that you're leaving behind you.

A stór mo chroi, when the evening mist
Over mountains and seas is falling,
Then turn away from the throng and list
And it's then that you'll hear my sad calling
For the sound of a voice that I'll sorely miss
For somebody's speedy returning.
Aroon, aroon, say you'll come home soon
To the love that is for ever burning.

When she had finished singing the people yelped and clapped and stamped their feet, and she left the circle and returned to her friends.

The musicians struck up again, blasting out a lively polka. I felt I just had to go over to the woman and say I had really enjoyed her song. She nodded and smiled and said thank you. Her fingers drummed on her bottle of beer and she shook her torso from side to side with the rhythm of the music.

'I'm Irish myself,' I said.

She turned to me and peered deeply into my eyes. 'Oh really?' She smiled. 'Can I ask you something?'

'Sure,' I said.

'Tell me,' she beamed, 'how's your ass for lovebites?'

I felt hot. She reached out laughing and touched my hand. The barman called for last orders. Just fine, I told her. Really, just fine. Never better actually. Honest to God.

I turned around and left and walked quickly back to my hotel through the wet streets of San Francisco with the sound of jigs and wild reels still buzzing in my ears. I had a plane to catch next morning, after all. The way I saw it, it really wouldn't do to get tied up at the last minute.

HISTORICAL BIBLIOGRAPHY

A number of Irish-American historians have done extremely thorough and dilligent work in the area of Irish immigration, settlement, internal migration, social customs and culture in the United States. Throughout this book I have repeatedly relied for historical insight and instruction on the writings of three scholars in particular; these are Kerby A. Miller, Lawrence J. McCaffrey and the late William V. Shannon.

Miller's *Emigrants And Exiles: Ireland And The Irish Exodus to North America* (Oxford University Press, 1985) is quite simply a masterful study, which for all its scholarly rigour and immense knowledge is eminently readable, deeply passionate and finally unforgettable. (The concluding bibliography of published and unpublished sources, particularly Irish-American emigrants' letters, is a towering achievement in itself. Many of the extracts from emigrant's letters which begin the chapters in *Sweet Liberty* are quoted from Miller's book.) I cannot recommend the book highly enough. McCaffrey's *The Irish Diaspora In America* (Indiana University Press, 1976) is a slimmer volume which is nevertheless essential reading for all those interested in the subject. Shannon's *The American Irish: A Political And Social Portrait* (University of Massachusetts Press, 1963) is more old fashioned and anecdotal, a cracking good story, but full of shrewd observation and profound insight. If *Sweet Liberty* contains anything of value to the amateur historian of Irish America, it is probably borrowed from Miller, McCaffrey or Shannon, to whom I immediately and enthusiastically refer the reader interested in further study. Needless to say, any mistakes of fact, interpretation or emphasis are my own.

Other recommended books are as follows:

Adams, John R., *Regional Sketches* (New Haven College and University Press, 1972).

Brown, Thomas N., *Irish-American Nationalism* (Lipincott Books, Philadelphia, 1966).

Curley, James Michael, *I'd Do It All Again: A Record Of All My Uproarious Years* (Prentice-Hall, New Jersey, 1957).

Darst, H. Jackson, *Dublin And The Darsts: A Portrait Of A Virginia Country Town And One Of Its Families* (Wilderness Road Regional Museum, Newhern, Virginia, 1992).

Duff, John B., *The Irish In America* (Wadsworth Books, California, 1971).

Krantz, Les, *America By The Numbers* (Houghton Mifflin, Boston, 1993).

Kriebel, H. W., *A Brief History Of Montgomery County Pennsylvania* [Including Dublin Pennsylvania] (Norristown, 1923).

Lipscombe, Mance and Alyn, Glen, *I Say Me For A Parable: The Oral Autobiography Of Mance Lipscombe, Texas Bluesman* (Norton, New York, 1993).

Marling, Susan, *American Affair: The Americanisation of Britain* (Boxtree Books, London, 1991).

Miller, Kerby and Wagner, Paul, *Out of Ireland: The Story Of Irish Emigration To America* (Aurum Press, London, 1994).

Nevins, Allan, (ed), *The Diary Of George Templeton Strong* (Macmillan, New York, 1952).

Nevins, Allan, (ed), *The Diary Of Philip Hone* (Dodd, Mead And Co., New York, 1927).

O'Connor, Nuala, *Bringing It All Back Home: The Influence of Irish Music* (BBC Books, London, 1991).

Pool, Elizabeth, *Pen, Brush, Chisel And Clef: Dublin's Halcyon Days* (Dublin New Hampshire Historical Society, 1992).

Quinn, David Beers, *The Roanoke Voyages 1584–1590* (Dover Publications, New York, 1991).

Reeves, Pamela, *Ellis Island: Gateway To The American Dream* (Crescent Books, New York, 1991).

Smith, Alfred E., *Up To Now: An Autobiography* (Garden City, New York, 1929).

Taylor, Philip, *The Distant Magnet* (Harper and Row, New York, 1971).

Wittke, Carl, *The Irish In America* (Russell and Russell, New York, 1970).